With every good wish.

Terence C.F. Prittie

*Whose
Jerusalem?*

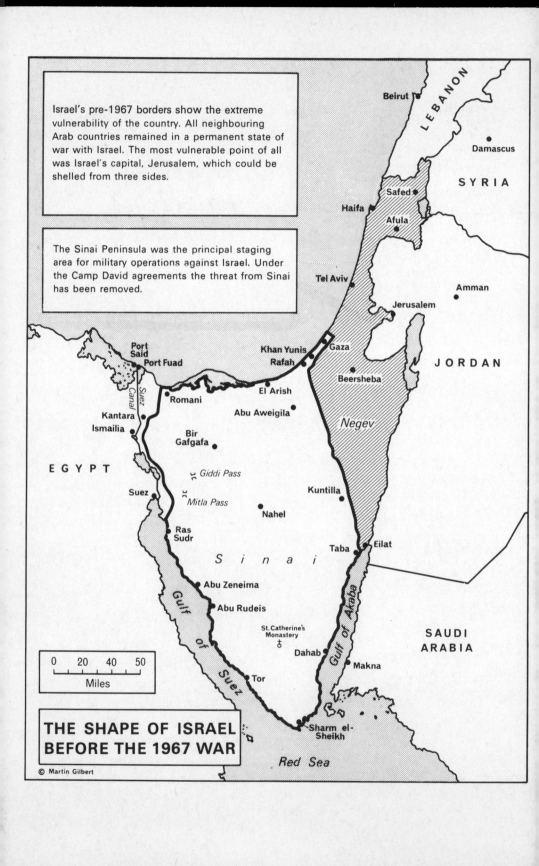

Israel's pre-1967 borders show the extreme vulnerability of the country. All neighbouring Arab countries remained in a permanent state of war with Israel. The most vulnerable point of all was Israel's capital, Jerusalem, which could be shelled from three sides.

The Sinai Peninsula was the principal staging area for military operations against Israel. Under the Camp David agreements the threat from Sinai has been removed.

LEBANON

Beirut

Damascus

SYRIA

Safed

Haifa

Afula

Tel Aviv

Amman

Jerusalem

JORDAN

Port Said
Port Fuad

Khan Yunis
Rafah

Gaza

Beersheba

Suez Canal

Romani

El Arish

Kantara

Abu Aweigila

Ismailia

Negev

EGYPT

Bir
Gafgafa

Giddi Pass

Kuntilla

Mitla Pass

Suez

Nahel

Ras
Sudr

S i n a i

Taba

Eilat

Abu Zeneima

Abu Rudeis

Gulf of Suez

St. Catherine's
Monastery

Gulf of Akaba

SAUDI
ARABIA

Dahab

Makna

Tor

Sharm el-
Sheikh

0   20   40   50

Miles

THE SHAPE OF ISRAEL
BEFORE THE 1967 WAR

© Martin Gilbert

Red Sea

Whose Jerusalem?

Terence Prittie

FREDERICK MULLER LIMITED
LONDON

First published in Great Britain 1981 by Frederick Muller Limited,
London, NW2 6LE

Copyright © 1981 Terence Prittie

ISBN 0 584 10440 5

Typeset by Computacomp (UK) Ltd,
Fort William, Scotland.
Printed in Great Britain by The Anchor Press Ltd., Colchester

Contents

List of Illustrations

(between pages 112 and 113)

Foreword

Jerusalem means a great deal to many people. No other city in history has evoked such profound emotions and such deep love. She has been fought over, conquered, destroyed, and rebuilt over and over again throughout the last 4,000 years.

From 1948 to 1967, Jerusalem was a divided city and her ecumenical character was fragmented and perverted. In the last fourteen years Jerusalem has again become one city, the Holy Sites are once again accessible to all who wish to visit and worship there, and the scars of war are gradually being erased.

Jerusalem, however, is also a city of peoples; in fact, she is today the largest city in Israel. Two thirds of her population are Jewish, the other third are Moslem Arabs and Christians who belong to well over thirty Christian denominations. Simplistic formulae of melting pot and integration do not apply in Jerusalem because Jerusalem is above all a mosaic of diverse national and religious communities, each of whom is determined to preserve its religious, spiritual and cultural heritage.

Terence Prittie has done yeoman service in painstakingly outlining the history of Jerusalem in the distant past and in recent times. He lucidly describes the disparate and, at times opposing, aspirations of the various peoples who live in Jerusalem and, at the same time, stresses the not inconsiderable degree of tranquillity which has existed in the city since its reunification in 1967.

The Mayor of Jerusalem cannot solve the problems of the Middle East or the Arab–Israel dispute; but we have attempted to create in Jerusalem an atmosphere of peace, of tolerance, and of mutual understanding in spite of the absence of political consensus. We are convinced that this will ultimately be conducive to the creation of conditions which will help lay the foundation for peace in the Middle East.

Terence Prittie's thorough research has produced a book which makes it immensely readable for those who are interested in Jerusalem. For the student of Jerusalem, it is surely required reading.

Mayor of Jerusalem

CHAPTER ONE

The Place
and the Problem

Dynamic, ebullient and at sixty-seven years of age working from six in the morning to ten or eleven o'clock at night, Teddy Kollek had by mid-1980 been Mayor of West Jerusalem since 1965 and of the reunified city since 1967. In his unremitting dedication to Jerusalem he had exemplified the deep, instinctive and total attachment of the Jewish people to the place that became their capital city 3,000 years ago and has remained that in their thoughts and hearts ever since. 'Jerusalem', as one Israeli expressed it recently[1] 'is not just for living. Jerusalem is *being*.'

To the Israelis, the reunification of Jerusalem – which could never have taken place had King Hussein of Jordan not attacked the city at the behest of President Nasser of Egypt in the Six Day War of 1967 – was quite simply an act of God, providential, irreversible, final.

There are two features of Teddy Kollek's modest office on the Jaffa Road which are symbolic. Its door is kept permanently open. This is not just for the benefit of his staff (who are well advised to enter quietly and state their business as briefly as possible), who can come and go without knocking or other formality. The open door signifies availability to all – Jews, Arabs, foreigners, Christians and Muslims. Kollek is prepared not merely to listen to their worries and complaints; he wants to hear them and deal with them. He sees himself as the representative of *all* of the people of Jerusalem – not of a single race, a single party, a single sector of society or strand of opinion.

The second feature of his office is a photograph which hangs often initially unnoticed by visitors who tend to begin examining and admiring the fifteen ancient maps of Jerusalem on the walls. Sooner or later the Mayor will draw the caller's notice to the photograph; it is of the infamous 'Berlin Wall', stretching away on either side of the barred Brandenburg Gate. In his own words: 'I keep this hanging here just to remind people what division means. What happened to the Berliners? Friends and neighbours, even families, were separated from one another and split asunder – husband from wife sometimes, mothers from their children. Does anyone *really* want this to happen again, here, in Jerusalem?'[2]

To Kollek – as to almost every Israeli citizen or Jew in the outside world, and to many Arabs too – the unity of Jerusalem is natural and normal. His own arguments in favour of permanent, inviolable unity are based on simple logic as much as on heartfelt attachment to the city. If sovereignty over Jerusalem were to be divided again, 'then the walls, the barbed-wire, the machine-gun nests and the armed sentries will return – who can doubt it?'[3] For these were the consequences of unnatural division between 1948 and 1967.

Nor does the Mayor see any reason why a united Jerusalem should not be able to function, even if its citizens speak Hebrew, Arabic, English and many other languages. 'Look at Switzerland, functionally one of the most successful countries in the world's history, yet with clear-cut dividing lines between French-, German- and Italian-speaking communities.' Jerusalem, moreover, *does* function: 'If anyone doubts it, let him come and see for himself. So very many people do come, and if they come to learn, they go away satisfied.'[4]

One group of 'learners' came in April 1980. Thirteen Mayors of American cities visited Jerusalem to attend a conference on the social problems of multi-racial cities, with Jerusalem as the classic test-case. Most of them had no political axe to grind – their own cities did not have substantial Jewish communities. The two black Mayors among them might possibly have been expected to adopt the critical attitude towards Israel usual in the black countries of the Third World. But the Mayors were unanimous in praising Jerusalem's open society and the sense and purposefulness of its administration. According to the Mayor of Minneapolis, Don Fraser, 'You leave Jerusalem with a clear smell of freedom and a sense of people who demonstrate compassion and a dedication to human dignity'; and Richard

Caliguiri of Pittsburgh put his thoughts in a single line: 'I stand in awe of your city'.

Two other statements were: 'I will not sacrifice conscience for expediency; we are with you', and 'Only a unified Jerusalem can provide security and opportunity for growth'. Was all this part of a back-scratching exercise of mutual admiration? But then the first of these last two statements came from George Voinvich of Cleveland, which has no significant Jewish community, and the second from the black Mayor of Cincinnati, Ken Blackwell. The likelihood is that they said exactly what they thought.[5]

Jerusalem, sadly, is today a bone of bitter contention between Israel and the Arab world. There are many reasons for this, but a chief Arab complaint is that Israel practises a racist policy of discrimination and oppression in the city. The Arabs have regarded Jerusalem as their own since the seventh century. The Arabs of East Jerusalem insist only that their part of the city belongs to them, by right of residence there, but the extremists of the Palestine Liberation Organization assert that all of Jerusalem belongs to the Palestinian people.

Israelis maintain that Jerusalem is their own natural and eternally destined capital city, that there has once again been a Jewish majority there for well over a hundred years past, and that in 1967 they were given a God-sent opportunity to end the unnatural division which had lasted a brief nineteen years out of its 3,000 years' existence. They had not sought this opportunity, but they were bound to welcome it and exploit it.

The outside Christian world, of course, claims a special interest and commitment in Jerusalem by virtue of the ministry and crucifixion there of Jesus Christ. Three world communities, then – Jewish, Arab and Christian – have a deep-rooted, long-lasting interest in the place. All three communities have valid, if differing reasons for this. All three, therefore, are intimately concerned with the city's future, and all have – or should have – an all-embracing belief in the survival of Jerusalem as a city of peace. If it could only become this, it could offer an epic example to the whole world.

Jerusalem, inevitably, is the most central, the most neuralgic point in the Arab–Israeli dispute. This was obvious in Israel's 1948 War of Independence, less so perhaps during the following nineteen years when the city was divided between Israeli and Jordanian sovereignty. But it became so again when re-unification took place in 1967. Total Israeli control aroused the bitter resentment of the Arab world, as well as Christian suspicions which owed much to 2,000 years of antisemitic tradition and teaching. Arab resentment was further fostered by the belief that the Arabs of East Jerusalem had become second-class citizens in what had been their own land.

Kollek has steadfastly maintained that he has done all that he could for the 100,000 or so Arabs among Jerusalem's population of about 400,000:

> Look at what is being done and what you can see, and look below the surface too. Hundreds of Arab homes are being built all the time; as many building-permits are being issued monthly as used to be granted in a whole year when they were under Jordanian rule. The richer Jerusalem Arabs are building country-houses outside the city. Much has been achieved in renovating the Christian and Armenian Quarters of the Old City, or in shoring-up houses in the Muslim Quarter which were in danger of collapse. In Jordanian times, shaky buildings simply *did* fall down. The Church of the Holy Sepulchre should have been repaired ages ago, after the earthquake of 1927 – instead, the work was continually postponed. It was left to us to make a serious start, in 1972.
>
> Then look, for instance, at the schools in East Jerusalem today. In a single Arab neighbourhood 750 boys and 860 girls are now going to school, where there used to be 400 and just 100. Arab mothers who were illiterate are coming forward and asking to be taught to read and write. Almost paradoxically, we Israelis are organizing courses for them in their own Arabic language. We have stepped up vocational and teacher training and introduced instruction in handicrafts – the Arabs of Jerusalem have to have an industrial base for their existence just as the rest of us do. I honestly believe that we have improved the quality of life for them, and we shall go on improving it.[6]

Of course, all that *could* have been done for Jerusalem's Arabs has not yet been done; the Mayor would be the first to admit it, and has indeed criticized Israel's Government for being 'miserly' in the granting of rights to the Arab community.[7] His view has always been that their rights needed to be carefully studied, and a way found of giving them practical assertion. Those who had lost homes and property should be encouraged to claim compensation; but 'compensation can only be given if it *is* claimed. A compensation scheme was tabled as long ago as 1964; active discussion of it was well under way by 1967. Then came war. A law on compensation was framed by 1973, and there were Arabs queuing up to claim. Then, war once more, and since 1973 the Arabs have hung back. Only two or three claims a month are coming in, and these are being settled.'[8] And where housing for Arabs was concerned, more still needed to be done. Kollek's view, in April 1980, was that 6,000 housing units for Arabs should be planned for the immediate future. But this entailed providing the appropriate infrastructure for roads and services – and money for all this was scarce.[9]

On the future of Jerusalem Kollek has been guided by four main principles. Two have already been mentioned, the indivisibility of the city and equality of treatment and rights for all of its citizens – equality of participation in the running of the place, too, if only the Arabs could be persuaded to join in the municipal administration. The third principle was that the 'Jerusalem Question' should be the last to be tackled in searching for a comprehensive settlement of the Arab–Israeli dispute, and should be treated as an intrinsic and integral part of that settlement. And the fourth principle is one to which any sane person would subscribe – that the 'Jerusalem Question', like every problem in the world's history, is not insoluble. Defeatism is the deadliest enemy of human progress, the biggest barrier to human happiness.

In a letter published in May 1980, Kollek hinted at the need for some sort of special status for Jerusalem.[10] The need was self-evident; Jerusalem – and this should be said over and over again – is a unique city and the question of its future demands a unique solution. Kollek was thinking essentially of the political problems involved – the city's status, its definition in accordance with the needs of its Jewish, Muslim and Christian inhabitants, and its future administration – when he wrote:

> I believe that the problems can only be constructively dealt with if Jerusalem is given a special status which would enable it to deal with all its most complicated problems, from housing to education, from health to social welfare – concerning a great variety of Jewish, Christian and Muslim communities – quickly and efficiently, with proper government supervision but without interference by the government in every little detail and the long delays inherent in the present system.
>
> This status would have to be formulated in a special Jerusalem Law ... In the framework of such a special status,

there is possibly room for a Minister for Jerusalem; without it, he would be a powerless bystander ... Jerusalem, which has singular problems, needs a special status.

In a personal interview, he explained this further:

It is fairly obvious that Jerusalem needs special arrangements – it's different from Tel Aviv and any other city in Israel. After all, cities of countries like Germany are already allowed to run their own affairs with a considerable degree of independence. This does not entail encroaching on matters which belong to government – foreign relations, defence, economic policies and so on. Jerusalem merits and requires special treatment more than any other city in the world.[11]

Kollek has made three other facets of his thinking about Jerusalem's future plain. First, its present municipal boundaries need not be substantially changed, although minor rectifications would always be possible. 'We took twenty dunams from Beit Jalla farmers, for instance, which we could give back if it depended on me.'[12] Israel has been accused of unilaterally extending the borders of the reunified Jerusalem, for sinister reasons of its own. Kollek has pointed out:

When we ended the division of Jerusalem, we found that King Hussein's Jordan had already drawn up its own plan for the creation of a Greater Jerusalem. It would have included the Arab townships of Ramallah, El Bireh, Beit Jalla and Bethlehem. We did not want to remove the inhabitants of these places from their Arab environment; in particular we believed that the Christian Holy City of Bethlehem should preserve its own identity. We gave the reunified Jerusalem the most logical borders which could be devised.[13]

But there was 'room for some give and take in final negotiation over boundaries', which were not, like Jerusalem itself, 'eternal'. 'They were drawn up thirteen years ago by political and military strategists, not by rabbis.'[14]

The formula of President Sadat of Egypt of an 'undivided city, divided sovereignty' was unacceptable. It was 'self-contradictory. If there is divided sovereignty, it is clear that there would be two sets of laws. This would mean two police forces and customs. In a month the minefields would be back.' Divided sovereignty meant, in practical terms, a city once again physically divided, and that 'would be to kill it'.[15]

Finally, a political solution had to be found for Jerusalem's Arabs. Israel and Egypt, he told the American–Jewish Committee, had been debating the question of autonomy for the Palestinians of the adjacent West Bank. It would be absurd for Jerusalem's Arabs to be excluded from the political rights which would be granted to their immediate Arab neighbours, so 'another solution must be found', and their rights must 'be enshrined in law' and not left dependent upon 'administrative practice which could easily be reversed'.[16] Thus, why should Jerusalem's Arabs not vote for representatives in the administration of an autonomous West Bank entity? Political rights included municipal rights, and Kollek has never ceased to express the hope that Jerusalem's Arabs can be drawn into participation in the administration of what, in their estimation, is as much their city as that of the Jews. He has concentrated that hope into a single sentence: 'I want to give everyone the feeling that Jerusalem is *his* city, that he will not be set upon by Israelis and that he will be treated with dignity'.[17]

Some of these same precepts were implicit in the speech made in Jerusalem by the French writer, Simone de Beauvoir, when receiving the Jerusalem Prize for defence of the freedom of the individual in society. She said:

> During this visit ... I was able to see the beauty of the reunited city and the sweetness of life which one can breathe deeply there. I am convinced of something else; the reunification of Jerusalem poses many problems, as it must be done in a way that will satisfy both communities, and this, of course, is very difficult. But it is even more important that any solution that does not preserve the unity of Jerusalem would suffer from unacceptable defects. On the other hand, I feel a solution will undoubtedly be found to the problem of Jerusalem and of preserving its unity.[18]

So, four guidelines from someone outside the immediate orbit of Arab–Jewish dispute – Jerusalem must stay united; all of Jerusalem's inhabitants must be helped to live as free individuals in the fullest sense; a fitting solution *will* be found to all of Jerusalem's problems; and Jerusalem already *works* today.

To these guidelines should be added one potentially sombre, even apocalyptic thought. The 'Jerusalem Question' is the most central and the most controversial issue in the Arab–Israeli dispute. That dispute is the most dangerous among the very many that have racked, and continue to rack, the whole Middle

East region, although it should be remembered, Iraquis fight with Syrians and Kurds, Syrian Alawite and Sunni Muslims fight among themselves, as do the traditionalists of the North Yemen and their Moscow-dominated southern neighbours, Ethiopia and Somalia are at loggerheads, and Iran has become a veritable witches' cauldron of sectional and regional hatreds, resentments and pretensions. Because of the world energy shortage and the immense importance of Arab oil, the basic interests of the only two genuinely 'great' powers – the United States and the Soviet Union – are inextricably interwoven with developments in the Middle East. That is why, if there is to be a third world war, it might be sparked off in that area. The whole Middle East, of course, is a tinder-box. The thought is inescapable that Jerusalem, for whose peace Jews, Christians and Muslims alike pray, is only just down the road from Armageddon.

REFERENCES

1. James McNeish, *Belonging*, Collins, London, 1980.
2. Teddy Kollek, in conversation with the author.
3. Ibid.
4. Ibid.
5. These quotes are from the *Jerusalem Post*, 11 April 1980.
6. Teddy Kollek, in conversation with the author.
7. In a speech to the American–Jewish Committee, Jerusalem, 11 February 1980.
8. Teddy Kollek, in conversation with the author.
9. Ibid.
10. *Jerusalem Post*, 4 May 1980.
11. Teddy Kollek, in conversation with the author.
12. *Jerusalem Post Magazine*, 1 February 1980.
13. Teddy Kollek, in conversation with the author.
14. Kollek to Abraham Rabinovich, *Jerusalem Post*, 14 May 1980.
15. *Jerusalem Post*, 2 February 1980.
16. In a speech to the American–Jewish Committee, Jerusalem, 11 February 1980.
17. In an interview with *The Times*, 8 April 1978.
18. Simone de Beauvoir, in a speech of acceptance at the Seventh Jerusalem Book Fair, April 1975.

CHAPTER TWO

City of Peace?

Among the 656 mentions of Jerusalem in the Hebrew Bible there are more than seventy epithets referring to its special nature. It is the 'City of Justice', the 'City of Eternity', the 'City of Truth', the 'City of Peace'; in a Christian hymn it is 'Jerusalem the Golden'. All of these epithets are efforts somehow to indicate a uniqueness accepted almost universally down the ages.[1]

Yet if there is one thing that Jerusalem has manifestly not been, it is a 'City of Peace'. It may have deserved the poetic imagery which has been lavished on it, its aura of gold, its radiant atmosphere, its air as sweet as wine, its hauntingly beautiful horizons; but it has been destroyed at least seventeen times and has probably witnessed greater bloodshed, brutality and bickering than any other city on earth. Virtually its entire population has been put to the sword, and when the city was under siege by the Romans in AD 70, up to 400 Jews are believed to have been crucified daily within sight of its walls.

It may be one of the oldest inhabited places on earth, vying with neighbouring, 7,000-years-old Jericho, but its origins are obscure. Jewish historians believe that Hebrew tribes lived there before it became the chief stronghold and holy city of the Jebusites, a small people who may have been of Indo-European origin and have come from the area of the Caucasus but who were certainly in possession of Jerusalem prior to 1000 BC. One Arab version is that all the inhabitants of Palestine were originally Arabs, living there from 9000 BC and including

Canaanites, Amorites and Jebusites – even the Philistines, arriving from the Aegean around 1200 BC, were supposedly 'assimilated' by the indigenous Arab population.[2] The Hebrew Israelites, according to the same authority, arrived only a century earlier, more than 2,000 years after the Jebusites had built Jerusalem and 'conferred sanctity' upon it; they were rootless, divided tribes, nomads who established themselves fully in Jerusalem for a mere seventy years. Abraham was an Arab, not an Israelite and did not speak Hebrew; hence 'The period of uncontested Arab habitation and rule in and around Jerusalem covers at least 8,000 years.'[3]

This is merest conjecture. What is sure is that Jerusalem was a principal city in Canaan in 1000 BC. The Bible gives its earlier name as 'Salem' when Abraham, returning from battle, was greeted by its king, Melchizedek, who 'brought forth bread and wine, and he was a priest of the most high God'.[4] In Accadian records, it was 'Urasalim', and in Egyptian 'Urushamen' or 'Rushalmam'. Jebus was well fortified and repelled the first Israelite attack, led by Joshua, but it was probably a relatively small place built on a single low ridge, chosen by reason of the water supplied by the Pool of Siloam. Its 'sanctity' was not unusual at the time; urban settlements acquired a holiness by virtue of being places of refuge and learning. Jerusalem's true sanctity would derive from a unique religious status conferred upon it by the Hebrew kings, David and Solomon.[5] David captured the city; Solomon built its First Temple and installed in it the Ark of the Covenant, that covenant between God and his chosen people. There is a clear implication in the Bible that the capture of Jerusalem may have been less violent and bloody than was usual in those times, for David bought a threshing-floor as the site for the Ark from Araunah the Jebusite.

Jebus had been a small tribal capital; Jerusalem became the political, religious and national capital of a whole people and of a state which for a short time looked like building up a dominant position in the whole populated area of the Middle East, from the borders of Egypt to the Euphrates. Geography was against the Israelites, however, and their story became one of a desperate struggle for survival in what amounted to a corridor of inhabited land between the Mediterranean Sea and the Arabian Desert, against immensely more powerful enemies. At the southern end of this corridor was Egypt, at the northern end were emerging nations with even greater resources. The Sinai Peninsula has often been described as the bridge between Asia and Africa at the world's most important intersection of trade-routes. It is, rather, a small barrier of desert. The bridge is the corridor which has become known as Palestine.

From the foundation of Jerusalem onwards the tribes of Israel were in very much the same position as the Jewish State of Israel from its foundation in 1948 until President Sadat of Egypt visited Jerusalem, and offered the first possibility of breaking the deadly crescent of enemies. David's kingdom, like present-day Israel, lay on a great highway. There were other enemies than Egypt to the south, and there were the Assyrians and Babylonians to the north. Desert tribes like the Moabites, Amalekites and Edomites sought a share in the more fertile land to the west of the Jordan, and the unprotected Mediterranean coast was wide open to invaders from the sea. In 928 BC the Assyrian King Sennacherib laid siege to it. In 587 BC Nebuchadnezzar, King of Babylon, captured and destroyed it, carrying virtually a whole people away into captivity.

When the Jews – more specifically the surviving tribe of Judah – returned forty-eight years later, they rebuilt the city and its Temple. They were determined to stay. Before, they had fought against Stone Age religions and the often perverse and brutal fertility-cults which emanated from them; now they would be confronted with more sophisticated religions spreading from Asia and with the bewitchingly attractive mystery cults of the Hêllenes. In 350 BC, it was the turn of the Persians to capture Jerusalem; then that of Alexander the Great eighteen years later. He brought more insidious enemies with him – the Grecian sense of beauty and the Grecian belief in life after death. Alexander's conquest of almost the whole civilized world left an evil legacy; for the next 150 years there was relentless Greek pressure on the Jews to modify their – as Greeks saw it – inflexible and constipated ethical and religious code.[6] Indeed, in 175 BC the Greek-oriented Antiochus Epiphanes set out to destroy the Jewish religion, robbing and vandalizing the Temple, banning Mosaic law, erecting heathen altars, defiling the holy places by offering pigs for sacrifice (the pig was judged unclean under Mosaic law and its flesh forbidden as food), and provoking the national uprising under the Maccabees.

Somehow the Jews survived in what had in their minds and hearts become, unforgettably and in perpetuity, their own city and the core of their being. But an even more ruthless enemy was about to arrive. The Assyrians and Egyptians had fought for control of an all-important trade-route, the Moabites and other desert tribes for land to cultivate, the Greeks as colonizers of the Mediterranean littoral and in order to assert values and beliefs which they regarded as the most civilized in the world. The yardstick of Roman policies was the expansion of imperial power, based on law, order and expertly imposed tyranny. This tyranny was, during the last three decades of the pre-Christian era, exercised indirectly through the satellite kingship of Herod the Great, who reconstructed the Temple and rebuilt the walled city. When he died, Roman rule became more direct and oppressive, under badly-chosen representatives of Caesar. Pilate, unlike the vacillating character depicted in the New Testament, was rigorous and brutal. Cumanus encouraged a Roman centurion to commit an act of indecency in the area of the Temple Mount and then massacred the protesting Jews. Florus was a thief, and by robbing the Temple in AD 66 provoked full-scale rebellion.

In this rebellion, which ended with the recapture, from the rebels, of Jerusalem by the Emperor Titus in AD 70, probably nearly one million Jews were killed, upwards of 300,000 of them by the tortures of crucifixion.[8] Roman bestiality was the product of a ruthlessness engendered by the philosophy of continuous expansion and the need to smash all spirit of resistance. The struggle against the might of Rome was epic, and actually enhanced the holy quality of Jerusalem in Jewish eyes. The Jews lived on in their wrecked capital city and worshipped their God on the Temple Mount. When the Emperor Hadrian sought to build a Roman fort on this holy site, the Bar Kochba rebellion broke out and was bloodily suppressed in AD 135. Jews were banned, on pain of death, from settling in Jerusalem, which was renamed Aelia Capitolina. Yet Jews continued to live as close to the city walls as they could and must often have entered Jerusalem – there is a record of a Rabbi Hanina Ben-Taradion preaching to his congregations 'in ravished Zion',[9] and by the third century a synagogue had been built on Mount Zion itself. By the fifth century Jewish persistence had paid off, and they were allowed – under Byzantine rule – officially to reside once again in Jerusalem.

At this stage, in spite of war, massacre and large-scale dispersion throughout the Roman Empire, the Jews probably still constituted a majority in what they never ceased to regard as their own land. The seventh century brought another unexpected and far-reaching change in their fortunes. By the beginning of that century Jerusalem had been for nearly 300 years under the rule of the Byzantine Eastern Roman Empire. Then in 614 the Persians conquered the city and gave the Jews a privileged position over its Christian inhabitants. The Jews were suspected of connivance with the Persian massacre of Christians, and were massacred in their turn when the Byzantines regained Jerusalem in 629. This, however, was only a brief turn of the tide; in 638 Jerusalem fell to the Arabian Caliph Omar and the followers of the Prophet Muhammad. They came, from the Jewish point of view, almost as friends, for the Byzantines had once again exiled the Jews from their holy city.

Now they were allowed back again. Their representatives petitioned for the return of 200 families. The Christian Patriarch opposed this and the Muslim conquerors struck a compromise; seventy families were allowed to return. They settled first close to the Western Wall, the only surviving portion of Herod's Temple, then in an area of the walled Old City between the still-existing Damascus and St Stephen's Gates. Next they bought land on the slopes of the Mount of Olives, with the aim of building a cemetery. What they could not immediately have foreseen was that religious rights were now to become a triangular struggle in Jerusalem. Since the beginning of the fourth century, when the Emperor Constantine and his mother Helena began building churches and other monuments, Jerusalem had become a primarily Christian city. Both the Empress Eudoxia and the Emperor Justinian added many more Christian buildings, while Christian schisms and heresies began to give the city a salient feature which has survived ever since – competing creeds and churches, of Ethiopians, Armenians, Copts, Nestorians, Syrian Jacobites and the Greek Orthodox congregation which became the most powerful of all. The cult of relics, tombs and other memorials of the dead took firm root. Money flowed in from Christian Europe; churches, monasteries and shrines sprang up, often in places connected with the life of Jesus, his disciples and other Christian saints. Judaism and Christianity had been rivals for centuries past; they were now joined by an Islam determined to make its own religious mark on Jerusalem and to stay there.

This was not at once apparent. Not only were the Jews allowed to settle in Jerusalem again, but it looked for a time as if they might re-establish their old religious supremacy there. They had piled stones on the Temple Mount, in readiness to rebuild the Temple, and they were temporarily given control of the Mount and allowed to celebrate the Feast of the Tabernacles there. But Muhammad had staked a religious as well as a physical claim to

Jerusalem through the legend passed down to his followers that he had ridden to the city on his celestial steed, Buraq, and had ascended thence to Heaven with the Archangel Gabriel. Jerusalem was given a deep Islamic significance by this event, almost certainly because of the Muslim faith's dependence on both Jewish and Christian legend and teaching and of its claim to be God's ultimate revelation to mankind (see Chapter 3). For this reason, Jerusalem had necessarily to become a Muslim holy city. Its claim took practical expression with the building by Abd al-Malik, between 691 and 697, of the Dome of the Rock on the Temple Mount, a monument which was turned into a mosque. His elder son, al-Walid, built the El Aqsa mosque close beside it.

It took the Muslim rulers fifty years to assert their religious claim in concrete form. Had it been otherwise, the history of the Middle East and indeed of the whole world would have been different. The Muslims already had two holy cities, Mecca and Medina. Unfortunately they were for a time in the hands of a rival while Omar was Caliph, and Jerusalem became virtually his capital. For a time, too, Muslims turned to Jerusalem to pray, although Mecca was soon substituted. Lacking a long religious tradition of their own, early Muslim rulers attached special importance to Jerusalem. Thus the writer, al-Muqaddesi: 'Mecca and Medina have their superiority by reason of the Kaabah and the Prophet, but on the Day of Judgement both cities will come to Jerusalem, and the excellencies of them all will be united!'[10] By the time the Dome of the Rock was built, it has to be remembered, the Muslims had conquered great areas of the civilized world. Ownership of Jerusalem was at least in some degree a matter of prestige.

In the triangular struggle for religious pre-eminence in Jerusalem the Muslims were not challenged for 400 years. Their holy book, the Koran, preaches religious tolerance, and Arab writers have invariably claimed that special tolerance was shown to the 'People of the Book', Jews and Christians, that tolerance had a practical value since it won more converts than the sword, and that all non-Muslims were asked to do in return was to obey the laws and pay their taxes.[11] Certainly, plenty of goodwill was shown but there were lapses too. A number of Christian churches in Jerusalem were sacked in 923; in 937 and 975 the Church of the Holy Sepulchre was damaged by Muslim mobs; and in the latter year the Orthodox Patriarch was burned alive as a Byzantine spy.[12] In 1009 the Caliph Hakim forbade pilgrimages and ordered the destruction of all churches and synagogues, save the Church of the Nativity in Bethlehem, although he was later to relent and amend his order.

Then in 1071 the Seljuk Turks captured Jerusalem and fighting in and around the city between them and the Egyptian Fatimids caused appalling devastation. The Seljuk conquest and the ensuing disorder was one of many reasons for the Crusades, which began with the wholesale slaughter of an estimated 10,000 Jews in the Rhineland in 1096 and led on to the sacking of Jerusalem in 1099, entailing the massacre of most of its Muslim inhabitants and almost all of its Jews, some of these burned alive in their synagogues. Crusader rule constituted one of the blackest periods of Jewish history in Jerusalem, yet there were still desperate efforts to maintain a presence there. In 1140 a Spanish-born Jewish poet, Judah Halevi, set out for Jerusalem via Cairo and was allegedly trampled to death by an Arab horseman when approaching the city walls. His example may have fired others, for when Benjamin of Tudela paid a visit in 1170, he found 'a dye-factory there, which the Jews rent yearly from the king, so that no man but the Jews shall do any dyeing work in Jeruslaem, and there are about 200 Jews living below the Tower of David at the limits of the city' – this in spite of the fact that a Crusader ordinance specifically banned Jewish and Moslem settlement in Jerusalem as 'profane'.[13]

Ordinances of this kind were bound to have a seriously adverse effect on the life of Jerusalem. Cardinal Henry of Albano, a legate of Pope Gregory VIII, depicted the capture of Jerusalem by the Crusaders as an act of redemption – the liberation of the Church of the Holy Sepulchre would lead to the recovery of the 'true' Jerusalem and to the salvation of the soul.[14] Christian bigotry even produced such theories as one proclaiming that the soil of the Holy Land had been 'polluted' by Muslim and Jewish presence, and that it had been 'bought' with Jesus' blood – surely an amazing and disgraceful misinterpretation of Christ's ministry. Under Crusader rule the population of Jerusalem dropped initially to about 3,000, an all-time low since the Romans razed the city to the ground. It had been as high as 200,000 before the destruction of Herod's Temple, had fallen to an average of about 80,000 under Byzantine rule and to about 30,000 after the Arab conquest. Its recovery was to be both slow and spasmodic after Saladin reconquered the city from the Crusaders in 1187.

A second consequence of Crusader rule was equally prejudicial to the city's future. The Greek Patriarchate had been unquestionably the leading Christian body in the city up to 1099. The Crusaders came from western Europe, and were to introduce three orders of knights. Two of them, the Templars and Knights of St John, were mainly French, and the Order of the Teutonic Knights was German. All of them were representatives of western Christianity, and the Latin Church established itself in Jerusalem with their help. It was to engage in incessant quarrels with its Greek rivals for the next eight centuries, weakening the Christian communities of Jerusalem and contributing to a European war in the Crimea. More immediately, the Latins showed their intolerance by renaming the Dome of the Rock and the El Aqsa Mosque the 'Templum Domini' (Temple of the Lord) and 'Templum Solomonis' (Temple of Solomon), by placing a large golden cross on the roof of the Dome of the Rock, and converting the Dome of the Chain into a Christian church.

Much has been made by some Jewish historians of the fact that, from the conquest of Jerusalem by the Seljuk Turks onwards, the city was never again under Arab rule. Strictly speaking, this is correct, but for a fleeting period of Arab Fatimid rule just before the First Crusade. The Seljuks were demonstrably not Arabs. Nor was Saladin; he was a Kurd, and the Kurds trace their descent from the Medes who shared in the making of the Persian Empire. From the middle of the thirteenth century until 1517, Jerusalem and the whole of Palestine were under the rule of the Mamelukes, directed from Cairo. From 1517 to 1917 they were a part of the Turkish Ottoman Empire. There followed only the British Mandate before Palestine was partitioned and the State of Israel came into being in one part of it. During the entire period Jerusalem never belonged to an Arab state and was never the capital even of a major province. Its importance – certainly in the eyes of the outside world – was purely religious. Its secular history, accordingly, was one of vicissitude, culminating in escalating isolation, atrophy and neglect. It would be conquered only twice more, before the most discreet conqueror of all, General Allenby, walked through its gates on foot in 1917 – by the Ottoman Turks, and by the Pasha of Egypt, Mehemet Ali, in 1831. When Napoleon invaded Palestine, via Egypt, in 1798, he ignored Jerusalem as being of no military significance. In every previous war it had been regarded as being of cardinal importance; it sat on the north–south main ridge through Palestine which was strategically more interesting than coastal roads which ran through marsh and sand-dune. But by

Napoleon's time, the coastal roads were more negotiable.

First, then, the Mameluke period. The Mamelukes founded several mausoleums, a religious court and centres of religious study, a library and other public buildings. They did much to embellish the Muslim buildings of the Temple Mount. The emphasis of Mameluke rule was to make Jerusalem a centre of religious study. This was understandable; as the Mamelukes saw it, Jerusalem and all Palestine was an appendage of Muslim rule which was centred on Cairo. Jerusalem was an outpost.

Jerusalem's Christian and Jewish communities suffered as a result, mainly because local governors were virtually independent and mostly inefficient, and there was no exercise of central authority. Jerusalem was a mere dependency of the Pashalik of Damascus, on a par with Nablus, Sidon, Gaza and Beirut.[15] Jerusalem was already a backwater; there is no shred of historical evidence to suggest anything to the contrary.

Yet the Mamelukes showed a certain, undefined liberality. In 1267 Rabbi ben Nahman, better known as Nachmanides, wrote to his family in Spain that there seemed to be only 2,000 inhabitants left in Jerusalem, including 1,700 Muslims, 300 Christians and exactly two Jews, brothers who were 'dyers by trade'. Nachmanides set out to revive the Jewish community of Jerusalem, and he achieved this after first founding a synagogue. He was of a practical turn of mind where concentrating Jewish population was concerned; his target was the Mount Zion area, taking in a corner of the Old City. Around 1505 the Mamelukes allowed Obadiah de Bertinoro from Italy to found a rabbinical college in Jerusalem. He was an inspiring leader and helped to encourage an influx of Spanish and Portuguese Jews. There are no exact figures of the numbers of Jews in Jerusalem at this time; two estimates were of about 500 in 1483 and of 200 families in 1495.

Certainly, the conquest of Palestine by the Ottoman Turks brought a further revival and expansion of the Jewish community. There were four reasons for this. In the first place, the Ottoman Empire was still in its first great era of expansion. Constantinople had fallen to the Turks in 1453, Serbia already in 1389 and Southern Greece by 1460, then the Crimea, the Caucasus, Albania and Wallachia, the southern province of what is today Romania. Within another twenty-five years the Turks had captured Hungary, Bosnia, Moldavia and Bessarabia, and stood on the slopes of the Northern Carpathians and at the gates of Vienna. This was a vigorous, innovative period of Turkish history and among the earliest acts of the ruler, Suleiman the Magnificent, were the rebuilding of the walls and gates of Jerusalem, the repairing of its roads and the renovation of its water supply.

Then there was an immediate expansion of trade. The Turks, like the Mamelukes, ruled Palestine through local governors. Those of the Mamelukes degenerated; they were lazy, corrupt and inefficient and their authority declined to such an extent that one finds the Emir of Jerusalem being chased into his palace and besieged there by Bedouin Arabs in 1480, while the city that he was meant to protect was comprehensively looted by these desert marauders. Turkish governors, during this period of history, were able and busy. Expanding trade brought closer contact with Western Europe, and in 1538 a treaty was signed with Francis I of France which concentrated entirely on trade – the only clause with any religious connotation provided merely for the right of Christian traders to practise their own religion.[16] Finally, the influx of Jews from Mediterranean countries continued, especially from Spain, which had expelled its entire Jewish population in 1492. Spanish 'Sephardi' Jews moved to North African cities and to Salonika, Constantinople and Adrianople. When, in the late sixteenth century, the Sultan Bayezid II invited Jews to settle in Palestine, they began to arrive from all the corners of the Mediterranean. Jews came from Western European countries, too, and in 1621 Rabbi Isaiah Halevy reported that there were 500 Sephardi families in Jerusalem, and a growing number of 'Ashkenazi' European Jews.

The Sephardi Jews built the imposing complex of the four synagogues grouped on the traditional site of the Academy of Rabbi Yohanan Ben-Zakkai, but the decline of the Ottoman Empire had inevitable repercussions on Palestine. Enjoying no sort of autonomy and split among different 'sanjaks' for administrative purposes, Palestine relapsed into a political and economic backwater. The Jews of Jerusalem suffered from heavy taxation: poll-taxes, gift-taxes, a tax on land, a watch-and-ward tax and a government-aid tax.[17] There was a measure of discrimination; as non-Muslims, Jews were 'dhimmis', entitled to protection but with the status of second-class citizens. They had to wear distinguishing dress – the first such prescribed article of wear was a yellow turban. Nor could they claim legal redress. There were occasional acts of violence caused by religious fanaticism; thus the Hurva synagogue in the Jewish Quarter of the Old City was burned down in 1721. (It was rebuilt only in 1837.) Otherwise, Jerusalem was a relatively safe place in which to live, but this did not apply to its immediate hinterland, where travellers were in perpetual danger.

In spite of periodic influxes of Jewish immigrants, Jerusalem's decline, and that of its Jewish community, continued steadily until almost the middle of the nineteenth century. As one historian put it: 'It was in the early part of the nineteenth century that the cumulative effect of centuries of neglect and destruction reached its culmination.'[18] The total population of Jerusalem fell to around 6,000, a third of it Jewish. For many of the Jews who made their homes in Jerusalem came there to pray and to die there and there was no natural increase of population. At least they obstinately refused to leave; according to one Jewish historian: 'There were periods of devastation and ruin in Jerusalem, as occurred in Safed; yet the Jewish population withstood the onslaught and settlement was never abandoned, even for a short period, as in Tiberias, or even for a few years, as in Safed.'[19] Jerusalem was regarded as a place of refuge by Palestinian Jews, and when there was a dangerous epidemic in Safed in 1812 virtually its whole population fled to Jerusalem.

By 1827 there were only 1,000 to 1,200 Jews in Jerusalem, and Jewish survival there must have seemed in doubt for the first time under Ottoman rule. Many of them lived under miserable conditions. The French writer Chateaubriand described them as 'covered with rags, seated in the dust of Zion, seeking the vermin which devoured them while keeping their eyes fixed on the Temple'.[20] Another traveller, Dr John Kitto, found that 'a large number of houses in Jerusalem are in a dilapidated and ruinous state. Nobody seems to make repairs so long as his dwelling does not absolutely refuse him shelter and safety. If one room tumbles about his ears, he removes into another, and permits rubbish and vermin to accumulate as they will in the deserted halls.'[21] Another facet of Jewish existence was described in these terms:

> What a painful change has passed over the circumstances and condition of the poor Jew that in his own city, and close by where his temple stood, he has to suffer oppression and persecution. In Jerusalem his case is a very hard one, for if he should have a little of this world's goods in his possession, he is oppressed and robbed by the Turks in a most unmerciful manner; in short, for him there is neither law nor justice.[22]

Indeed, as another writer makes plain, Turkish failure rubbed off most painfully on the 'dhimmi', the second-class citizen. The word 'Jew' had become the lowest term of abuse in Arabic, the Arabic form of the word 'Ashkenazi' became synonymous with 'coward', while Jews in general were referred to as 'the children of death'.[23] In 1816 the Jewish population was limited to 2,000, on pain of death to those late-comers constituting the surplus. Yet a seventy-six-year-old Jew who arrived at the time could write: 'I am now seventy-six years old and yet I have lived only two days. I have begun to live from the moment that I set foot upon the holy ground – and that was two days back.'[24] *

In fact – for this statement was made in the 1840s – a significant moment in Jerusalem's history had already been passed. In 1838 the British Government, with the permission of Egypt – Palestine was under Egyptian rule from 1831 to 1840 – appointed a Consul to Jerusalem. The Ottoman regime which regained control of Palestine in 1840 was in reforming mood; it relaxed restrictions on non-Muslim subjects and consolidated the status of foreign consulates. These consulates provided advice, help and even protection to the nationals of their countries who settled in Palestine, including Jews. The consulates, too, brought foreign investment in their train; this contributed to the development of communications. During the middle of the nineteenth century Jerusalem became linked with the coast by new roads and a railway, and Lloyds steamers began to ply between European ports and Palestine. Jerusalem began to emerge from the near-isolation of centuries.

The effect on Jewish immigration was instantaneous. One observer wrote: 'The influx of Jews has been very considerable of late. A fortnight since, 150 arrived here from Algiers. There is now a large number of Jews here from the coast of Africa, who are about to form themselves into a separate congregation.'[25] A prominent and philanthropic British Jew, Sir Moses Montefiore, after making the first of many visits there in 1827, was injecting capital into Jerusalem for the building of homes and workshops.

---

* In *The Modern Traveller* (London, 1830) James Conder recounts the experiences in Palestine of the French writer, François Auguste, Vicomte de Chateaubriand. He found Jerusalem 'a labyrinth', gloomy and 'fraught with infection', with 'a few paltry shops which expose nothing but wretchedness to view', a place of unpaved streets, dust and loose stones. The two good features of Jerusalem were Christian monks and Jews, who accepted degradation and insult, 'living as slaves and strangers in their own country', but surviving with immense determination, worshipping their God and increasing their learning and that of their children.

A commercial future, in addition to spiritual satisfaction, became possible for the new immigrants, as western-financed hostels, shops and hotels opened. Jerusalem became a steadily increasing tourist attraction. By 1848 the population of the city had risen to 15,000, with at least 5,000 Jews, 6,000 Muslims and 4,000 Christians, most of them Arabs. Indeed, the *Encyclopaedia Britannica* of 1853 assessed the Jewish population of Jerusalem in 1844 at 7,120, making them the biggest single religious group in the city. The same publication put the Jewish population at 10,600 in 1872, compared to 5,300 Christians and 5,000 Muslims, giving for the first time for perhaps 1,400 years an overall Jewish majority.

There is a widely held view that 'the' Jews 'left' their native country, en masse, when the Romans captured Jerusalem, and only 'returned' after the First World War, when Zionism – in effect, Jewish irredentist nationalism, as many Arabs saw it – had been endorsed by a British government. Zionist propaganda, denounced by enemies of the idea of a Jewish state, made the cardinal and elementary mistake of lending support to this view, by writing of 'the Return' as if it were a sudden and miraculous event which made the creation of a Jewish state possible. In reality, the only miracle was the achievement of the Jewish people in maintaining, against all the odds, a continuous presence in what they believed to be their own land – always filtering back whenever they could. Up to the fourth century they managed to maintain a majority there. Christian oppression drastically diminished their presence, but thereafter they returned, singly or in batches, when opportunity offered. Zionism, therefore, was not irredentist; it gave fuller expression to a sense of identity and of association with the Jewish homeland which had never been lost.

In the 1870s the Zionist idea, preached by men like Moses Hess in his book *Rome and Jerusalem*, published in 1862, took practical shape in the 'Lovers of Zion' movement ('Hovevei Zion'). Its members, living in the Jewish 'Pale of Settlement' in western and southern Russia, organized small groups of pioneers, who set out for Palestine determined to work the soil with their own hands, and build up a community which belonged to the fullest possible extent in and on the land. As one early settler put it, 'We wanted to build Israel with our own hands. We believed that the community which we would help to create would be 80 per cent farmers. Our whole philosophy was contained in the phrase "back to the soil".'[26] The pioneers owed a big debt to Baron

Edmond de Rothschild, who in the 1880s took up the mantle of Sir Moses Montefiore, rescued struggling Jewish settlements, invested money in them and others of his own creation, and introduced more systematic and profitable methods of farming. They owed much, too, to the propagation of the Zionist idea by Theodor Herzl, the driving force behind the holding of the First Zionist Congress at Basle in 1897. There, Herzl called for the purchase of land in Palestine, the granting of a Jewish loan to the Ottoman Sultan in return for his patronage, discreet planning of Jewish immigration, and Jewish development of the soil of Palestine.

Herzl died in 1904, but his work was carried on by Chaim Weizmann, the first Jewish leader to pin his hopes firmly on Britain as the country which could make the creation of a 'Jewish home' in Palestine possible. Weizmann felt sure that the Ottoman Empire was ripe for dissolution. Britain was established in Egypt and the Sudan, in Aden and on the Persian Gulf, and was the obvious power to move into a position of dominance in the Middle East. Weizmann also believed in British institutions and the British way of life and he made good and influential friends in Britain. His key meetings with the British Foreign Secretary, Mr Arthur Balfour, occurred during the First World War, although he had first met him as early as 1906. Later Weizmann would say that:

> I went to Balfour alone; but behind me there stood eighty generations of Jews. The forces accumulated during thousands of years spoke through me, not money, but the voices of our sages, fighters and heroes who rest in the holy soil of Eretz Israel. Eminent statesmen listened to these voices. It was the voice of history that spoke through my mouth.[27]

The upshot of these meetings was the Balfour Declaration of 2 November 1917. It promised British help in creating a 'national home for the Jewish people' in Palestine, subject to the reservation that 'nothing shall be done which may prejudice the civil and religious rights of existing non-Jewish communities'.

This is to jump ahead of the story of the consolidation of Jerusalem as a predominantly Jewish city. Back in 1843 Dr John Kitto had remarked that 'although we are much in the habit of regarding Jerusalem as a Moslem city, the Moslems do not actually constitute more than one-third of the entire population'.[28] Fifty years after he wrote this, there were over

28,000 Jews in a total population of 45,000. In 1905 there were 40,000 Jews, compared to 13,000 Christians and only 7,000 Muslims, and at the outbreak of the First World War the Jewish population was over 48,000, out of a total of 75,000. The development of Jerusalem, as a religious centre attracting tourism and trade, was the one bright spot in the contemporary history of Palestine, still no more than a backward and neglected province of the Ottoman Empire and with a total population not much more than three times that of its one great city. The Jewish contribution was beyond doubt. One commentator wrote at the time:

> If numerical superiority be a criterion of possession, and achievement a measure of power; if the higher civilization be that of the more effective philanthropy, and true part and lot in the soil be that of him who restores it to cultivation; then, mysterious as may seem to us the workings of God's providence, the deep tragedy of their existence, the dark problem of their destiny, is approaching solution, and Jerusalem is for the Jews.[29]

The shape and general configuration of Jerusalem had changed radically by 1914. Up to 1850 virtually the whole population was contained within the walls of the Old City. In the next thirty years building outside the walls was a patchwork affair of small Jewish, Christian and Muslim settlements, dotted across the rocky landscape mainly to the north-west and south-west. From 1880 onwards the main building development was to the west of the Old City in a broad belt running along the Jaffa Road and principally to the north of it. The sector of this belt adjoining the Old City was Arab, the more distant and larger sector Jewish. Other, much smaller Arab districts were beginning to take shape to the north and south of the Old City; here, smaller Jewish pockets of settlement intermingled with them.

The war cut short all immediate further development. The population fell by 25,000 or one-third, that of the Jewish majority by nearly 50 per cent. The Jewish community suffered particularly because of its low birth rate, the end of all immigration, the deportation of many thousands for forced labour elsewhere in the Ottoman Empire, and the movement of others seeking succour in the direction of the advancing British armies. There were additional causes. In an official army report of 4 May 1918, Major William Ormsby-Gore wrote that:

> The present condition of the Jewish population of Jerusalem is bad. They now number about 25,000, of whom about 20,000 are in need and receipt of some form of help. Sixty per cent are infected with malaria, a large number are weakened by extreme poverty, hunger and the after-effects of typhus. The mortality of all ages of the Jewish Community in Jerusalem during the year 1917 was 2,084. Typhus fever was responsible for this tremendous loss of life.

This depleted community faced an uncertain future. But there were certain factors in its favour. First there was the pledge implicit in the admittedly somewhat obscure Balfour Declaration. At least it was evidence of British goodwill, even if this goodwill began to wear thin even before the three years of British military government ended and the British Mandate entered into force in 1922. The question whether Britain 'betrayed' the Arabs by pledging help to create a Jewish 'national home' will probably never be finally settled. Field-Marshal Lord Kitchener had given an undertaking during the war to the Sherif Hussein of Mecca that there 'would be no intervention in Arabia'. As one historian has pointed out, this could have meant almost anything, for no Arab nation existed at the time and Arabia was a sub-continent without defined boundaries.[30] Of much greater potential importance was the detailed correspondence which took place between July 1915 and January 1916 between Sir Henry McMahon, the British High Commissioner in Egypt, and Sherif Hussein. In answer to Hussein's request for a definition of the frontiers of a future Arab state, McMahon expressly excluded from it 'the districts of Mersina and Alexandretta and portions of Syria lying to the west of the districts of Damascus. Homs, Hama and Aleppo cannot be said to be purely Arab and should be excluded ...' Palestine, and Jerusalem, were not mentioned, and Arab spokesmen have persistently maintained that this meant they should have become part of the Arab state.

Three points may be relevant when considering this claim. In the first place, if the yardstick for inclusion in an Arab state was that a place was 'purely Arab', Jerusalem and many other places in Palestine would inevitably have been excluded, for they were obviously far less Arab than Homs, Hama and Aleppo. In the second place, a British High Commissioner in Cairo could not possibly have pledged great areas of the Middle East to a hereditary ruler in Mecca in the middle of a world war, or negotiated a peace settlement unilaterally when other allied countries would be involved. Finally, McMahon himself, in a letter to the London *Times* of 23 July 1937, would say that Palestine was excluded from any pledge that he gave. In a statement to the House of Commons on 11 July 1922, Winston Churchill, then Colonial Secretary, said that not only was Palestine excluded from all pledges but that the Emir Feisal, designated to be the first head of an Arab state created by Britain, had most explicitly accepted his explanation of this.

Still, British promises undeniably caused confusion and bitterness. This was particularly true of the Balfour Declaration, although Sherif Hussein evidently accepted an undertaking given in January 1918 by Commander D. C. Hogarth of the British 'Arab Bureau' in Cairo, that the Declaration did not conflict with earlier promises to the Arabs.[31] Feisal, Hussein's third son, who took a far greater part in peace negotiations than his father, appeared mollified. At the Paris Peace Conference in February 1919 he declared that: 'The Jews are very close to the Arabs in blood, and there is no conflict in character between the two races. In principle, we are absolutely at one.' But the Palestinian Arabs have ever since complained, understandably, that Hussein and Feisal were not entitled to make decisions for them or accept British explanations. The Balfour Declaration concerned them, and them alone of the members of the Arab world. Nor have they ever accepted such a view as that of the historian James Parkes, who later wrote:

> The failure [of the Mandate] has *not* been due to the criminal character of the basic enterprise. The British were not 'giving away' a country which did not belong to them, nor forcing upon its 'owners' an alien immigration of people who had no right to be there. Even apart from the Jewish question, Palestine for nearly two thousand years had not 'belonged' exclusively to those who dwell in it. Christians have rights in it which successive Muslim rulers have recognized, and Muslims of other countries have rights in it which the lawlessness of local sheikhs and fellaheen do not override. But in addition Jews have rights in it, which Muslim rulers have likewise recognized, and which they have never ceased to exercise up to the shrinking limits of the country's absorptive capacity. The Balfour Declaration 'gave' them nothing. It recognized rights which already existed.[32]

However balanced such a view may be, Arab bitterness grew

like a forest fire. It was fanned less by Jewish statement or action than by attitudes in the outside world. Thus President Woodrow Wilson received the following recommendation from his own American delegation at the Paris Peace Conference: 'It is right that Palestine should become a Jewish state, if the Jews, being given the full opportunity, make it such. It was the cradle and the home of their vital race ...'[33] And in the House of Commons Winston Churchill, on 1 July 1922, reaffirmed the promises made in the Balfour Declaration, and supported 'the further development of the existing Jewish community, with the assistance of Jews in other parts of the world, in order that it may become a centre in which the Jewish people as a whole may take interest and pride'. The Jewish people 'should know that it is in Palestine as of right and not on sufferance'. A year earlier, in the Imperial War Cabinet, he had gone further than this in an exchange of question and answer:[34]

Mr Meighen: 'How do you define our responsibilities in relations to Palestine under Mr Balfour's pledge?'

Mr Churchill: 'To do our best to make an honest effort to give the Jews a chance to make a National Home there for themselves.'

Mr Meighen: 'And to give them control of the Government?'

Mr Churchill: 'If, in the course of many years, they become a majority in the country, they would naturally take it over.'

Here was the real fear for the Palestinian Arabs, that they might be 'taken over' by the more active, efficient Jewish community. Churchill, of course, visualized a state of peace, prosperity accruing from sound British administration, and an influx of population which might offer the Jews the chance of founding a state of their own. Lloyd George implicitly endorsed his views, with 'The notion that Jewish immigration would have to be artificially restricted in order to ensure that the Jews should be a permanent minority never entered into the heads of anyone engaged in framing the policy.'[35] Both men were instinctively, perhaps inexplicably, inspired by the Zionist dream, and Churchill had boldly gone into print: 'If, as may well happen, there should be created in our own lifetime by the banks of the Jordan a Jewish State under the protection of the British Crown, which may comprise three or four millions of Jews, an event will have occurred in the history of the world which would from every point of view be beneficial.'[36] *

* Churchill made a great many other statements of his belief in Zionism. In March 1921 he told Arab petitioners, during his visit to Palestine, 'You have

Churchill was both idealist and pragmatist. In March 1921 he sanctioned the detachment of all areas east of the Jordan and the creation of 'Transjordan' under the Emir, Abdallah, another son of Sherif Hussein. These areas had been explicitly assigned to the Palestine Mandate on 23 December 1920.[37] What was no more than a provisional arrangement was made permanent on 25 May 1923, but a formal agreement was signed only on 20 February 1928. Even so, it left Transjordan within the Mandatory area. Long before Churchill's action, the Syrian Congress declared in July 1919 that Palestine was 'the southern part of Syria'.[38] The Palestine Arabs were left more isolated than ever; by the time that the British Mandate entered into full force, it must have seemed to them that no one was ready to help them.

The Palestinian Arabs had no more than a semi-fledged sense of political identity at this stage in their long history of total subjugation. The Jewish community was very differently placed. The 'return to the land' had produced the unique 'kibbutz' experience, of communal farming and living based on the principle of total co-operation. These kibbutz settlements which began to burgeon from just before the First World War were tightly-controlled enclaves of productive Jewish endeavour. They spent much of their time reclaiming barren soil, and they put it to the best use. The Jewish community could claim other successes. In 1907 it had created the 'Hashomer' watchmen's organization, purely for local self-defence against Bedouin and other raiders. This would in time develop into the 'Haganah', a well-trained communal militia which would, in turn, form a base for Israel's armed forces. The Jewish National Fund, acting through the 'Keren Hayesod' Foundation Fund, was the operative body in sole charge of land purchase in Palestine, where it had its own immigration office and agricultural settlement department. In 1920 the community formed its own trade union structure, the 'Histadrut' and a year later the

asked me to repudiate the Balfour Declaration and to veto immigration of Jews into Palestine. It is not in my power to do so, nor, if it were in my power, would it be my wish.' And on the same visit he told a Jewish audience at the Hebrew University: 'We owe to the Jews a system of ethics which even if it were entirely separated from the supernatural would be the most precious possession of mankind – worth the fruits of all other wisdom and learning together.'

Of economic development carried out in Palestine by the Jews, Churchill told the House of Commons on 4 July 1922: 'I am told that the Arabs would have done it themselves. Who is going to believe that? Left to themselves, the Arabs of Palestine would not in a thousand years have taken effective steps towards the irrigation and electrification of Palestine.'

Twelfth Zionist Congress in Carlsbad set up a thirteen-man executive for Palestine which became the Jewish Agency, representing the social, cultural, political and economic interests of the Jewish community in Palestine. Meanwhile the foundation-stone of the Hebrew University had been laid. With effective help from abroad, the Jewish community, soon to launch its own political parties, was creating the fabric of a state. One acute observer, Norman Bentwich, had found little of a Jewish-state idea during pre-1914 visits,[39] but under British administration, all things seemed possible: 'Before 1914 you wondered how anything ever got done. After 1919 you expected the most grandiose plans to be carried out in a night and a day.'

This was precisely what the Palestinian Arabs feared; the pace of both Jewish immigration and communal development was alarming. Between 1922 and 1944 the Jewish population of Jerusalem almost trebled, from 33,000 to 92,000. The Arab population barely doubled, from 28,000 to 59,000. The most rapid growth came after 1930 and in the Second World War the city was not, as in the First, depopulated – it became a British military and communications centre of considerable importance. There has been a tendency among some Arab writers to claim that the growth of the Jewish population of Jerusalem was some kind of dark plot, hatched with British collaboration. In fact the Arab population of Jerusalem increased by 37 per cent between 1922 and 1931, while in purely Arab towns like Nablus and Gaza it was up by only 7 per cent, and in Gaza actually decreased by 2 per cent.[40] The British had turned Jerusalem into a major administrative centre; this, in turn, stimulated trade and industry. A growth of population inevitably followed.

Arab objections to the increasing Jewish presence in Jerusalem were founded on a number of arguments. One was that the Jews had no 'historic right' whatever to be in the country, because 'Palestine is the homeland of the Palestinians who, as the descendants of the Philistines, Canaanites and other tribes, inhabited the country from the dawn of history until 1948.'[41] The same writer argued obliquely in favour of the maintenance of the Jewish status as subjects of the Arabs, on the grounds that they 'have lived in peace and harmony with the Arabs throughout centuries and the persecutions which the Jews had suffered during their history were not committed by the Arabs'. Both arguments were fallacious. Even an isolated island like Britain has been conquered by Celtic tribes, Romans, Angles,

Saxons, Jutes, Danes, Norsemen and Normans. Palestine was a thronged corridor of land between centres of population and power, and movement through this corridor of peoples who conquered and settled there was incessant. As for the matter of persecution of the Jews, all that can be said is that the Arab record was conspicuously better than that of Christian Europe, but that there is a long list of fully-documented Arab persecutions too.

Jerusalem was bound to become a flash-point for Arab unrest. In 1920 communal riots which were certainly started by the Arabs resulted in the deaths of five Jews and much destruction of property. In 1928 trouble began over Jewish worship at the Western Wall, the only surviving part of Herod's Temple. Because they segregated women from men in prayer, the Jews set up a screen in the narrow cul-de-sac running along the short, exposed section of the Wall. This was inadvertently pointed out to Arab religious officials by the British District Commissioner, and at Arab request the British removed the screen.[42] The Arabs, under the instructions of their highly combative Grand Mufti, Haj Amin el-Husseini, thereupon turned the cul-de-sac into a thoroughfare by knocking down a wall, and organized regular and noisy calls to Muslim prayer from a nearby roof-top. They also published faked photographs showing the Jewish flag, with the Star of David, flying from the top of the Dome of the Rock. The British authorities unwisely endorsed the conversion of the cul-de-sac into a thoroughfare. By so doing they turned it from a place of prayer into a hive of contention and potential violence.

In the following year a Jewish boy was stabbed to death after kicking a football into an Arab garden and trying to retrieve it. On 22 and 23 August 1929, Arab mobs attacked Jewish worshippers and passers-by. Six Jews were killed; the troubles spread to places outside Jerusalem too, producing a Jewish death-toll of 133, with another 339 wounded. All of them were the victims of Arab rioters, whereas 110 Arabs were killed in battles with the British police and only six in an isolated Jewish counter-attack. Nearly 4,000 Jews had to leave their homes. The next bout of rioting took place from 1936 to 1938. The Jewish community lost twenty-seven dead; hundreds were injured and there was massive damage to property. Typical of Arab incitement to violence was this leaflet: 'O Arab! Remember that the Jew is your strongest enemy and the enemy of your ancestors since olden times. Do not be misled by his tricks, for it is he who tortured Christ and poisoned Muhammad. It is he who now endeavours to slaughter you as he did yesterday.'[43]

The British, as has happened so often in their colonial history, were left in the uncomfortable position of pig-in-the-middle. It was hardly surprising that, after futile efforts to secure co-operation between Arabs and Jews, they turned their minds to the possibility of partitioning Palestine. In July 1937 the commission led by Earl Peel reported in favour of a plan which would have created a small Jewish state in Galilee and a part of the coastal plain, while more than three-quarters of Palestine would be linked with Transjordan in a sovereign Arab state. Jerusalem would have been the centre of a permanent British Mandatory zone, including Bethlehem and a narrow corridor to the sea at Jaffa. The Peel Plan was shelved, and in 1938 the Woodhead Commission put forward three sets of alternative proposals, tempered by a general recommendation against partition on the grounds that the two proposed states would not be viable. Jerusalem, again, would have been the centre of a separate enclave, somewhat bigger this time and with room for an airfield as well as a corridor to the Mediterranean.

Since they were inconclusive, the Woodhead Commission's proposals too were shelved. In 1938 the Jewish Agency came up with plans of its own, this time relating to Jerusalem only. The thought behind it was that, if a compromise could be reached over Jerusalem, an equitable plan could be devised for partitioning Palestine. Under the Jewish Agency plans, the Jewish suburbs of Talpiot, Arnona, Mekor Hayim and Ramat Rahel would be surrendered, as would – very surprisingly – the Jewish Quarter of the Old City. Jewish Jerusalem would, however, have included a narrow corridor linking West Jerusalem with Mount Scopus and the buildings of the Hebrew University.

This proposal was never discussed with the Arabs or the British. It was overtaken by the British White Paper of May 1939 which limited Jewish immigration into Palestine during the next five years to 75,000, and the Jewish portion of Palestine's total population to one-third. The White Paper envisaged the creation of an independent, unified Palestinian state within the next ten years, with guarantees of security and free access for the Holy Places of Jerusalem. The Permanent Mandate's Commission reported to the League of Nations that the White Paper was not in accordance with the terms of the British Mandate – the main objection was to abandonment of Christian control of their own Holy Places. No sympathy was spared for the Jews of Germany, Austria and Czechoslovakia, suffering under brutal Nazi persecution and vainly seeking a safe-haven. A lone voice in Britain was Winston Churchill's; he told Parliament on 23 May that the Balfour Declaration had been abandoned and the Jews betrayed.

The Jewish community in Palestine was appalled by the White Paper, yet sensibly decided to co-operate to the full in the war against Nazi Germany which broke out three months later. The war, inevitably, brought an end to political planning for the time being and the history of its six years' duration has, with one exception, no part in this book. The exception was provided by the struggle over the Mayoralty in 1944. It presaged the far grimmer struggle which was to come as soon as the war was over.

In 1944 the population of Jerusalem was nearly 61 per cent Jewish, 21 per cent Muslim and 18 per cent Christian. But, under the Mandate, there had always been a Muslim Mayor, at the head of a Municipal Council of six Arabs and six Jews. In 1944 the Arab Mayor, Mustafa Bey al-Khalidi, died; not unreasonably, the Jewish leaders suggested that the new Mayor should be more representative of the majority of the city's inhabitants – should, in fact, be a Jew. The suggestion was greeted with grave consternation by the Arabs. The British High Commissioner, aware of democratic processes in his own country, was still unable to swallow this proposed breach of tradition, however short-lived. He offered a compromise; the dead Mayor's place on the Municipal Council would be filled by another Muslim, while two British representatives would be added to it. Two pigs-in-the-middle, instead of one! The British, in this last, lean phase of colonialism, were apparently unable to learn. The High Commissioner proposed, in addition, that there should be an annual rotation of Mayors – Muslim, Christian and Jewish, in that order.

The Jewish leaders accepted, with the provision that the Mayoralty should last two years and that the first Mayor, under the new system, should be Jewish. As so often in the history of the British Mandate, the Arabs refused all idea of compromise, and in March called a general strike and boycotted their own Municipal Council. The British answer was to appoint a six-man, British commission to carry on the city's administration – from July 1945 until the end of the Mandate.

In the meantime the Chief Justice in the Mandatory administration, Sir William Fitzgerald, was asked to conduct an independent inquiry into the future administrative configuration of Jerusalem. His report was published on 28 August 1945. It was short, and to the point. Sir William reluctantly accepted that Arab–Jewish co-operation in the municipal field could not longer be expected. Jerusalem was, however, 'indivisible', and so 'over that Jerusalem I propose to spread a cloak to cover all contending parties'. Jerusalem, Sir William went on, should become 'an administrative county, under the general control of an administrative council on the analogy of the London County Council', entailing the creation of Arab and Jewish boroughs. In case it might be thought that this was the brain-child of an insular Briton, it should be mentioned that Sir William was an Irishman, from County Limerick.

The Fitzgerald Plan delineated borough boundaries with total impartiality. It foresaw only the two boroughs, but with each divided into six wards. Each of the two boroughs would send four representatives to the Administrative Council, where they would be joined by two members nominated by the British High Commissioner. The Administrative Council would exercise the minimum functional control over the two boroughs, which would be virtually self-governing, but it would have special powers and responsibilities with regard to all Holy Places, and it would look after the walled Old City, which was excluded from the borough system.

The Fitzgerald Plan had some admirable features. The borough system removed Jerusalem from the battlefield of Arab and Jewish nationalism. Borough boundaries were correctly drawn, as contemporary maps showing Jewish and Arab settlement demonstrate. Mount Scopus and the Hebrew University were left out of the reckoning, as they fell outside the boundaries of the 'administrative county'. But Sir William would doubtless have found a felicitous solution for this Jewish enclave too. The best feature of his plan was its simplicity. The only flaw was extraneous; the plan presupposed that Britain would continue to supervise it. This basic assumption was already in doubt, and the plan – like so many others – was shelved. But the concept may not be dead; it had a relevance, even in 1980, thirty-five years later.[44]

All British planning was already prejudiced by the fact that the post-war British Labour Government had literally no idea what it could do, or even wanted to do with Palestine. Back in 1931 the Labour Party leader, Ramsay MacDonald, had written to Chaim Weizmann that 'The obligation to facilitate Jewish immigration and to encourage close settlement by Jews on the land remains a positive obligation of the Mandate, and it can be fulfilled without prejudice to the rights and position of other sections of the population of Palestine.'[45] This typically and urbanely optimistic assessment had not been fulfilled. British policy and administration were already moving into their chaotic death-throes. The British colonial era was not quite over. But where colonial rule survived, it was because Britain still had a role to play as protector and friend. In Palestine, both Jews and Arabs were heartily sick of British rule: the Jews because they felt it impeded the creation of a state of their own in the land that they had always regarded as their own, and the Arabs because they mistakenly believed that the British presence was the only obstacle to their now ingrained desire to thrust the Jews out of their country, and into the sea.

Because of the abject futility of British policy in the last three years of the Mandate, its consequences need not be described in detail. In April 1946 an Anglo-American Committee began examining the situation and advised retention of the Mandate by Britain until a United Nations trusteeship could be devised. It asked for 100,000 Jewish immigrants to be admitted – a modest request in view of the fact that all details were now known of Hitler's mass-murder of six million Jews, and that hundreds of thousands of homeless Jewish survivors were sitting in Europe waiting for their salvation. The Prime Minister, Clement Attlee, demurred; he appointed yet another 'expert' commission, led by one of his own Ministers, Herbert Morrison, and Henry Grady of the United States. It proposed partition, with the southern Negev desert as well as the Jerusalem area to remain British-administered. The United States President, Harry Truman, rejected the plan. This was in July, and in September 1946 Britain and the states of the newly created Arab League met in London, where the Arabs insisted on the creation of a unified Palestinian state in which the Jews would have one-third of the parliamentary seats, with a ban on further Jewish immigration.

Britain's Foreign Secretary, Ernest Bevin, was warm-hearted, short-tempered and unamenable to argument. He deeply resented American pressure for the acceptance of Jewish refugees into an area in which the United States had no responsibility. He was displeased by American acceptance of the Jewish Agency plan for radical partition in October 1946. He was irritated by having the advice of experts, like Oxford's Professor Reginald Coupland, quoted at him. Coupland, the most active member of the Peel Commission, poured scorn on the 'unitary illusion – the illusion that two peoples with no purposes in common could be forced by institutional compulsion to form a single statehood'.[46] From November 1946 until September 1947, much influenced by the argument of the Imperial General Staff that Palestine should be held as a British military base against the impending Soviet menace, Bevin made efforts, sometimes vigorous but mainly spasmodic, to salvage something of the Mandatory regime and system. He gave up only when the findings of the UN Special Committee, formed in June, were about to be announced. Predictably, they recommended the partition of Palestine, with a special international regime for Jerusalem, and guaranteed freedom of access, visit and transit for all Holy Places, without distinction as to creed or nationality. With very minor modifications, their report was approved by the General Assembly of the United Nations in the historic vote of 29 November, by 33 to 10, with 10 abstentions.

Bevin had much more to compete with than conflicting opinions. During the last years of the British Mandate there was a state of incipient civil war in Palestine. Jewish efforts were directed towards securing the entry into the country of emigrants from Europe who had survived the Nazi concentration camps. It was unthinkable to Jews in Israel, and outside it, that these people should be left marooned in central Europe, with the reek of the charnel-house still in their nostrils. Yet their immigration was declared illegal, and the Jewish response included acts of violence like the blowing up of the King David Hotel in Jerusalem, in which ninety Britons, Arabs and Jews were killed.

By November 1947 it was clear that serious trouble lay ahead. Jewish leaders accepted the United Nations Partition Plan; the Arabs utterly rejected it. War was certain; Jerusalem, in the front line, was bound to bear the brunt of it and, in all probability, to suffer most of all. Responsibility for this miserable situation was, to some extent, divided, but one eminent authority had no doubt where it lay. Professor Reginald Coupland's view was:

> The Palestine problem arises from a conflict of 'right with right', and of promises with promises. A just solution, therefore, cannot be achieved without concessions on both sides. By acquiescing in Partition, Dr Weizmann and his colleagues have shown a willingness to compromise; but the Mufti and his colleagues maintain their original demand for 100 per cent, namely, the stoppage of Jewish immigration

and the subjection of the National Home to an Arab majority in an independent Palestine.[47]

Coupland was one of many advisers whom the British Government recruited and whose advice was then totally ignored. British colonial thought and practice were dying at the time; even so, one Middle East expert has asked how it was that 'His Majesty's Government continued for thirty years to pursue so doggedly a policy recognized by many … as leading inevitably to trouble and strife'.[48] There seems to have been only one answer, the British refusal to realize that, with the colonial era coming to an end, Palestine could not in any event have been held. That stubborn refusal, in its turn, owed most to the argument of the military establishment, that Palestine's strategic position was of cardinal importance. Bevin's last struggle to avert partition took place when Egypt was as good as lost and Palestine looked to be more important than ever.

REFERENCES

1. Pinchas Peli, in 'The Meaning of Jerusalem in the Jewish Religion', *Israel Digest*, Jerusalem, 18 May 1979.
2. A. M. Aamiry, *Jerusalem: Arab Origin and Heritage*, Longman, London, 1978.
3. Ibid.
4. Genesis, Chap. 14.
5. Professor Yehoshua Ben-Arieh, lecture to Geography Department of York University, 1975.
6. Christopher Hollis and Robert Brownrigg, *Holy Places*, Weidenfeld, London, 1969.
7. Professor Yehoshua Ben-Arieh, see above, note 5.
8. Josephus. He gave the death-toll at 1,100,000. Quoted by Charles Gulston, *Jerusalem: The Triumph and the Tragedy*, Zondervan Publishing, Grand Rapids, Mich., 1978.
9. In the Lament 'Cedars of Lebanon', by Arzei Levanon, quoted by Dr Menashe Harel, *Jerusalem Post*, 3 June 1970.
10. A. L. Tibawi, *Jerusalem: Its Place in Islam and Arab History*, Institute of Palestine Studies Press, Beirut, 1969.
11. Ibid.
12. The Rev. Dr J. M. Parkes, *Whose Land?*, Penguin, Harmondsworth, 1970.
13. Dr Menashe Harel, loc. cit.
14. Walter Zander, *Israel and the Holy Places of Christendom*, Weidenfeld, London, 1971.
15. The Rev. Dr J. M. Parkes, op. cit.
16. Walter Zander, op. cit.
17. Dr Menashe Harel, loc. cit.
18. The Rev. Dr J. M. Parkes, op. cit.

19. Yitzhak ben-Zvi, quoted by Dr Menashe Harel, loc. cit.
20. F. A. de Chateaubriand, *Travels in Greece, Palestine, Egypt and Barbary during the years 1806 and 1807*, London, 1811.
21. Dr John Kitto, *Modern Jerusalem*, London, 1947.
22. John Lothian, in 1843. Quoted by Martin Gilbert, *Jerusalem: Illustrated History Atlas*, Macmillan, New York, 1977.
23. Dr Tudor Parfitt, in the *Jewish Chronicle*, 2 April 1976.
24. Ibid.
25. Rev. F. C. Ewald, letter to *Jewish Intelligence*, 30 November 1943.
26. The late Levi Eshkol, Prime Minister of Israel, in conversation with the author.
27. Chapter by Blanche Dugdale, in *Chaim Weizmann*, ed. Meyer Weisgal, Dial Press, New York, 1944.
28. Dr John Kitto, op. cit.
29. Miss A. Goodrich-Freer, *Inner Jerusalem*, London, 1907.
30. Richard Aldington, *Lawrence of Arabia*, Collins, London, 1955.
31. J. C. Hurewitz, *Diplomacy in the Middle East*, vol. 2, Van Nostrand, New Jersey, 1956.
32. James Parkes, *A History of the Jewish People*, Penguin, Harmondsworth, 1964.
33. J. C. Hurewitz, op. cit.
34. Imperial War Cabinet Minutes, quoted by David Lloyd George in *The Truth about the Peace Treaties*, vol. 1.
35. David Lloyd George, *The Truth about the Peace Treaties*, vol. 2.
36. Winston Churchill, in *Illustrated Sunday Herald*, 8 February 1920.
37. J. C. Hurewitz, op. cit.
38. Ibid.
39. Norman Bentwich, in personal conversation with the author.
40. From *The Middle East: A Handbook*, ed. Michael Adams, Anthony Blond, London, 1971.
41. Ibid.
42. Christopher Sykes, *Cross Roads to Israel*, Collins, London, 1965.
43. Jerusalem Arab Students' leaflet, 11 September 1929.
44. *Report by Sir William Fitzgerald on the Local Administration of Jerusalem*, by Government Printer, Palestine, 28 August 1945.
45. David Lloyd George, op. cit.
46. Abba Eban, *An Autobiography*, Weidenfeld, London, 1978.
47. Coupland Papers, Rhodes House, Oxford.
48. Sir John Richmond, in *International Affairs*, January 1980.

CHAPTER THREE

'Nine Measures of Beauty'

According to the rabbinic sages 'Ten measures of beauty came into the world, and nine of them were given to Jerusalem'.[1] A more mundane saying was: 'Whosoever has not seen Jerusalem in its splendour, has never seen a lovely city'.[2] In the English Bible Jerusalem is mentioned 850 times, 750 of them in the Old Testament.

The depth and strength of Jewish attachment to Jerusalem has lasted for 3,000 years and has never wavered. The Psalmist called the city 'the perfection of beauty'.[3] To the prophet Isaiah it was 'the faithful city, full of justice, in which righteousness lodged'.[4] Three thousand years ago King David collected the materials for the Temple that Solomon would build, local copper and stone, cedar wood from Hiram, King of Tyre, gold and silver from farther afield. The Temple was to be the symbolic dwelling-place of the God of Israel in the heart of his Land and People, and this symbolic truth would of itself be eternal and indestructible.

Of the eighteen Hebrew Blessings, the tenth is 'Sound the great horn of freedom, raise the ensign to gather us from the four corners of the earth. Blessed art thou, O God, who gatherest the dispersal of thy People Israel.' And the fourteenth reads: 'And to Jerusalem, Thy city, return in mercy and dwell therein: rebuild it soon in our days as an everlasting building and specially set up therein the Throne of David.' Driven into exile in the sixth century BC, the Jews took a sacred oath:[5]

If I forget Thee, O Jerusalem
Let my right hand forget its cunning.
Let my tongue cleave to the roof of my mouth
If I remember Thee not,
If I set not Jerusalem above my chiefest joy.

Still in exile, Jews would pray at the Passover ceremony 'Next year in Jerusalem'. The Jews of Eastern Europe contrived to build their homes facing towards Jerusalem and prayed for rain in October – as they would have done in Jerusalem, but after the harvests had already been gathered in where they were living. For any Jew in exile, to be buried in the Holy Land was to be in a condition of resurrection. It is coincidental, but surely apt, that when one looks up 'Jerusalem' in Stevenson's *Book of Quotations*, one finds the reference under 'Heaven'.

One of the most impressive passages in the Bible is in these words of Isaiah's:[6]

For Zion's sake, I will not keep silent,
And for Jerusalem's sake I have set watchmen on Thy walls.
Take ye no rest and give Him no rest
Until He establish Jerusalem and make it a praise.

There are endless quotations of this kind which illustrate the special place that Jerusalem has in every Jewish heart, and its centrality in Jewish existence. One historian, James Parkes, explained this attachment in simple but evocative terms: 'The whole religious significance of the Jewish Bible ties it to the history of a single people and the geographical actuality of a single land ... For Jews the Land is a Holy Land in the sense of being a Promised Land, the word indicates an intensity of relationship going beyond that of either of the other two religions (Christianity and Islam)'.[7] Jerusalem was Zion, a place in that Holy Land and yet embodying the whole of it. The same writer referring to the essential unity of Jewish belief, focused on Jerusalem, says: 'From one point of view Israel is, and always will be, a land of many cultures; but from another, Israel is basically a land of only one culture, because there is only one Judaism, only one Bible, one Talmud, one historic tradition, even if it has widened out in modern times like the estuary of a great river with many channels and islands'.[8] In this sense, the Jewish faith was unique.

The eternal nature of Jewish attachment to Jerusalem is bound up with Messianic belief, that this is where the Messiah, sent from

Heaven to found God's Kingdom on earth, would eventually arrive. Jerusalem, therefore, must always remain holy in Jewish hearts. The Hebrew scholar Maimonides was thinking of this when he wrote: 'Why do I say that the Temple area and Jerusalem are still in their first sanctity while the rest of the Land of Israel, for the purposes of the sabbatical year and so forth, did not keep its first sanctity? The sanctity of the Temple and of Jerusalem is based on the Divine Presence, and the Divine Presence never left them.'[9] As Maimonides saw it, there was, so to speak, a chain of divine command; it passed into the Temple from its inner Holy of Holies, where only the High Priest could enter on the Day of Atonement, and it passed from the Temple to the whole of Jerusalem and to the whole of the Land of Israel.[10] The Divine Presence would be reasserted, dramatically, on the Day of Judgement. But it was implicit in the very stones of Jerusalem, and if the stones were taken away, it would be implicit in its indestructible soil. Two sober, non-Jewish writers found Messianic prophecy to be much more than a dream: 'Today no one could deny the reality of the feelings of those who equate the state of Israel with the Messianic fulfilment of Judaism. It is possible to lay text to text, through the Law and the Prophets, to support the cause of Zionism.'[11]

As the heart of the Jewish people, Jerusalem was bound to become the heart of any Jewish state which contained it. Because the Land and the People were one, and because Jerusalem was the core of both, no other capital could be envisaged for the State of Israel. In Jewish eyes the marriage of the secular and the religious, in Jerusalem, was a perfect marriage, and a perfect marriage will last for ever. For Jews, interest in Jerusalem was primary, but most Jews would readily admit that it is of abiding interest to two other creeds too, Christianity and Islam. Only, they would insist, Christian interest is secondary – based on the 'New Covenant' provided by Jesus and embracing world-wide Christian communities with no connection with the Land of Israel – while Muslim interest is tertiary – Islam's holy city is Mecca, and Medina is next in importance. For both of these faiths the sacredness of the Land and of Jerusalem is derivative, while the direct link with God through the Temple and its Holy of Holies does not exist at all for them. An essential difference was explained by one theologian as follows:

For Christians and Muslims that term [holy sites] is an adequate expression of what matters. Here are sacred places, hallowed by the most holy events, here are the places for pilgrimage, the very focus of highest devotion. But Judaism is different ... The sites sacred to Judaism have no shrines. Its religion is not tied to sites but to the Land, not to what happened in Jerusalem but to Jerusalem itself.[12]

Christianity did not aspire to so basic a belief in the sanctity of Jerusalem and the Land around it. An illustrative story is that of an English clerk, Philip of Lincoln, who set out on a pilgrimage to the Holy Land in 1129. On his way, he stopped at the Abbey of Clairvaux, met the Abbot and decided to stay there permanently. The Abbot wrote to the Bishop of Lincoln and explained why: 'He has entered the holy city and has chosen his heritage ... He is no longer an inquisitive onlooker but a devout inhabitant and an enrolled citizen of Jerusalem.' But this Jerusalem, 'if you want to know, is Clairvaux. She is the Jerusalem united to the one in Heaven by whole-hearted devotion, by conformity of life, by a certain spiritual affinity.'[13]

Jerusalem, for Christians, was 'the New Jerusalem, in Heaven', whereas the Jews had always believed that it was the spiritual as well as the geographical centre of the world.[14] Some Christians thought differently from their fellows; thus Englishmen like Lord Byron, Isaac Newton, William Cowper and that 7th Earl of Shaftesbury who was chiefly responsible for the establishment of a British Consulate in Jerusalem in 1838. They dreamt of the rebuilding of the Temple and the fulfilment of the prophecies. But the terrestrial Jerusalem was, at best, a mere temporary and transient appendage to the heavenly Jerusalem. This concept owed much to the teaching of the New Testament that, not the Temple, but Christ in person was the centre of religious belief and experience. This resulted in partial 'de-territorialization',[15] although a special veneration and sentimental affection were reserved for those places where Christ's feet had trod.

St Jerome, although spending much of his life in Bethlehem, declared that 'the heavenly sanctuary is open from Britain no less than from Jerusalem, for the Kingdom of God is within you'.[16] Martin Luther inveighed against pilgrimages, and John Milton felt the same way:

> Here Pilgrims roam, that strayed so far to seek
> In Golgotha him dead, who lives in Heaven.[17]

William Blake appealed in gloriously evocative terms for the building of Jerusalem 'in England's green and pleasant land'.

Christian hymns and prayers, indeed, are almost exclusively heavenly, although beliefs lingered obstinately that Jerusalem was the centre of the cosmos and that it would be at Jerusalem that history would reach its apocalyptic finale.[18]

Nevertheless, Christian interest in the Holy Places of Jerusalem has always existed and has at times become very strong. For three periods in its history the city was under Christian rule – under the Byzantines from 324 for three centuries, under the Crusaders from 1099 for less than one, and under the British for just over thirty years up to the foundation of the State of Israel in 1948. A continuous Christian presence was maintained without a break from the death of Jesus down to the present. It was disfigured by perpetual bickering between different Christian Churches. Perhaps one significant date in this sad story was 1054, when the schism between the Eastern and Western Churches led to the ambassador of Pope Leo IX placing a Bill of Excommunication of the Greek Patriarch Michael Cerularius on the altar of Haghia Sophia in Constantinople. The deep rift between Greeks and Latins was the principal struggle in the centuries which followed, but Copts, Ethiopians, Syrian Christians and others played their parts, and the Greeks and Latins were periodically rent by internal disputes.

Only these two last sought to achieve dominance in Jerusalem as a whole, and in the Churches of the Holy Sepulchre and the Nativity in particular. At one stage, between 1630 and 1637, control of the sanctuaries changed hands six times, with the Greeks in charge at the beginning and end of the period. During the eighteenth century the Latins were more often in a dominant position, and the struggle intensified in the 1840s. In 1848 Pope Pius IX gave a vicious twist to the conflict by issuing his encyclical *In Suprema Petri*, enjoining the 'strayed sheep' of the Eastern Churches to return to the communion of St Peter's Holy See in Rome. The Patriarchs of Constantinople, Alexandria, Antioch and Jerusalem, in return, denounced the Church of Rome for heresy.

According to one authority,[19] the Ottoman authorities played off the Greeks and Latins against one another. In 1604 their edict, or 'firman', confirmed the Latins in control of the Holy Places, but this was reversed by the firman of 1637. In 1740 the Latins were in favour again, but in 1757 it was the turn of the Greeks. The 1852 firman confirmed an uneasy status quo of shared rights – by this stage 'Holy' Russia was taking an active interest, while the Latins had long since identified themselves completely with the Church of Rome and were more aptly regarded as Catholics. At one stage there was hand-to-hand fighting between monks of rival orders, using candlesticks and crosses as weapons. At another, the silver star in the Grotto of the Church of the Nativity, the property of the Catholics, was stolen. The disgraceful confrontation in Bethlehem contributed to the more serious secular confrontation between Russia and France, which in turn led on to the disastrous, bloody and unnecessary Crimean War. Seldom in history have Christian differences produced a more futile example of disregard for human life and civilized behaviour.

The Ottoman authorities may well have wished to avoid having to intervene in these unintelligible disputes. What was more operative from their point of view was that a great deal of money was invested in Jerusalem, for long centuries mainly in churches and shrines but, during the nineteenth century, increasingly productively in hospitals, schools and hostels. During the same period trade and tourism increased too. A balance of interest, at least, was maintained between Christian congregations and Muslim rulers down to the British capture of Jerusalem in 1917.

Fortuituously, this roughly coincided with the Russian Revolution, an event which would have a considerable effect on the balance of external interest in Jerusalem. The Muslim Ottomans were ousted; now a Communist and atheist Russia abandoned all interest in the religious affairs of Jerusalem. One of the chief contestants for dominant influence dropped out, and there was only a brief period of jockeying for religious control before Britain assumed it as an intrinsic part of the duties of the Mandatory Power. France's Prime Minister Georges Clemenceau agreed with some reluctance to the full exercise of British powers under the Mandate, but in 1920 his successor, Paul Cambon, tried in vain at the London Conference to assert a French right to a 'protectorate' over the Holy Places. Christian countries, it seemed, would never learn. The French demand was blocked with the help of Italy's Prime Minister Francesco Nitti, which may not altogether have pleased the Vatican. In June 1921 Pope Benedict XV was complaining in his encyclical *Causa Nobis* that the trusteeship of the Holy Places was in the hands of 'alien non-Catholic Christians' (the British!), and that the creation of a Jewish National Home in Palestine would 'deprive Christendom of the position which it had always occupied in the Holy Places'.[20] The disturbing possibility yawned of another Christian conflict, this time between the Vatican and the British Mandatory Power which, perhaps unwisely, had indicated readiness to protect the interests of the forlorn Eastern Churches. (The Greek Government offered a loan to its indigent Patriarchate in 1919, but it was not taken up.)

One must return, over a long span of time, to the thoughts and interests in Jerusalem of the third great monotheistic religion, that of Islam. But first, a brief digression on Christian involvement, of a less serious but still worrying kind. Judaism is non-proselytizing. Not only that, but it is, in fact, extremely difficult for a non-Jew to be accepted as a Jew. Even in the supposedly enlightened atmosphere of the twentieth century, he or she must go through an extended initiation. Islam has conquered, and in the wake of conquest offered conversion as the alternative to inferior status. Christianity, particularly during the nineteenth century, sought to convert peacefully.

The 'London Society for Promoting Christianity among the Jews' was established in 1808. Judaism has given a basic religious concept to Christianity, as well as Jesus, whom Judaism may eventually come to regard as the greatest of its prophets. There was something weirdly incongruous about this well-meaning London group setting out to bring ultimate enlightenment to the one people who had made Christianity possible. It was well-meant, for sure. The Society sent out a Swiss, Mr Tschudi, in 1820, to set up a permanent post. He failed, and so the Society's next envoy, Dr Nicholayson, went out and succeeded in 1833. He was a Dane, and perhaps a minor doubt might set in, that a London society kept drawing on people from, in the insular British idiom, 'abroad'. Perhaps it was wise to do so; a Protestant Bishopric was established in 1841, with a 'Bishop in Jerusalem', not 'of' – so that no offence could be given to the Greek Patriarchate. In 1849 the first Protestant church was opened in Jerusalem. In 1851 the Church Missionary Society of London took a hand. It may, providentially, have equated Jews with benighted heathens; for it busied itself with building schools and charitable institutions, and in encouraging pilgrimage.[21] Proselytization now took second place.

American missionaries were hard at work too, and according to one estimate of the 1850s it cost an American Protestant missionary up to 5,000 dollars to convert a single Jew.[22] The missionary wave brought aberrant Christians in its wake, to settle in Jerusalem and try to work out their salvation. One old English lady claimed to know that the Messiah would arrive during a certain ten-day period of the year, and during those ten days regularly took tea for two up to the Mount of Olives. An eccentric of a different kind arrived in 1898 in the shape of Kaiser Wilhelm II. For his visit, all buildings were scrubbed and all dogs sent into temporary exile. Even this did not entirely satisfy the Kaiser, who insisted on riding into Jerusalem like a conqueror; a compromise was achieved by knocking a hole for his passage through the walls of the Old City, so that he did not at least ride through a main gate.[23]

The Muslims, like the Christians but unlike the Jews, believed in the conversion of 'infidels'. But the policies of Islam were coloured by a degree of tolerance of the two other monotheistic faiths to which it owed so much. As one Israeli writer put it:

> Islam regards itself as the last, and the purest divine revelation, which came in order to purify and to complete the older Jewish and Christian revelations. Since, in the Islamic view, the Jews and the Christians corrupted the original Divine word and introduced innovations and alterations into it, Mohammed was sent as the last Prophet and the last Messenger, to bring the real word of God to humanity.[24]

Islam therefore regarded itself as heir to the two religions which preceded it, and to all Holy Places belonging to them. In asserting the principle of inheritance, Islam was merely emulating Christianity, but it went much further, claiming not only to have taken over the Covenant with God but actual bricks and mortar. The Muslim claim became total in the concept that 'there had never been any other sanctity than the Islamic one, since Judaism and Christianity at their roots are in fact Islam'.[25] The totality of this claim, based on sincere belief, is breathtaking.

Jerusalem, as the city holy to both Jews and Christians, was inevitably included in this Muslim claim. Its Islamic rulers renamed it 'Al Kuds', or 'Al Kuds ash-Sharif', the Holy and Noble City. Jerusalem is not mentioned by name in the Muslim Koran; indeed why should it have been, for Muhammad's ministry was in Mecca and Medina and Jerusalem was a faraway city which he had never seen? But in the first verse of Chapter 17 of the Koran there is what has since been claimed to be an indirect reference to the El Aqsa Mosque in Jerusalem: 'Glory be to Him, who carried his servant by night from the Holy Mosque [of Mecca] to the Further Mosque'. Muhammad allegedly was carried on the back of a celestial steed, al-Buraq, in the company of the angel Jibril (Gabriel) from Mecca to Jerusalem in a single night. From the Temple Mount he ascended to Heaven by means of a celestial ladder, and communed with God. There is, of course, an insuperable difficulty of time and place; if the 'Further Mosque' was the El Aqsa, then this journey would have had to have taken place more than half a century after Muhammad's death, when the El Aqsa was built. The 'Further Mosque' would, like the steed and the ladder, have had to have been celestial.

What is sure is that Muhammad ordered, for a time, that his followers should turn to Jerusalem in their prayers, as was the custom of the Jews. At the time, he was intent on befriending and converting the Jews of the Hejaz. But he made virtually no converts from among them, and in 623 instructed the faithful to turn to Mecca as the 'Qibla', or direction, of their prayer. So it has remained ever since. Nor did Muhammad prescribe pilgrimage to Jerusalem. Pilgrimage to Mecca was a primary and fundamental duty of every believer in Islam, but Jerusalem was to be a place of 'ziharah' or brief sojourn, not of 'hajj' or pilgrimage. Islam's second holy city was Medina. Theoretically, Jerusalem ranked third, but there were later to be other places of Muslim pilgrimage than Mecca and Medina. For the Shi'a Muslims, there were Qum, Meshed, Kerbala and Najjaf, which 'were almost as important, if not co-equal with, Mecca. None of them spoke of Jerusalem, El Kuds, or sought to go there.'[26]

One writer has claimed that:

> The sanctity of Jerusalem was born as a result of political necessity during the early Umayyad period (661–750), when Islam had to struggle both ideologically and politically, mainly against Christianity in Syria ... Even after the sanctity of Jerusalem had been established in Islam, and reached, towards the beginning of the eighth century, its final stages of development, it was in reality a conditional sanctity. This means that Jerusalem became the focus of Moslem religious sentiments and emotions, and its Islamic sanctity was accentuated and stressed, only when some other, non-Islamic Christian or Jewish political entity claimed it or held it. When the city was safely in Moslem hands, one hardly heard of it; religiously speaking, it fell into oblivion.[27]

If this judgement may sound harsh, Jerusalem was certainly of essential interest to Islam only intermittently. For a time in the seventh century the Caliph Omar made the city his headquarters, while Mecca and Medina were in the hands of a rebellious rival. The 'Dome of the Rock' was built on the Temple Mount towards the end of the century by the Caliph Bad el-Malik. By a curious dispensation his name was erased from the inscription on one of the Mosque's gates nearly 150 years later, and that of the contemporary ruler Abdullah al-Ma'mun substituted. But the wording of the inscription was not otherwise altered, so making al-Ma'mun the founder of the mosque at a time when his own father had not yet been born![28] The mosque housed the great rock, upon which Abraham was said to have prepared to sacrifice his own son, Isaac. Abraham was claimed as a direct ancestor by Muhammad, and Abraham, Moses, Elijah and others were claimed as Islamic prophets. As one historian has noted, Islam simply 'appropriated' Jewish and Christian historical figures, traditions and shrines wholesale – a mosque was even built, as a sign of possession, within the fortified area of St Catherine's Monastery in Sinai. Yet twice in the thirteenth century, when Christian Crusaders captured the Egyptian river port of Damietta, the Egyptian Emir of the day offered to 'trade' Jerusalem for it. Even so, Muslim veneration of Jerusalem remained basically sincere.[29] One Arab writer believes that, in order to describe Muslim feelings about Jerusalem, 'history would need to borrow from religion its deepest feelings, and from poetry her sweetest terms'.[30]

Jerusalem certainly gained in importance in Islamic eyes as a result of the Crusades. A new kind of literature began to flourish whose nature, one writer suggested, was almost 'Zionist' – the praises of Jerusalem were sung endlessly and enthusiastically.[31] The principal reason for this was clear: Islam was engaged in a desperate and courageous struggle to regain what it regarded as an important part of its inheritance from the Christian invaders. The new attachment to Jerusalem, won through the shedding of blood, owed something to the personality of Islam's greatest soldier, then or thereafter, Saladin. His courage and chivalry were epic. The subsequent stagnation of interest in Jerusalem also has a psychological explanation: for more than seven centuries Muslim control of Jerusalem was never seriously challenged.

Reference has already been made to the Islamic attitude towards the non-Muslims under Muslim rule during these long centuries. Such people, Jews and Christians, were theoretically under Muslim 'protection' as 'People of the Book'. But, as James Parkes points out, it was:

unfortunate that Christians and Jews, in the hope of securing better treatment for their fellows under Muslim rule by the flattery of Muslim authorities, should have created out of Koranic tolerance ... the legend of the favourable treatment of Christians and Jews. It might indeed be said of the Turkish authorities that they exhibited the toleration of indifference when suitably paid to do so. But, apart from this, the legend ... has no support in the Muslim history of the last thousand years, apart from the brief period of the Osmanli Sultans.[32]

Even under slow-moving, ostensibly benign Turkish rule, Jews who strayed into Muslim quarters of Jerusalem were liable to abuse and even assault, while 'for a Jew or a Christian to enter the enclosure of the Dome of the Rock was punishable by death'.[33]

Those 'protected' under Muslim rule were 'dhimmis'. It was pure fable that they were automatically well treated.

From the time of Umar the second caliph (634–644) dhimmi peoples could reside in Islamised lands only if their work was beneficial to the maintenance and expansion of Arab-Islamic rule. Later, the theory was developed into a system of legalised economic exploitation and oppression based allegedly on divine will ... The indigenous peoples of the Middle East and North Africa were gradually reduced – through pillage, ransom, exploitation, oppression, dispossession, forced conversion, famine and physical elimination – from majorities to helpless minorities. Their everyday life was governed by countless oppressive rules and it became a religious obligation to humiliate and to revile them. Lifting a hand against a Muslim, even in a case of legitimate defence, was a capital offence. In an age of injustice, their sworn testimony was refused by Muslim courts ... Their blood was considered of an inferior quality to that of Muslims and could be shed lightly.[34]

The same writer went on:

Dhimmis were often considered impure and had to be segregated from the Muslim community. Entry into holy Muslim towns, mosques, public baths, as well as certain streets was forbidden them. Their turbans ... their costumes, belts, shoes, the appearance of their wives and their servants, had to be different from those of Muslims in order to distinguish and humiliate them; for the dhimmis could never be allowed to forget that they were inferior beings. The humble donkey was generally the sole beast of burden permitted them and then only outside the town and on condition that they would, as a sign of respect, dismount on sight of any Muslim ... In the street, dhimmis were obliged to walk on the left, or impure, side of a Muslim. Their gait had to be rapid and their eyes lowered. Their graves had to be level with the ground so that anyone could walk on them.[35]

Muslim religious leaders crystallized, anchored and sought to perpetuate the image of the dhimmi as a second-class citizen. They resented the measure of emancipation won during the nineteenth century, as a result of growing European involvement in the Middle East and European territorial conquest in North Africa. In Palestine, when Turkish rule ended, a special danger arose, of territorial usurpation, and it was unthinkable that this should be achieved by Jews. For, 'The special relationship between Palestine and the Jewish people motivated a persecution which was crueller there than elsewhere. Never was a nation so systematically humiliated and destroyed in its national expression (demography, history, language and culture) than was the Jewish remnant in its own homeland.'[36]

Muslim dominance was asserted by the establishment of their own shrines where those of Jews, Christians and others had stood, or continued to stand. This happened at the Tomb of Jethro at Kfar-Hittim, the Altar of Elijah on Mount Carmel, the Tomb of the Patriarchs in Hebron, the Tomb of Gamaliel at Yavneh and the Tomb of Samuel just outside Jerusalem. In Jerusalem itself a Muslim minaret was built alongside the Church of the Holy Sepulchre, as 'protection' of it, but the supreme Muslim take-over was of the Temple Mount. It became an article of faith with the Muslim leadership that attempts by the Jews to worship, in their own fashion, outside the Western Wall of the Mount were tantamount to a conspiracy to seize the whole Mount and rebuild their own Temple upon it. This argument was advanced time after time during the British Mandate, and it is a sad reflection that British administrators allowed it to influence their decisions. But many times before the Mandate, Jewish religious observance at the Wall had been rigorously curtailed. In 1839 a Jewish proposal to pave the muddy alleyway along the Wall was turned down, as a 'preliminary to their ultimate aims'.[37] In 1840 the Jews were forbidden to 'raise their voices' in prayer at the Wall or to 'proclaim doctrines'.[38] And in 1911 they were refused permission to bring chairs for the aged, in case they should 'claim possession'.[39] For Muslim possession was total, irreversible and eternal, as exemplified by the authority of the Waqf, the Muslim administrative foundation whose ownership rights were endorsed by God. 'It is unlawful for any governor, official or tyrant to abolish the waqf ... or endeavour to abolish it or part of it. He who does so ... disobeys God and rebels against Him, and deserves His curse!'[40] It would be hard to find a more sweeping definition of property rights.

The Jews, of course, did not suffer alone. As one writer has explained:

> The fundamental problems of the Christian churches in the Holy Land could be summed up briefly as follows. Ever since the seventh-century Muslim conquest, and with but a relatively brief interruption, the relationship between the civil power and the churches has been one of conflict. The need to guard continually against multiple oppression and hostile cunning, particularly pernicious during the four centuries of Ottoman rule, mercilessly eroded the churches' membership, always threatening to sap their evangelical vitality, and reduce them to mere quasi-ethnic communities on the margins of society which they already were in law. Only in the dying years of the Ottoman Empire could a relatively substantial increase be observed in basic rights and liberties.[41]

Muslim resentment that a Christian power was once again in control of Jerusalem and its Holy Places was intense; such a circumstance had automatically warranted a 'jihad' or holy war in the past. It was much worse, even unbearable, that the claim to succession to a British Mandate which would, it was hoped, be of limited duration was now contested by the Jewish subject-race. Underlying religious feeling had much to do with the iron and absolute Arab intransigence during the Mandatory period, and it was in no way surprising that it should have crystallized in the person of the Grand Mufti of Jerusalem, the chief religious leader. For leaders in other Arab countries the situation of Jerusalem was unfortunate. But the Syrians hoped eventually to reinforce their claim to the whole of Palestine, as 'southern Syria', and the Emir Abdallah of Transjordan had the British-officered Arab Legion at his beck and call and a treaty of friendship with Britain in his pocket – he must have hoped that his time would come, when the future of Jerusalem came to be finally decided. For the Mufti and his religious followers, the situation of Jerusalem was utterly unacceptable. The removal of complete Islamic control over the city was the reversal of the teachings of the Prophet, a blasphemy.

To the Mufti it must have seemed peculiarly intolerable that the Jewish dhimmis should have political pretensions in the country where they had been subject to Islam since the days of Muhammad. It was even worse that their political aims should include the demand for religious equality and the fullest possible access to their holy places. But the Mufti was not alone in his forebodings. The Vatican had a dual reason for concern: physical control of the Holy Places was now vested in a British Protestant power and the Jews were being allowed to infiltrate into the Holy City. Wise in the ways of diplomacy, the Vatican decided to concentrate its fire on one of these enemies at a time.

A Vatican statement, made in a letter to the League of Nations of 15 May 1922, accordingly dropped previous objections to Britain being the Mandatory power in Palestine, but complained that the Jews were being given 'an absolute preponderance in the economic, administrative and political field to the detriment of other nationalities'. The Vatican refused to accept the findings of a single commission of inquiry set up by Britain to adjudicate religious claims and differences; instead, it demanded that voting power in any such commission should be reserved exclusively to Catholics, as the true guardians of the Holy Places. This was amended, in a memorandum sent by Cardinal Gasparri of 15 August, to the stipulation that commissions should have a built-in Catholic majority. In addition, all rights in the Holy Places which had already been acquired by Catholics should be inviolable. The Vatican's demands, which to say the least were importunate, boomeranged; the Mandatory authorities dropped their proposal of a neutral commission and assumed full responsibility themselves.

Subsequently the Vatican sat back to watch disconnected and increasingly chaotic events in Palestine and bide its time. For the Pope and his advisers three thoughts must have been paramount. The British were steadily losing their grip of the situation; this meant that a unitary solution, through the creation of a single Arab–Jewish state, was becoming increasingly unlikely. In the second place, any kind of dismemberment of Palestine could open the way to the creation of a special status for Jerusalem. Finally, now that Russian interest in Jerusalem had evaporated, there was every chance of the Roman Catholic Church gaining lasting, paramount influence in and over Jerusalem.

As far back as 1841 Prussia, of all improbable countries, had proposed the internationalization of the Holy Places of Jerusalem, Bethlehem and Nazareth. This would be regulated under the terms of an international agreement and statute, and the Christian populations of the three towns would be given local self-government.[42] Here was the germ of the idea of a special status for Jerusalem, and the idea was immediately taken up when plans for the partitioning of Palestine were first mooted. Thus the Peel and Woodhead Commissions both proposed the separation of Jerusalem from whatever Arab and Jewish states were created. So did the Morrison–Grady Plan and so, finally, did the United Nations Special Committee in its report which was approved by the General Assembly, on 29 November 1947.

The Vatican held its hand until October 1948, when the Arab–Israeli war which began in May had ended in a total Israeli victory. The course and significance of that war will be described later; for the moment, the operative consideration was Jerusalem and how its future was affected.

Under the United Nations partition plan it was to have become a 'corpus separatum', an enclave with its own statute, which would be drawn up and approved by the UN Trusteeship Council. The enclave would have measured about twelve miles from north to south, and ten miles from east to west, and would have included Bethlehem, with its 'sister towns' of Beit Jalla and Beit Sahur, as well as about fifteen villages, almost all of them Arab. It would have had a population of about 210,000, evenly balanced between Jews and Arabs, although the Jewish population of the Jerusalem Municipality alone was nearly 100,000, against 65,000 Arabs. Jewish acceptance of the internationalization of Jerusalem was based on two precepts. The first was that it was better to have half a cake than none at all – something which the Palestinian Arabs consistently refused to understand. The second was that the UN plan provided for a referendum to be held, after ten years, to seek the views of all residents as to whether the international regime should continue or be modified. Perhaps surprisingly, the Jewish leaders were convinced that devotion to Jerusalem would ensure a Jewish majority by that time. For the Arab birthrate was much higher than the Jewish.

In the first half of 1948 efforts to secure Arab and Jewish co-operation under a UN Trusteeship Council broke down. France and the United States then proposed a temporary international regime, but this was rejected by the UN General Assembly in May. Jerusalem was left as a 'corpus separatum', in theory, but with no administration. An element of farce, apparent thus early in the history of the UN, was provided by the appointment of an American Quaker, Dr Harold Evans, to be Special Municipal Commissioner in Jerusalem. For a Quaker was bound by his conscience not to accept military protection, and Dr Evans waited forlornly in Cairo for the fighting, now in full swing, to come to an end. When it did, a situation had been created of de facto Israeli and Jordanian military occupation of Jerusalem. The Israelis held the whole of West Jerusalem, or about two-thirds of the built-up areas of the whole city. The Jordanian Army occupied East Jerusalem, including the walled Old City, but Mount Scopus remained as an enclave in Israeli hands on the north-eastern edge of the city. Although Jerusalem was for much of the war cut off from all other Israeli areas and was under siege, the Israelis lost only the treasured Jewish Quarter of the Old City and one or two small areas during the fighting. They gained most of southern Jerusalem and overran Arab settlements on the western fringes of the city and in the 'corridor' which was opened to connect it with the main territory of the State of Israel and the Mediterranean.

In October 1948 Pope Pius XII's encyclical *In Multiplicibus Curis* called for the establishment of an international regime for Jerusalem. It made no provision for the rights or wishes of its inhabitants. At Easter 1949 a further encyclical, *Redemptoris Nostri*, restated the demand for internationalization, adding that there should be Roman Catholic precedence in, and control of, the Christian Holy Places. Momentarily, it looked as if internationalization was still a possibility; by the autumn of 1949 a number of Arab states, previously opposed to it, had switched to support of internationalization. They included Egypt, Iraq, Syria and Lebanon, in fact all of the Arab states geographically nearest to Jerusalem save Jordan and Saudi Arabia. Supporting internationalization, too, were the Soviet Union and thirteen other states, mainly of the Soviet bloc. In December 1949 the United Nations General Assembly reiterated the demand for internationalization.

A new proposal came in January 1950 from Roger Garreau, the French President of the UN Trusteeship Council. This was that Jerusalem should be divided into three zones, Israeli, Jordanian and international. The Temple Mount would be in the Jordanian zone, and all Christian Holy Places in the international zone. Like so many other plans, this foundered; the Catholic Patriarchate was in favour of it, not so the Greek Orthodox and Armenian. Without the support of the Churches themselves, no Christian 'mini-enclave' could be made to work. This latest proposal, and the reactions to it, shared one singular feature: 'None of their statements [of the Christian Churches] to the United Nations concerning Jerusalem and the Holy Places refers with a single word to the fundamental rights of the local populations, the principles of self-government and democracy, or even the most elementary human freedoms.'[43] In sharp contrast, the Commission of the Churches on International Affairs, a mainly Protestant body, declared: 'Our primary concern is with *people*, not *places*, and we have therefore stressed first of all the rights and freedoms of all men'.[44]

Abba Eban, the chief Israeli representative at the United Nations, had established a close working relationship with Garreau. In his view: 'As a French government official, he was committed to internationalization, but as a Frenchman of lucid intelligence, he could not believe that internationalization was anything but a fantasy. So we went through the motions of drafting a constitution for an international government of Jerusalem that would never come into existence – and of defining the powers of a high commissioner who would never be appointed.'[45] Eban himself saw nothing against 'functional internationalization' of the Holy Places, governed by some charter of rights and responsibilities, but he regarded territorial internationalization with contempt. In his words

The spiritual ideals conceived in Jerusalem are the moral basis on which democracy rests. Would it not be incongruous if the United Nations were to advance the course of democratic liberty everywhere and yet prevent self-government from taking root in the very city where the democratic ideal was born? Our vision is of a Jerusalem wherein free people develop their reviving institutions, while a United Nations representative fulfils the universal responsibility for the safety and accessibility of the Holy Places. This is a vision worthy of the United Nations. Perhaps in this as in other critical periods of history, a free Jerusalem may proclaim redemption to mankind.[46]

Eban was prepared to pledge Israel to conclude agreements with the United Nations on functional internationalization, giving the UN commissioner the fullest possible control and even, where possible, conceding some measure of extra-territoriality. But this would affect an area of one and a half square miles only, and not the 100 square miles envisaged by the UN draft statute. With solemn lack of all positive purpose, the drafting of the statute was completed, and on 1 April 1950, the UN Trusteeship Council, with equally solemn vacuousness, approved its endorsement of the creation of a 'corpus separatum' of Jerusalem and surroundings. The General Assembly voted on 15 December, but there was no two-thirds majority and the statute was shelved. The Soviet bloc changed sides, for the Soviet Union had come to the conclusion that the spread of authority and influence in the 'corpus separatum' would be altogether too ecumenical. As an atheist state, the Soviet Union itself would be left out in the cold.

The UN General Assembly discussed the question of internationalization once more, in 1952, without result. The lessons to be drawn from this protracted and purposeless exercise should be clear. Jerusalem had been the bone of contention between so-called 'great' powers in the past, and they had never reached useful agreement, due primarily to contending, selfish interests. The opinions and interests of UN members were legion and multifarious. Had their attention been focused on the creation of limited, functional internationaliz-ation of as small an area as possible at the outset, something might have been achieved.

As it was, the collapse of British Mandatory rule in Palestine, the Arab–Israeli war which followed and the futile deliberations of the United Nations left Jerusalem, for the first time in its entire history, a divided city – apparently irrevocably and for an indefinite period of time. There are breaches which may be closed, wounds which may be healed. But this one looked as irreparable as the division of Berlin. Each dividing-line ran, not just between two parts of a city or merely between two nations, but between two different worlds – in popular parlance, between East and West in Berlin, and in Jerusalem between the Arab world and a Jewish state which it regarded as an outpost of alien European civilization.

For the Jews, the outcome of their War of Independence – where Jerusalem was concerned – was in one sense a source of great sadness, but in another an act of providence, a gift from

God. The jewel of Jewish existence in Jerusalem – possibly a humble jewel in an ocular sense or in the philosophy of Mr Worldly Wiseman – was the Jewish Quarter of the Old City. Its inhabitants had fought their hardest, but they included a high proportion of the old and infirm, and of religious Jews whose way of life was utterly divorced from the use of arms. A walled city may be a difficult place to capture, but a minority within its walls, fighting for its existence against an overwhelming majority, is doomed. The Jewish Quarter had been built up as close as possible to the Western Wall of the Temple Mount. The Jews are not worshippers of shrines as such, but their relationship to the Temple Mount is a part of their belief in life itself, and has been an inspiration for their hold on life during centuries of oppression. The loss of the Jewish Quarter was bitter indeed.

Against this loss was the dispensation – who should blame any Jew if he believed it to be divine? – under which most of Jerusalem became part of the State of Israel. After the war was over, there were demarcated, demilitarized zones and agreed, empty, and hideous, sectors of 'No Man's Land'. But two-thirds of the city which comprises nine measures of beauty in Jewish thought and belief remained in Jewish hands. The infant State of Israel had never asked for this, and had accepted the UN partition plan, with the internationalization of Jerusalem.

For the Arabs, the outcome of the 1948 war was a sense of dreadful outrage. Part, indeed the most vital part, of Jerusalem had been saved. The Dome of the Rock and the El Aqsa Mosque remained under Muslim control. The Jordanian Arab Legion fought with gallantry, and with some of Saladin's peerless chivalry, to maintain the Arab presence in Jerusalem. It had, in addition, been better trained, officered and armed than the volunteer Jewish contingents which opposed it. But the overall outcome of the Arab–Israeli war was a terrible blow to Arab pride. It represented the victory of outcasts over the elect. It was unbearable. This automatic Arab gut-reaction became thereafter one of the most cogent factors in a developing situation.

REFERENCES

1. Kiddush 49 b, of the Talmud.
2. Sukhot 51 b, of the Talmud.

3.   Psalm 50: 2.
4.   Isaiah 1: 21.
5.   Psalm 137: 5, 6.
6.   Isaiah 62: 1.
7.   James Parkes, *Whose Land?*, Penguin, Harmondsworth, 1970.
8.   James Parkes, 'The New Face of Israel', Brodetsky Lecture, Leeds University Press, 1964.
9.   Quoted by Professor Ze'ev Falk, in the Jerusalem Interfaith Symposium, January 1972 (*Christian News from Israel*, vol. XXIII, no. 1).
10. Ibid.
11. Christopher Hollis and Robert Brownrigg, *Holy Places*, Weidenfeld, London, 1969.
12. Professor Krister Stendhal, *Harvard Divinity Bulletin*, Autumn 1967.
13. *The Letters of St Bernard of Clairvaux*, ed. Bruno Scott-James, London, 1953.
14. Harold Fisch, *The Zionist Revolution*, Weidenfeld, London, 1978.
15. Professor Zvi Werblowsky, 'The Meaning of Jerusalem to Jews, Christians and Muslims', Charles Strong Memorial Lecture, Australia, 1972.
16. Ibid. (quoting Epistle 58).
17. John Milton, *Paradise Lost*, III, 476–7.
18. Professor Hugh Nibley, *Jerusalem in Christianity*, Keter Publishing, Jerusalem, 1973.
19. H. Eugene Bovis, *The Jerusalem Question*, Hoover Institution Press, Stanford University (Calif.), 1971.
20. Walter Zander, *Israel and the Holy Places of Christendom*, Weidenfeld, London, 1971.
21. James Parkes, *Whose Land?*
22. Norman Kotker, *The Earthly Jerusalem*, Scribner, New York, 1969.
23. Ibid.
24. Moshe Sharon, 'How Jerusalem became Al-Kuds', *Jerusalem Post*, 3 August 1979.
25. Ibid.
26. Sir Michael Hadow, *Jerusalem*, Anglo-Israel Association, May 1975.
27. Moshe Sharon, loc. cit.
28. Moshe Sharon, 'History in Stone', *Jerusalem Post*, May 1979.
29. James Parkes, op. cit.
30. A. L. Tibawi, *Jerusalem: Its Place in Islam and Arab History*, Institute of Palestine Studies Press, Beirut, 1969.
31. Professor Zvi Werblowsky, loc. cit.
32. James Parkes, op. cit.
33. Dr Tudor Parfitt, 'Jerusalem before Zionism', *Jewish Chronicle*, 2 April 1976.
34. Bat Ye'or, 'Oriental Jewry', lecture at Jews' College. London, 5 September 1976.
35. Ibid.
36. Bat Ye'or, *Aspects of the Arab-Israeli Conflict*, Wiener Library Bulletin, vol. XXIII, new series 49–50.
37. A. L. Tibawi, op. cit.
38. A. L. Tibawi, *The Islamic Pious Foundations in Jerusalem*, Baskerville Press, London, 1978.
39. A. L. Tibawi, *Jerusalem: Its Place in Islam and Arab History*.
40. A. L. Tibawi, *The Islamic Pious Foundations in Jerusalem*.
41. 'Our Jerusalem Correspondent', *The Tablet*, 8 March 1980.

42. Walter Zander, op. cit.
43. Ibid.
44. Ibid.
45. Abba Eban, *An Autobiography*, Weidenfeld, London, 1978.
46. Ibid.

CHAPTER FOUR

City Divided:
The Role of Jordan

Chaim Weizmann, who had played a crucial part in the creation of the State of Israel and became Israel's first President, addressing Jerusalem's Jews when the 1948 War of Independence was over, declared:

> In addition to the historical connection between us and Jerusalem, in addition to the unbroken chain of Jewish settlement in this city, in addition to the fact of our being a majority in it, your supreme bravery in defending the city gives us the right to proclaim that Jerusalem is ours and shall remain ours. Where are all those who spoke high-sounding phrases about the spiritual significance of Jerusalem to the entire civilized world? Did they raise a finger to protect Jerusalem ... against the shells of the Arabs? Did they do anything when the Jewish quarters of the Old City with their revered synagogues were turned into rubble-heaps by Arab cannon and were desecrated after the surrender? Did they protest by one word that for over a year Jews have been prevented from approaching the Wailing Wall which is the holiest of our Holy Places?[1]

Weizmann spoke with deep feeling in Jerusalem. The Jewish part of it had suffered bitterly during the War of Independence and the era of escalating chaos which preceded it. The United Nations vote in favour of the partition of Palestine resulted in an Arab campaign of terror in the city. Thus the Jewish 'commercial centre' was looted and burnt on 2 December 1947. The shopping district in Ben Yehuda Street was devastated by a bomb explosion on 22 February 1948, with fifty-two people killed and hundreds wounded. Another bomb, planted in the headquarters of the Jewish Agency, killed thirteen people on 11 March 1948 (the complicity of pro-Arab British soldiers was suspected but never proved). By March a regular blockade of Jerusalem had been instituted by Arab guerrillas, supported by Syrian, Iraqi and Jordanian troops. In theory, Palestine was still administered by Britain, and British troops were responsible for keeping the peace. They were powerless to do so.

In the six weeks before the final British withdrawal from Jerusalem on 15 May 1948, the Arabs made strenuous efforts to make the blockade fully effective, operating from fortified hill villages on either side of Jerusalem's only 'escape-route', the road to Jaffa and the sea. Jewish military activity was directed with two aims in view, self-defence in the city itself and sallies down the road to Jaffa to keep it open for supply convoys. The main Arab bases for offensive action along the road were at Kastel, Latrun, Kolonia, Deir Ayub and Deir Yassin. On 9 April a commando of the Irgun, an extremist paramilitary group which was completely separate from the main Haganah defence militia, was sent from Jerusalem to take Deir Yassin. According to its own officers, their column was fired on by Palestinian Arab irregulars, after a demand to surrender had brought the hoisting of a white flag. The Irgun men thereupon killed more than 250 people, including virtually the whole population of the village. Their action was condemned by the Haganah and the man who became Israel's first Prime Minister a month later, David Ben-Gurion. Four days later Arab guerrillas slaughtered seventy-eight Jewish doctors and nurses who were on their way to the Hadassah Hospital on Mount Scopus. This was one of a whole string of Arab atrocities.

The departure of British troops and the proclamation of the State of Israel on 14 May brought intensified Arab efforts to capture Jewish Jerusalem. Syria, Egypt, Lebanon, Iraq and Jordan (still officially 'Transjordan' but shortly to become the Hashemite Kingdom of Jordan) all officially entered the war against Israel. It was the Jordanian 'Arab Legion', armed, trained and commanded by British officers, which would play the leading part on the Arab side in the battle for Jerusalem. Its commanding officer was Brigadier-General John (later Sir John) Bagot Glubb, known affectionately by his troops as Glubb Pasha.

Here was an extraordinary situation. Glubb has since maintained that 'The Jordanians only entered the Arab state, which they found already invaded by the Israelis'.[2] In the first place, there *was* no 'Arab state', for the representatives of the Palestinian Arabs had refused the one offered by the United Nations in November 1947. In the second place, the UN plan had designated Jerusalem as a 'corpus separatum', and this was the position when the Legion attacked the city. Finally, the Legion failed to penetrate into West Jerusalem only because of the determination of its Jewish defenders. A number of offensive thrusts against West Jerusalem by the Legion were, indeed, repelled. But the most paradoxical feature of the situation was that Transjordan was under British protection and a Treaty of Alliance had been signed between the two countries on 15 March 1948. Britain therefore stood by while its ally attacked a small neighbouring state which had been created by a vote of the United Nations, and which had offered the hand of friendship to all Arab neighbours in its initial Declaration of Independence. If Transjordan was guilty of an act of naked aggression, it was abetted by Britain.

In his book *A Soldier with the Arabs*, Glubb has made a whole string of damaging admissions.[3] Thus he has suggested that the proposed Jewish state would be unviable and that this justified all-out opposition to its creation. Then he admitted that the Arab League instructed member states to attack Israel the moment that the British Mandate ended – he was indeed carrying out its orders. He admits too that Britain allowed a situation of 'authorized anarchy' to develop, presumably in order to bring down the Israeli state in ruins. He sent the Legion to attack the Jewish settlements at Etzion, ten miles south of Jerusalem weeks *before* the Mandate ended; there, about 150 Jewish villagers were killed, the last fifteen of them murdered in cold blood after capture and having been photographed by their captors. Etzion had strategic importance. It commanded the Jerusalem–Hebron road.

Glubb admits, too, that 'The greater part of the military units of the Arab Legion were already in Palestine before the British Mandate came to an end'.[4] They were withdrawn at the last moment; in fact there were elements of the Legion on both sides of the River Jordan on 14 May. In reality this was no more than camouflage, for units were held in readiness 'to move to the area which the Arab Legion was expected to defend after the 15th of May'.[5] This was Jerusalem and parts of what is now the West

Bank. Glubb had no doubt about what his main objective was: Jerusalem was 'on the ridge of the mountains. The Holy City was therefore not only of immense moral and religious value. It was the key to the military situation.'[6] Such a statement makes it pretty plain that Glubb intended to capture the whole of Jerusalem, if he could.

His book contains accounts of even stranger calculations. Thus: 'When hostilities in Palestine became inevitable, I sent a personal signal direct to the [British] Commander-in-Chief, Middle East, asking him to dispatch immediately to Aqaba a ship containing specified types of ammunition. The C-in-C *rose to the occasion*, and the ship was duly loaded.'[7] This amounted to a request for British intervention, and later in the war Glubb even suggested that the RAF should be used in action against the Israelis.[8] The requested ship suffered an opera-bouffe fate; its cargo was seized by the Egyptians in transit, and impounded! Glubb's repeated efforts to have the ammunition passed on again failed, but he had a minor triumph: 'In the evacuation, the British Army were unable to clear all their small-arms ammunition and *were glad to dispose of it to us*'. Once again, one is amazed by such barefaced collusion, and one should recall that the Transjordanian–British treaty was purely defensive – Britain was committed to help only if its ally were attacked. This had not happened.

The Arab Legion fought well in the battle for Jerusalem. Glubb has repeatedly insisted that it was badly outnumbered, and that its real strength was not the 7,400 full-strength figure but 'only' about 6,000. What is sure is that the Legion was a well-trained, regular army unit; the Jews defending Jerusalem were civilians put into uniform. The Legion had artillery weapons and armoured cars, according to one estimate, 24 and 45 respectively.[9] The same source gives overall Arab armaments available for use against Israel at 152 artillery weapons, 150 armoured cars, 20–40 tanks and over 50 fighter aircraft. These weapons could be transferred from one part of the front to another; Jerusalem, on the other hand, was defended by men armed with rifles, machine-guns and one or two light mortars, and it was under siege. The Arab Legion, finally, could 'live off the land; in Jerusalem the daily ration dropped to under 900 calories and there was a serious shortage of water.

An independent observer in Jerusalem at the time saw things very differently from Glubb. The British journalist, James Cameron, reported:

The surrounding Arab nations made no secret of their intentions. In the south an Egyptian armoured brigade of 4,000 men was camped just across the border. Three regiments of the Syrian Army were ready in the north. The Lebanese Army was trifling, but it was standing by to enter Galilee. The Iraqis were moving a mechanized brigade towards the Palestinian frontier to work with the Arab Legion, with heavy armour and artillery that the Haganah could never hope to oppose. This was not to speak of Fawzi el-Kawkji's [Palestinian] Liberation Army ... Against all this was now mustered a Jewish militia of rather fewer than 30,000. Of these a third had no weapons at all.[10]

In addition, 'Jerusalem was a deplorably difficult place to organize'. The Haganah was 'conspicuously weak' there, and the high proportion of deeply religious Jews disbelieved in armed struggle, 'insisting that the duty of the male youth in the schools was to recite the Scriptures and reflect on abstruse theology, not to scurry about usurping God's function with a gun'.[11]

The truth was that, if the Arab Legion fought well, Jerusalem's Jews fought better, not merely because it was a battle for survival but because it was their own Holy City that was at stake. The 1,500 or so organized but poorly armed Jews put up an epic resistance. Paradoxically, had the Legion and other Arabs never blockaded or attacked Jewish Jerusalem at all, it might never have become the capital of Israel or come under exclusive Jewish control. The blockade forced the Jews to create a corridor to the sea. It sounded the knell of doom for Arab towns like Ramleh and Lod, and was responsible for more than 100,000 Arabs being driven out of the so-called 'triangle' of which Jerusalem was the apex, and into refugee camps. Months after the siege had been lifted, Israel's Government decided by a 5–4 vote in August 1948 that the internationalization of Jerusalem was preferable to its division, even though the major part of the city would become a part of the State of Israel.[12] Not for the last time, the Jews would discern the 'hand of God' in a mistaken Arab decision.

Glubb's Legionaries were spat on in Ramallah and other towns of the West Bank by Palestinians who had played no part in the fighting. Those responsible for their woes were their own leaders who refused to accept an independent Palestinian state – for the first time in Palestinian existence – under the UN Partition Plan, and in addition those Arab states that attacked Israel, and Arab spokesmen like Azzam Pasha, Secretary General

of the Arab League, who vowed that 'This will be a war of
extermination and a momentous massacre, which will be spoken
of like the Mongolian massacres and the Crusades'.[13] The truth
was that the setting-up of a state by what had been regarded in
the Islamic world as a subject race could only be regarded as a
catastrophe. The attack upon Israel by five neighbouring Arab
states was in the nature of a 'jihad', a holy war, waged to
obliterate undying shame and insult.

Certainly, it had little to do with Palestinian rights and
liberties. For Jordan proceeded to annex the West Bank,
including East Jerusalem de facto, although annexation was
formally promulgated only in April 1950. This Jordanian
annexation was not merely in defiance of the United Nations; it
was against the wishes of the Arab League and was denounced
by its members. Only two countries, Britain and Pakistan,
recognized the annexation of the West Bank, only Pakistan that
of East Jerusalem. The legality of Jordanian annexation was, to
say the least, highly dubious, and Jordan could cite only four
arguments in favour of it. The first was that, with the Palestinian
state rejected by the Palestinians themselves, Jordan was in effect
moving into a political vacuum. Then the Jericho Conference of
Palestinian notables in December 1948 gave quasi-legal
authorization for annexation by recognizing Jordanian
sovereignty, while the Arab League accepted de facto Jordanian
occupation in May 1950, although at the same time censuring
King Abdallah and laying down the condition that some other
final settlement of the Palestinian question should not be pre-
empted. Lastly, the 1949 Armistice Agreement with Israel
effectively protected Jordanian occupation by prohibiting Israel
from initiating action to displace Jordan.[14]

The Jordanians showed the same lack of respect for Jerusalem
as they did for Palestinian rights. While the battle for Jerusalem
was taking place, the Arab Legion showed a callous disregard for
both buildings and non-combatants. On 18 May its artillery took
up positions on the Mount of Olives and from its commanding
heights bombarded the Jewish Quarter of the Old City
mercilessly. The Legion's commander, Abdallah el-Tal, made no
bones about it:

> The operations of calculated destruction were set in motion. I
> knew that the Jewish Quarter was densely populated with
> Jews who caused their fighters a good deal of interference
> and difficulty. I embarked, therefore, on the shelling of the

Quarter with mortars, creating harassment and destruction. Only four days after our entry into Jerusalem the Jewish Quarter had become a graveyard. Death and destruction reigned over it ... As the dawn of Friday, 28 May 1948, was about to break, the Jewish Quarter emerged convulsed in a black cloud – a cloud of death and agony.[15]

Independent observers like the French Consul, M. de Neuville, confirmed that the Arab Legion shelled both the Old and New City and caused widespread destruction.[16]

The Jordanian performance was even worse after the Jewish Quarter surrendered. It had been defended by about one hundred Israeli soldiers, a contingent which managed to penetrate into the Old City when fighting started, with spasmodic help from some of the civilian population of about 2,000. Appeals were made in vain to the United Nations to declare the Old City to be an 'open city' and stop its destruction. The Arab Legion to its credit, allowed some of the civilian population to be evacuated, and gave the remainder protection when the Quarter surrendered. But many hundreds, including children and old people, were kept prisoner until March 1949 before being returned to Jewish Jerusalem.[17]

Meanwhile the Quarter was being largely laid waste. In its 22 acres were thirty-five synagogues and twenty-three other places of worship or religious study. All but one of the synagogues were ransacked, and twelve were totally destroyed. The famous four connecting synagogues of Istanbul, Yohanan ben Zakkai, Hanavi and Haemtzai, were stripped of all their possessions, so defaced that they ceased to resemble places of worship, and turned into Arab slum dwellings, crowded and insanitary. The Karaite synagogue was converted into a scrapyard, and the Ramban synagogue into a cheese factory, while the Ohel Shem synagogue became a goat-pen.[18] The great Hurva synagogue, perhaps the pride of the Quarter, was razed to the ground. More than 3,000 memorial plaques of marble, on which were recorded details of the foundations of the many places of worship, were systematically pilfered.

Nor, sad to relate, can there be the slightest doubt that all of this was done deliberately. The mob was given *carte blanche* in the initial looting, when scrolls and vestments were disgustingly defiled, prayer books ripped to pieces and the library of the Misgav Ladach synagogue and its 10,000 rare volumes consigned to the flames. Abdallah el-Tal described in his memoirs how the

Hurva synagogue was methodically blown up by Jordanian sappers acting under his personal orders.[19] Later examination of the sites of the destroyed and badly damaged buildings showed that they had mostly been dynamited.[20] That this was meticulously planned is beyond doubt, for in a closely built-up area such an operation would require extensive security precautions.

More poignant in its way was the wholesale Jordanian desecration of the millennial Jewish cemetery on the slopes of the Mount of Olives, for this could be watched by Israeli look-outs on Mount Zion. Jordanian spokesmen have since claimed that the terrible damage wreaked in the cemetery was the work of Israeli artillery during the fighting. In the first place the cemetery was out of range of gunfire from any Jewish position, save perhaps Mount Scopus, where there were no artillery weapons. Nor were there any worthwhile targets in the cemetery during the fighting, save the occasional sniper. When this has been pointed out, the Jordanian second line of defence has been that the cemetery was really only a hundred years old, that the land belonged to the Muslim Waqf, and that the lease of it to the Jewish community had expired some years ago. All of this is nonsense; the cemetery has been in constant use for over a thousand years, and by 1948 there were already more than 50,000 tombs in it; while plots of ground had been bought by Jewish families since time immemorial.[21]

The desecration of the cemetery began in earnest early in 1949; until then, stones had only been removed haphazardly by Arab householders for their own purposes. From 1949 onwards Jewish tombs were systematically despoiled and desecrated – a by-product of the removal of stones for more or less intelligible purposes seems to have been the smashing of many of those left behind. A detailed report on the uses to which tombstones were put was compiled after the Israeli capture of East Jerusalem in 1967, and after these tombstones had been located in all sorts of improbable places:[22]

(a) Paving of the broad Jericho–Jerusalem highway which was built slap through the middle of the cemetery. There was no difficulty in locating tombstones there!

(b) Paving of an access road to the Intercontinental Hotel, which the Jordanians brashly erected on the very top of the Mount of Olives, beyond doubt one of the most important of all Christian Holy Places (for wherever Golgotha may have been, the Mount of Olives remains where it always was).

(c) Use in Jordanian military camps. One example was the Arab Legion camp at Bethany. There, tombstones were used to pave paths, and one such path led to a camp latrine. Jordanian army boots trod perpetually over Hebrew inscriptions in stone, in reassertion of the rights of Islam over a subject-race.

(d) Exposure of graves to dig communication-trenches and fox-holes. This happened during the fighting; some military men, admittedly, would excuse or even approve this action.

(e) Building houses over graves and using tombstones in their construction. There were a few examples, only, of this, including that of the official 'caretaker', Sadar Khalil, a sad reflection on Jordanian officialdom.

(f) Using headstones as material for military emplacements, stables and chicken-coops. There is a revealing photograph of a Rabbi Nigrin of Jerusalem surveying, from a squatting posture, his own mother's gravestone, in a former Jordanian emplacement.

(g) Sundry other uses. In more than one place, the Jordanians cleared a large burial plot and levelled it, for use as a car park. In other places, the Jewish cemetery was used as a garbage-dump. More felicitously, trees were planted on top of graves, but certainly not to embellish the site, rather as a source of gain.

The case of Sadar Khalil, the caretaker of the cemetery, appointed by the Jordanian authorities, deserves a footnote. During the 1967 war he fled, with good reason, to Jordan. His son, Halil, was treated by the Israelis with courtesy, for he was not pressed about the construction of the family home. The following dialogue took place:[23]

Question: 'What was your father's job?'

Answer: 'He had to make sure that private persons did not take away stones and tombstones without the *Government's approval*. Some merchants had a *concession to traffic in stones* from the cemetery – everyone else we would chase away.'

Question: 'How were the graves destroyed?'

Answer: 'Labourers would demolish by day, and at night the Legion's trucks would come, load up and move off.'

It is beyond doubt, then, that the desecration of the cemetery was not merely countenanced, but was organized by the Jordanian authorities. The Jewish presence was to be utterly banished from East Jerusalem and all traces of it obliterated. The removal of tombstones was an operation which did not need to be hurried, as 'practical' uses had to be found for them. But after the capture of East Jerusalem by Israel in 1967 it was found that 38,000 tombstones out of 50,000 had either been removed, defaced or smashed. A mosque was built, squarely in the middle of the ancient cemetery, as a symbol of Muslim possession.

In the United Nations General Assembly Israel's representative, Yosef Tekoah, declared:

> Again the world stood by in silence. Nobody raised his voice. Where are the Security Council resolutions about the destruction of Jewry's Holy Places and religious sites in Jerusalem? Where are the Security Council resolutions condemning the desecration of the cemetery on the Mount of Olives? Where are the Security Council interventions about Jordan's refusal to allow free access to Holy Places and to the humanitarian institutions on Mount Scopus, in accordance with the General Armistice Agreement? When has the Security Council called on the Jordanian invaders stationed on the Old City walls to desist from keeping Jerusalem's population under constant menace, from firing indiscriminately, from satisfying the lust for blood in the murder of children, innocent archaeologists, unsuspecting tourists?[24]

Here were a number of accusations regarding matters other than the pillaging and destruction of the Jewish Quarter and Jewish Holy Places. First, then, the matter of access to the Holy Places and to Mount Scopus.

Article 8 of the 1949 Israeli–Jordanian Armistice Agreement was explicit. It laid down that there should be 'free access to the Holy Places and to cultural institutions, and use of the Jewish cemetery on the Mount of Olives'. Instead, the Jordanians hermetically sealed the frontier which ran through the middle of Jerusalem. The result was that 'for the first time since the Roman conquest of Jerusalem in the first century, Jews were barred from their holiest of places – the Wailing (Western) Wall, and from any rewarding access to the cultural, educational and religious sites on the Mount of Olives and Mount Scopus'.[25] The two main institutions on Mount Scopus were the Hebrew University and the Hadassah Hospital. They lay empty and derelict from 1948 to 1967, and the Israeli Municipality in West Jerusalem was obliged to build a new university and a new hospital. The President of the UN Trusteeship Council, Roger Garreau, did make an attempt to resolve the question of freedom of access to holy places but reported failure in 1950. He added:

> At least there is still ground for hope that the understanding and benevolent attitude of one of the two governments concerned [Israel] toward the legitimate demands of all the parties concerned for a just and lasting solution ... will finally persuade the other Government [Jordan] ... to take the wishes of the United Nations into consideration and to collaborate loyally in ensuring justice, peace and permanent security in the city of Jerusalem as well as the protection of, and free access to the Holy Places.

Not so; the Jordanians remained adamant and the frontier remained closed. It was not only the Jews who were deprived of access to their holy places; Israel's Arabs, who grew from a population of 150,000 to over 500,000 in the course of the next three decades, were unable to visit the Dome of the Rock and the El Aqsa Mosque, or to make the pilgrimage to Mecca. The closed frontier inflicted much human hardship too, just as the infamous Berlin Wall does today: friend was separated from friend, relative from relative. The Arabs of Israel became a forlorn and isolated community, through no fault of their own. Indeed, they were the best of Arab patriots, since by staying in their homes, they maintained an Arab stake in that part of Palestine.

The religious centres of these Israeli Arabs were scrupulously respected, in sharp contrast to what happened to those of the Jews in East Jerusalem. But there was Jordanian discrimination against the Christian Churches too. Christian Arabs tended on the whole to be better educated – they had church schools to thank for that – as well as being generally more prosperous than Muslims; because of this there were constant and absurd rumours that the Christian Arabs were intent on acquiring all of the valuable land in Jerusalem. The Jordanian Government took these rumours sufficiently seriously to pass legislation in 1965, blocking the acquisition of land or houses in Jerusalem by Christian institutions, whether through purchase, legacy or gift.[26] In 1958 Christian schools were forced to close on Fridays, the Muslim day of rest – Christian tradesmen had already been obliged to close their shops on that day. In the same year, members of the Brotherhood of the Holy Sepulchre, who had always been of Greek nationality since the order was founded in the fifth century, were obliged by law to become Jordanian nationals. Christians, throughout the nineteen years of

Jordanian rule, had the right to stay away from work on Sunday only up to 10 o'clock in the morning.

In 1953 a law was passed restricting the ways in which the funds of Christian organizations could be used. Christian schools came under restrictions too; they had to teach all subjects in Arabic, and no Christian religious instruction could be given to non-Christian pupils – because of their excellent standards, church schools took in plenty of pupils from the richer Muslim families. Christian children had to be instructed in the Koran. In 1966 church institutions had their customs and privileges, covering in particular medicines and medical equipment, withdrawn. There was a further injection of 'Islamization' into the syllabuses of church schools, and further steps in this direction were forecast. By 1967 a critical situation was reached over education, and only the outbreak of the 1967 war averted a real show-down. Had it come, church bodies would have probably fought their battles singly and with little or no help from outside the country. For Christian churches competed for converts and clung desperately to their existing, dwindling congregations. In 1964, incidentally, Jordan banned the activities of Jehovah's Witnesses on the grounds that their sect was over-friendly to Jews.

The Christian communities were dwindling for other reasons than religious ones. There was discrimination against Christians over all sorts of appointments, especially in government services and the armed forces. For reasons which cannot be satisfactorily explained, there was an influx of inhabitants of Hebron into East Jerusalem. The Hebronites, guardians of the Tomb of Abraham, are fiercely Muslim, and Christian Arabs must have regarded their increasing influence as a threat. Significantly, only one out of eight Jordanian Governors was a Jerusalemite. Of even greater importance to the hard-working and intelligent Christian community was Jerusalem's economic stagnation. Of course, this was partly due to the physical division of the city and the closed frontier with Israel; both East and West Jerusalem were at 'the end of the line' and trade could be carried on only with half a hinterland. But Jordanian governments undoubtedly neglected Jerusalem – it was too near the 'front line' and virtually all industrial development was carried out to the east of the River Jordan. Amman grew from a large village of 20,000 to a sprawling city of 300,000. Not so East Jerusalem.

Its population in 1948 was about 65,000. Twenty years later, it was almost exactly the same. Stagnation was illustrated by the absence of construction of public housing, and by inadequate services, with 60 per cent of households without running water, 30 per cent without electricity and four out of every five lacking reasonable sanitation. Lack of economic and social progress affected the Christian Arabs most of all, and they declined disastrously in numbers. In 1948 they numbered 25,000; twenty years later there were 10,795 left. Their birth-rate was lower than that of the Muslims, but emigration was the main cause of this sensational decline. Put another way, the Christians made up 38 per cent of the Arab population of East Jerusalem in 1948; in 1967 they comprised just under 15 per cent.

Perhaps it would be unfair to blame King Hussein of Jordan for what happened. Apart from strategic considerations, he could hardly be expected to trust the Palestinians; they were, after all, responsible for about half of the dozen or so attempts made on his life and they killed his grandfather, Abdallah, in 1951, when standing only a few feet away from him. Even in Jordan 'proper', that is to the east of the River Jordan, Hussein was afraid of the thrifty, able Palestinians acquiring an undue share of power, and relied upon the support of the Bedouin tribes which were utterly loyal to his Hashemite dynasty. The King built an 'East Ghor Canal' to the east of the Jordan and parallel with it, but not the 'West Ghor Canal' which had been projected. The east bank of the river became the country's market garden, while the west bank remained arid desert.[27] The King rarely went to Jerusalem – he was seen far more often at Aqaba, water-skiing – and only in the last years before the 1967 war did he begin building a 'summer palace' just off the Jerusalem–Ramallah road, the one part of East Jerusalem where some ribbon-development building had taken place. It was still not finished when war broke out. Hussein built a university in Amman, none in Jerusalem. This was a singular disservice to the Palestinians of the West Bank, who preferred to study in Cairo or Beirut, rather than Amman.[28] Every year there were around 2,000 Palestinian students in these 'foreign' universities, and only a handful from the West Bank at Amman's.

By the time of the 1967 war the only real signs of prosperity in East Jerusalem were the tourist industry and its principal financiers, the banks. There were only two firms employing more than fifty people, and the average workshop had an employ of only five. There were 2.4 persons to every room against 1.6 in West Jerusalem, and only one family in five had a refrigerator, against 77 per cent of West Jerusalem householders.

Unemployment was chronic. There were proportionately only half as many cars in East Jerusalem, and per capita income was about one-quarter of that in West Jerusalem, although prices and taxes were lower.[29] Yet East Jerusalem had the West Bank on its doorstep and the Jordanian market only forty minutes drive away; West Jerusalem was at the extreme end of a narrow corridor of Israeli territory, and the Arab blockade of the state meant that most of Israel's markets were several thousand miles away, in Europe and America.

Jordanian policies made Jerusalem very often a dangerous place in which to live. It was, as a future Mayor pointed out, 'a half-city' where one 'constantly sensed an atmosphere of war'.[30] The situation was 'uniquely difficult. Half the time your drove down a road or a side street, you ran into a sign reading: STOP! DANGER! FRONTIER AHEAD!' The Jordanian Army laid minefields through the heart of the city, established machine-gun nests, set up barbed-wire entanglements. Trigger-happy Jordanian frontier guards continually fired shots into West Jerusalem, and the Jordanian authorities would apologetically tell United Nations officials who inquired into such incidents that 'a soldier went mad'.[31] In April 1953, shooting went on for over twenty-four hours; in July 1954 it lasted intermittently for three days. There was a whole spate of such incidents in 1962 and 1963. Sometimes Israelis were attacked by Arab infiltrators, and hardly a month went by without a West Jerusalemite either being killed or wounded. One victim was a Baptist clergyman who went out to help a Christian Arab boy through a minefield, and had one of his legs blown off. On their side, the Israelis built protecting walls in places which drew down snipers' fire. The protecting walls themselves would then often be used by the Jordanians for target practice. An unpleasant feature of Jordanian tactics became fully apparent only after the 1967 war. The Israelis found that the minarets of the Dome of the Rock, the El Aqsa Mosque and the mosque at Sheikh Jarrah had all been used as snipers' positions, that part of the precinct of the Dome of the Rock had been used for storing military equipment, and that the Holy Cave beneath that building had been an ammunition dump.

In an open letter to the UN Ambassador of the Kingdom of Jordan, Monsignor John Oesterreicher, a Catholic prelate, remarked that King Hussein had lately proclaimed: 'My people and I regard ourselves as the guardians and custodians of Jerusalem on behalf of the entire Muslim world, as well as on behalf of the Christian and Muslim population of the city and all

Palestine.'[32] The Monsignor suggested that this claim was 'illegitimate and unacceptable'. He detailed the misdeeds of Jordanian rule in East Jerusalem, and took particular exception to the fact that 'with the help of Pan American Airlines, Jordan built the Hotel Intercontinental – a plush hotel on the hill of Jesus' agony!' (the Mount of Olives). He pointed out, too, that even his fellow Arabs had joined in uprisings against his rule in Jerusalem: thus in April 1963 several demonstrations took place and in the course of them eleven demonstrators were killed and over 150 wounded, including seventeen girl students. He utterly rejected King Hussein's claim to be Jerusalem's guardian and protector.

The Monsignor could have added that again, in 1966, there were no fewer than seven demonstrations against Jordanian rule in Jerusalem and West Bank towns, when more than a score of Palestinian Arabs were killed. It is curious that events of this kind attracted so little attention, whereas any affrays in which Israelis were involved automatically made headline news and have continued to do so. The reasons for this, at least where Britain was concerned, are clear. Jordan was the successor state to Transjordan, which was a British dependency, which Britain created unilaterally in 1922 and by so doing, detached three-quarters of the Mandatory area from Palestine west of the Jordan. There has always been a feeling of 'special relationship' between Britain and Jordan, and this feeling has been heightened by King Hussein's personal courage and charm and by his obviously anglophile sympathies. To his credit must be the fact that, alone among Arab rulers, he offered full citizenship to Palestinian refugees. In Jerusalem his representatives showed a degree of patience and skill in dealing with internal Christian feuds. But Jordanian trusteeship of East Jerusalem, from 1948 to 1967, could not possibly inspire confidence in the ability of King Hussein's government and country to fulfil a similar role in the future.

REFERENCES

1. Article by Martin Gilbert, from *Jerusalem Perspectives*, ed. by Peter Schneider and Geoffrey Wigoder, Furnival Press, London, 1976.
2. Sir John Bagot Glubb, *Peace in the Holy Land*, Hodder & Stoughton, London, 1971.
3. Sir John Bagot Glubb, *A Soldier with the Arabs*, Hodder & Stoughton, London, 1957.

4.   Ibid.
5.   Ibid.
6.   Ibid.
7.   Ibid.
8.   Sir John Bagot Glubb, *Peace in the Holy Land.*
9.   Edward Luttwak and Dan Horowitz, *The Israeli Army*, Allen Lane, London, 1975.
10. James Cameron, *The Making of Israel*, Secker & Warburg, London, 1976.
11. Ibid.
12. Meron Benvenisti, *Jerusalem: The Torn City*, Isratypeset, Jerusalem, 1976.
13. Speech at Arab League meeting, Cairo, 15 May 1948.
14. Elihu Lauterpacht, *Jerusalem and the Holy Places*, Anglo-Israel Association, October 1968.
15. Abdallah el-Tal, *Disaster of Palestine*, Cairo, 1959.
16. UN Security Council minutes, 22 May 1948.
17. *Rebuttals of Jordanian Misstatements about Israel's Administration of Jerusalem*, Israel Foreign Ministry, October 1972.
18. Ibid.
19. Abdallah el-Tal, op. cit.
20. *Rebuttals of Jordanian Misstatements.*
21. Ibid.
22. Ibid.
23. Ibid.
24. Yosef Tekoah, *Barbed Wire shall not return to Jerusalem*, extracts from speeches at the UN, Israel Information Services Publication, New York, 1968.
25. *Rebuttals of Jordanian Misstatements.*
26. Ibid.
27. Peter Snow, *Hussein*, Barrie & Jenkins, London, 1972.
28. Michael Krupp, in *Christian News from Israel*, vol. XXIII, no. 1, 1972.
29. Meron Benvenisti, op. cit.
30. Teddy Kollek, *For Jerusalem*, Weidenfeld, London, 1978.
31. Ibid.
32. Monsignor Oesterreicher, pamphlet of Anglo-Israel Association, November, 1971.
33. Ibid.

CHAPTER FIVE

The Road to Reunification

In a sense the division of Jerusalem from 1948 to 1967 was symbolic – its true and lasting unity can only be established when there is both peace and friendship between Jews and Arabs. The latter use the word 'salaam', meaning peace in a conventional sense. A different Arabic word, 'sulh', expresses the deeper meaning of peace allied to reconciliation. Such a condition has never existed in Jerusalem since the Roman conquest divided the city between master and subject races. The Muslims merely prolonged this state of affairs.

Israel had accepted Jerusalem's internationalization when the United Nations proposed it as part of a package agreement for the settlement of the whole Arab–Israeli dispute. This was the same reaction as that of the true mother of the child whom King Solomon ruled could be divided in two, if the two contenders for its possession could not settle their differences. Initial Israeli acceptance of internationalization was dictated by love of the city which had played a unique part in Jewish existence. Peace was its paramount need.

The war, and its outcome, meant that Israel would settle down to doing the best that it could with what remained of Jerusalem in its hands. There can be no doubt, however, that there was deep disillusionment over what had been lost. It included the whole of the Jewish Quarter of the Old City, the Western Wall – holiest place of all – the Mount of Olives cemetery, the Bath of Rabbi Ishmael and the Pool of Siloam, and the tombs of Absalom, Zachariah and Simon the Just (the last was turned into a stable by the Jordanians). About the only important Jewish holy place which remained in Israeli hands was the Tomb of David.

On all sides West Jerusalem was surrounded by hostile Arab territory, save to the west, where a corridor barely five miles wide linked the city with the rest of the State of Israel. Its frontiers with the Arab state of Jordan were hermetically sealed. The only 'peep hole' was at the so-called 'Mandelbaum Gate', between the West Jerusalem religious quarter of Mea Shearim and the 'American Colony' in East Jerusalem. The Jordanians permitted passage through this ramshackle apology for a customs-house only to Christian pilgrims and other tourists – one-way only, for having left Israel they were not allowed to return there – diplomats, personnel of the United Nations truce supervisory commission, and the fortnightly 'relief' contingents of Israeli police which looked after the enclave on Mount Scopus.

West Jerusalem certainly suffered from its position as an outpost. The pulsating heart of Israel was in Tel Aviv, and Haifa, sitting proudly on its beautiful bay, could well have claimed to be Israel's second city. Truncated West Jerusalem suffered from poor communications. The old main road to the coast was cut at Latrun, which remained in Arab hands, and the relief road rambled over hill and dale. It took the best part of two hours to drive from Jerusalem to Tel Aviv – when the new highway was built in the 1970s the time taken was halved – and the rail journey took well over three hours. West Jerusalem had no hinterland; its supplies had to travel up from the coastal plain and it was next to impossible to create competitive industries for its inhabitants. In some respects, West Jerusalem was worse placed than West Berlin, for the latter began its life in geographical isolation with efficient industries and with East European markets prepared to take its goods and services.

One observer described its 'small town character' when, even in 1965, it was still 'a provincial border town'. Members of parliamentary committees often preferred meeting in Tel Aviv, and spending the 'long week-end' out of Jerusalem was axiomatic for them and many government servants: 'Tourists came up in the morning for sightseeing and returned to their Tel Aviv hotels in the afternoon. The new Israel Museum was floodlit so that those who chanced to stay overnight would have something to look at after the sun went down.'[1] Jerusalem had been proclaimed a 'development town', but the percentage of its population employed in industry was barely half the national average, and 'there was not even a bank in town that could provide business loans of any size, and merchants had to travel down to Tel Aviv for their credit needs'.[2]

West Jerusalem's immediate salvation lay in it becoming Israel's main administrative centre. The Prime Minister's office moved there from Tel Aviv on 16 December 1949. All other principal government offices, with the exception of the Ministries of Defence, Police and Foreign Affairs, followed on 1 January 1950. Israel's Parliament, the Knesset, had already moved to Jerusalem on 26 December 1949, and on 23 January 1950, Jerusalem was proclaimed as being, and having always been, the capital of Israel.

The office and residence of the President would be transferred only in 1952, and the Ministry for Foreign Affairs a year later. The delay over moving them was for diplomatic reasons. The heads of foreign missions had to present their credentials to the President, and as long as the notion of Jerusalem as a 'corpus separatum' persisted, it was awkward for them to do so. Even after 1952 an exception was made for the Italian Minister, whose own government's intimate links with the Vatican were embarrassing, for the Vatican still explicitly recognized Jerusalem as a 'corpus separatum'. The Minister was therefore allowed to present his credentials to President Ben-Zvi when the latter was visiting Tiberias, in Galilee. Diplomats had to do much of their business with the Ministry for Foreign Affairs, and so an appropriate and 'diplomatic' reason was given for moving it to the capital – it was 'convenient' that it should not be cut off from the office of the Prime Minister and other government departments.[3] But, in order to make allowance for delicate sensibilities, a Foreign Ministry liaison office was maintained in Tel Aviv until 1962. The Ministry of Defence, for its own security, stayed there for good.

The conversion of West Jerusalem into a fully functioning capital city was a shot in the arm for its inhabitants. It brought jobs and trade. More important, it reduced the feeling of isolation and exposure and it certainly helped that over twenty foreign embassies and a number of other foreign missions moved in, thereby risking Arab displeasure. It encouraged the building of numerous institutions. The new Hadassah Hospital was set up near Ein Kerem, to the west of the city, and the new Hebrew University on the Givat Ram campus below the growing complex of government office-buildings. These would be followed by the Israel Museum, the National Convention Centre and a new National Library. The building began of residential suburbs at Beit Hakerem, Kiryat Hovel and Bayit Vegan. In the middle of the city the Histadrut (Trade Union) headquarters and the Chief Rabbinate were established; outside the city, a national cemetery and place of mourning was established on Mount Herzl, with a military cemetery and the Yad Vashem memorial centre dedicated to the 6,000,000 Jews murdered by the Nazis.

The religious importance of Jerusalem to the Jewish people was bound to be enhanced. Save during the short period of the British Mandate, the Jewish religion had existed and functioned on sufferance only for the best part of two thousand years in Jerusalem. Now it exercised its own rights in its own city. The religious quarter of Mea Shearim was long-established; now two more, smaller religious quarters were built to the north and west of the city, at Kiryat Mattersdorf and Givat Shaul. A number of religious colleges were built, and the Ministry for Religious Affairs established a new religious centre round the Tomb of David. Two new cemeteries were opened to compensate for the loss of the main cemetery on the Mount of Olives.

New shops, supermarkets, banks, cinemas, theatres, post offices and telephone exchanges were opened. Large sections of West Jerusalem began to take on the appearance of a thoroughly modern city, although slums remained, especially along and just off the Jaffa Road stretching westward out of the city. Several small industrial estates were built, and hotels to serve the slowly expanding tourist industry: there was not much to bring foreign tourists other than Jews, for the most important Christian holy places were all in East Jerusalem. But a number of new hotels were built, roughly doubling the number of hotel rooms to something under 4,000 by 1967.

The water problem was dealt with successfully. In 1934 the British authorities began to bring pumped water from the Ras-el-Ayn springs, in the coastal plain, but during the 1948 War of Independence the Arab Legion and Iraqi troops occupied the main pumping station and cut off Jerusalem's water supply. An appeal made by the UN Truce Supervisory Commission on 20 May 1948, to allow the water supply to Jerusalem to be restored, was categorically turned down by the Jordanian Government.[4] It was left to a Hebrew University professor, Leo Picard, to propose deep drillings in and around Jerusalem.[5] His suggestion was taken up; twenty-seven drillings took place, with the result that local water supply was raised to over 11 million cubic metres. West Jerusalem's additional needs, estimated at about 13 million cubic metres, were supplied by the National Water Carrier, which brought water from the upper reaches of the Jordan and the Sea of Galilee.

Public parks and gardens, and a Biblical zoo, were opened. Sport lagged behind and there were few swimming-pools or football fields. It took several years to build the University sports stadium; tennis courts were barely heard of, and the Jerusalem cricket team had to play their matches on opponents' pitches. West Jerusalem's was a quiet, reflective atmosphere, and there were relatively few restaurants and virtually no night-life. The big religious element in the city was partly responsible for this. By the mid-1960s there were increasing numbers of clashes between religious groups and their opponents over observance of the Sabbath. No public transport operated on the Sabbath, but religious districts objected to private motorists too. Mea Shearim demanded the right to barricade all of its streets and this was conceded, with police manning the barricades. The religious communities went further; they wanted all motor transport banned on the Sabbath. This provoked a counter-action; a 'League against Religious Coercion' was formed and organized one massive motorcade in November 1965, which tried to enter Jerusalem from the west and demonstrate in its streets.[6] The motorcade was halted by the police on the outskirts of the city, and hundreds of drivers and passengers thereupon lay down on the main road, blocking all traffic for over three hours.

The religious communities objected strongly, too, to 'unseemly' dress, which included shorts and sleeveless blouses. Tourists were liable to be stoned – motorists too, as one coach-load of astonished Spanish pilgrims discovered.[7] There were furious protests against a municipal swimming-pool, because women were allowed in at the same time as men. The religious communities also forced the closure of a youth club close to the Jordanian border, because it was too 'near' Mea Shearim and because it was attended by both boys and girls. The club's excellent aim had been to keep these same boys and girls off the streets. There were even attempts, which failed, to blockade the main road out of Jerusalem, to prevent people from heading out to the seaside on the 'seventh day'. Maurice Samuel wrote, 'The Jewish people loves and hates itself, admires and despises itself, with pathological intensity. It is either God-selected or God-rejected.'[8] The activities of the extreme religious groups in Jerusalem were, and remain a case in point. Often they caused the authorities more problems than did the Jordanians.

Like every major city of the free world, Jerusalem was eternally short of money, indeed, more so than most, for Israel, carrying a huge defence burden and economically boycotted and blockaded by all of its neighbours, had at the same time to settle, house, train and employ more immigrants than its own 1948 population. Little money could be expected from the government, yet money was very badly needed. In 1952, according to one authority, 'we couldn't buy books, records or newspapers from abroad'.[9] The population rose from 100,000 in 1948, to 160,000 in 1960, and 195,000 seven years later. Moreover Jerusalem had a high birth-rate, and the biggest proportion of any Israeli city of children and old people combined. Really good municipal government was as badly needed as money.

This was not immediately forthcoming. Municipal staff had been used to Arab-controlled administration, since the Arabs had always provided the Mayor down to the dying days of the British Mandate. Tax collection was slack, and so was payment of rates, especially in the fairly extensive slum quarters. An uneasy coalition of political parties controlled the first two municipal administrations, and the second was dissolved by the Ministry of the Interior in 1955. For a time administration was carried on by a committee of officials appointed by the Ministry. Then in 1955 a Mapai (Labour Party) Mayor was elected, and he and his immediate successor presided over Labour-led coalitions for the next ten years. Their record was adequate but not, on the whole, inspiring. To save money, the Municipality scrapped badly-needed road-building projects; to make money, it approved high-rise buildings which would cause much dissension later on. There was a continuing, if understandable failure to stop neighbourhoods near the Jordanian border and former city centre from deteriorating. The westward orientation of West Jerusalem increased the rift between the already separated East and West Jerusalem; at the same time, it increased the sense of separation and isolation.[10]

In 1965 came a turning-point in the affairs of West Jerusalem. The municipal elections appeared to have produced a stalemate. But one of the candidates was Teddy Kollek, a former Mapai member who had left his party, largely out of deference to Israel's first and greatest prime minister, David Ben-Gurion, who had quarrelled with the party leadership and formed his own 'Rafi' breakaway group. Largely by virtue of his own ebullient personality, Kollek won 20 per cent of the votes, twice as much as Rafi's average following in the country at large. This gave him only five out of twenty-one seats on the municipal council. Mapai also had five, along with experience in office and potential allies in the shape of parties which had served in its previous coalitions. But Kollek's personality was worth more than these apparently decisive advantages; astonishingly, he mobilized sixteen out of the twenty-one members to form what he modestly called a 'workable' coalition.[11]

Kollek combined the quick wits and charm of Vienna, where he had been brought up, with the energy and stamina of a fighting bull. He had worked very hard in his previous post, as an adviser in the office of the Prime Minister; now he embarked on a round-the-clock routine which displayed yet another characteristic, which had perhaps not been so obvious before, a deep and abiding dedication to Jerusalem. Non-religious himself, he was still acutely conscious of the religious tradition of the city and determined to maintain it. Later he would write: 'More synagogues and religious schools were built during my term than in any other period of the city's history; more roads in religious quarters were closed to Sabbath traffic; and incidents of incitement by purposely driving through an Orthodox quarter on a Sabbath have stopped.'[12]

He was very much aware of the magnitude of his task when he took over. In an interview at the time he declared:

> Jerusalem seems to me to be just as much a problem as the whole of Israel. It is being built without adequate planning and without architectural concepts. Big ugly blocks of flats have been put down anywhere; straggling suburbs are sprouting up all over the place. Building, which is going on unceasingly, is done without regard to surroundings, without regard to whatever has already been built or to the people living in the place. One of the first things I discovered was a large-scale project already under way which would wreck the Beit Hakerem suburb.
>
> The road-building plans are hopelessly behind schedule. Road-making has been sadly mismanaged, and a dozen new roads have been built badly, opened prematurely, and then closed. There is a staggering amount of dirt, confusion and mismanagement, and the people of Jerusalem are already beginning to lose pride in their own neighbourhoods. My four years as Mayor are going to be years of frustration, of wasting time on the undoing of shoddy work and wretched planning.[13]

There were three reasons why his pessimism was not borne out by events. The first was his own indefatigable enthusiasm and pertinacity; he simply refused to admit that a battle was ever lost. The second was his aptitude for obtaining money, the outcome of his skill in arguing his case. Later he would write about Israel's Minister of Finance, the man who needed most convincing:

> As to Jerusalem, Sapir supported many of its institutions but not the city itself. Whenever I claimed that Jerusalem was not getting its share, he showed me long lists of industrial and educational institutions that had been showered with funds. He had no understanding of the fact that when you invest hundreds of millions of pounds in a university, for example, you have also to invest an appropriate amount at least in building the roads leading to it.[14]

Pinhas Sapir was a hard nut to crack, but Kollek certainly got more from him than any previous Mayor had done; and he collected from all and sundry, especially from Jewish communities in other countries, where he was a welcome and immensely convincing speaker and where his case was always given deferential attention.

The third reason why his pessimism proved to be unfounded was the outbreak of the 1967 war, just half-way through Kollek's first term in office. The Six Day War of June 1967 was to be of historic importance in Jerusalem's history.

It began on 5 June, and the events leading up to it need not be described in detail here. They followed an unmistakable pattern of Arab planning to attack and annihilate Israel. On 13 May the Soviet Union informed Egypt's President Nasser that Israel was concentrating 'huge armed forces of about eleven to thirteen brigades' on the Syrian border.[15] This was utterly false but on 15 May the Egyptian Army began to advance through the Sinai Peninsula towards the Israeli frontier, for Nasser disregarded an assurance sent to him by Israel's Prime Minister, Levi Eshkol, that Israel had no intention of initiating any military action.

On 16 May Egypt demanded the withdrawal of the UN Emergency Force, which had been patrolling the Egyptian–Israeli border and preventing armed clashes. The first UNEF post was occupied by Egyptian troops on 17 May and the last by 23 May. On 22 May Nasser announced that the Straits of Tiran, connecting the Gulf of Aqaba with the Red Sea, would be closed to all Israeli shipping. Most of Israel's oil came from Iran, through the Straits to the port of Eilat. On 24 May the Cairo newspaper *El Ahram* stated that the Straits had already been closed by laying mines in its narrow channel and mounting artillery weapons at the fort of Sharm el Sheikh. In a broadcast, Nasser said bluntly 'The Arab people want to fight. We have been waiting for the right time, when we would be completely ready. Lately we have felt that our strength is sufficient.'

On 27 May the Soviet Ambassador to Israel, Chuvakhin, called on Eshkol in the middle of the night and warned Israel against firing the first shot. This was sheer effrontery; had the Soviet Union wanted to help, it would have corrected its own false reports of Israeli troops massed on Syria's frontier and would have urged Nasser to abandon the blockade of the Straits of Tiran. On 28 May Nasser declared that 'Israel's existence is in itself an aggression' and that a state of war against Israel already existed. Egyptian troops were indeed already firing across Israel's frontier. On 30 May King Hussein of Jordan flew to Cairo, signed a military pact with Egypt, and put his army under Egyptian command. Iraq undertook to join the pact five days later, while Syria was already in full military alliance with Egypt.

On 4 June Nasser stated: 'We are facing you [Israel] in battle and are burning with desire for it to start in order to obtain revenge ... This will make the world realize what the Arabs are and what Israel is.' The 'Voice of the Arabs' radio station promised two Tel Aviv girls for every Arab 'conqueror', and Radio Damascus issued a final call to arms: 'Fight, Arabs! Let them know that we shall hang the last imperialist soldier with the entrails of the last Zionist!'[16] War began, in a formal sense, between Egypt and Israel on 5 June when Israeli planes attacked ten Egyptian airfields and destroyed the greater part of the Egyptian air force while its planes were still on the ground.

This still did not mean there would be war in Jerusalem. Teddy Kollek, no starry-eyed optimist, wrote: 'We were pretty confident Jerusalem would be spared ... After all, we thought, Jerusalem is a holy city.'[17] But, 'suddenly, while it was still morning, the shelling started in Jerusalem. We could hear it and see it. There was no other fighting, no soldiers shooting rifles; just shelling from the Arab side.' The shelling was sporadic and ill-directed; even so, in three days nearly one thousand houses in West Jerusalem were hit.

One Arab historian has claimed that 'Israel began a simultaneous surprise attack on three Arab states, Egypt, Jordan and Syria'.[18] To say that Israel's attack on Egypt was a 'surprise' is true only in so far as its exact timing was concerned – Egypt had already declared itself to be in a state of war with Israel, had marched a considerable army across the Sinai Peninsula to Israel's borders, and was blockading Israel's coast. It could be argued that no counter-action by Israel could reasonably be regarded as a surprise.

Where Jordan was concerned, the facts were as follows:

At 9 a.m. Eshkol sent a message to the UN chief observer, General Odd Bull, to transmit to King Hussein. He promised that there would be no Israeli action against Jordan, 'if Jordan did not attack Israel'. This message was duly transmitted.

At 9.58 a.m. Jordan Radio broadcast: 'Israel's end is in your hands! Strike at her everywhere, until victory!'

At 10.20 a.m. Jordan began to shell West Jerusalem.

At 10.20 a.m. a second message from Eshkol, promising once more that there would be no Israeli action if Jordan did not attack Israel, reached the head of Jordan's delegation to the Mixed Armistice Commission, Colonel Muhammad Daud. He sent the message on to King Hussein, who received it around 11 a.m.

At about 1 p.m. Jordanian troops advanced on Government House, the UN headquarters standing on neutral ground, which they captured.

During all this, the only action taken by Israel was to order its forces in Jerusalem to return fire when fired upon, but to take no other action. Israeli restraint was remarkable, and the troop commander in Jerusalem, General Uzi Narkiss, has since admitted to having been beside himself with impatience.[19] He had only a single brigade, with fifty tanks, under his command. He knew that Jordanian armour would be moving up from the valley of the Jordan and had to be halted before it reached the city. To do this, his own troops, which would otherwise be seriously outnumbered, had to link up with the small detachment of Israeli defenders on the commanding heights of Mount Scopus, overlooking the road up the steep hillside from Jericho. Only in the late afternoon was he told that he could counter-attack, and then initially only towards Jordanian-occupied Government House.

The situation was saved only by the dilatory movement of the Jordanian army, almost certainly because of indecisive Egyptian command. The Jordanian armoured columns moved at a snail's pace up the road from Jericho, and Jordanian troops already in Jerusalem made no serious effort to capture the weakly held

Mount Scopus – there were only 100 armed Israelis there, with old Bren guns. Narkiss's men arrived there before either of the Jordanian forces and from then on the result of the battle for Jerusalem was not in doubt. In the latter stages of the fighting, Narkiss's main problems arose from the order given to avoid damaging the Old City and its holy places at all cost. The consequence was the sacrifice of the lives of many of his young soldiers, who had to fight their way through the narrow alley-ways of the Old City without artillery support. On 7 June the whole of East Jerusalem was in Israeli hands.

King Hussein's role was a sorry one. In his memoirs, he fully admitted that he received Eshkol's pledge of peace. But 'By this time, we were already fighting in Jerusalem, and our planes had just taken off to bomb Israeli air bases. So I answered Odd Bull: "They started the battle. Well, they are receiving our reply by air".'[20] In a newspaper interview, Hussein was rather more explicit: 'On 5 June after the fighting had already started, the Norwegian General of the UN, Odd Bull, handed me a communication from the Israeli side to the effect ... that if we would refrain from attacking we would escape the consequences that would otherwise be inevitable. By that time, however, we had no choice. We had to do everything to assist our allies.'[21]

In his autobiography, Abba Eban remarks that Hussein's sole ostensible excuse for attacking Israel was that Israel had 'unleashed' war against Egypt and that he was in honour bound to come to Egypt's assistance.[22] If so, it must have been one of the most foolishly quixotic acts in the history of war; Hussein would have done better to reflect that he had been most unwise to put his troops under Egyptian command, that he would commit himself to all-out attack if he moved them across the Jordan, and that Nasser's boastful and utterly false claim that Egypt had already destroyed 75 per cent of the Israeli air force should have been treated with the gravest suspicion. Hussein may have been quixotic; he was certainly glaringly gullible into the bargain.

Abba Eban has written that 'Israel has no cause to regret that even under Jordanian fire she gave King Hussein the opportunity of prudence'. As he made clear, it required courage in the cause of keeping the peace in Jerusalem to do this. For, 'the Jordanian Prime Minister, Sa'ad Jum'a, had said in his morning broadcast: "For many years we have been waiting for this battle which will wipe out the shame of the past". In a contrary spirit, it could be said that Israel, for many years, had nourished the hope that Arab–Jewish coexistence would find its first expression in a settlement with Jordan'.[23] So it was, for 'even in wars, an unspoken assumption of ultimate accord hovered over the relations between Israel and Jordan.'[24] This was something that Hussein forgot, or failed to appreciate.

One should seek to understand Israeli reluctance to counter-attack after the Jordanians had gone to war in Jerusalem. The Judgement of Solomon should be recalled once more. If the 'child' had been politically bisected, it was still alive – Jerusalem had not been destroyed when it was divided in 1948. Jerusalem had been through so many perils and vicissitudes, that there was no good reason, as Jews saw it, to abandon hope for its salvation. Jerusalem, then, had to be spared the horrors of war; Uzi Narkiss's men did their utmost to ensure this and Narkiss kept the use of artillery to the minimum and refused to call in the air force. But Jerusalem, once re-won and reunified, became a different sort of proposition. Here are several views:

General Narkiss reported to the first Cabinet meeting after the Jordanian shelling began. The implications of a battle being fought – and a successful battle at that – in and over Jerusalem were perfectly appreciated at the meeting; one member of the Cabinet, the Minister of the Interior, Shapira, remarked that, 'If we get into the Old City, we shall not be able to leave again'. Narkiss's reflection was: 'I then had to ask myself – what should we do if we reach the Wall? I had no answer to that question. The subject was imponderable and we have still not absorbed the full impact of the Wall being re-won.'[25]

Teddy Kollek had much the same thought: 'To advance on the Jordanian-held sector of Jerusalem was, of course, more of a political risk than a military one. Each of us knew in his heart that once we took the Old City, we could never give it up.'[26] In the preliminary discussions, Kollek refused to give a view on whether the Israelis should counter-attack on the ground and seek to occupy East Jerusalem. A soldier like Narkiss had no doubts; he and his men had to reach Mount Scopus, for there was no hope that the tiny Israeli garrison there could hold out when the main force of the Jordanian army arrived. Narkiss feared that Hussein might offer a localized truce in Jerusalem, after capturing Scopus. From a military point of view, its heights were of vital importance; for Jordanian artillery emplaced there would dominate virtually the whole of West Jerusalem.[27]

Abba Eban agreed with Kollek's view:

It was well understood that the defence of western Jerusalem would involve the need to capture the eastern part; that once an Israeli army entered the Old City it would be historically and emotionally impossible to relinquish it to Jordanian hands again; and that unlike any other sector of the front, this one involved international repercussions which would carry the war far beyond its regional context.[28]

The now aged but still prescient David Ben-Gurion remarked to Kollek: 'This is not the end of the war. The Arabs cannot take such a defeat and such humiliation. They will never accept it.'[29]

This was perfectly and painfully true. The shock of defeat was, for the Arabs, appalling, traumatic. In six days Israel smashed the armies and air forces of Egypt, Syria and Jordan. Israel's armies occupied the whole of the Sinai Peninsula, all Jordanian-held territory west of the River Jordan, and in the north the supposedly almost impregnable Golan Heights with the plateau beyond them. All three Arab countries must have realized that their capitals lay wide open to capture. But no humiliation was to them so profound as the loss of East Jerusalem. Its Mayor, Rouhi el-Khatib, had made a compact with some of his friends that they would all, within two days of the outbreak of war, drink coffee together in the Tel Aviv Hilton Hotel.[30] Instead, they saw, to their horror, the Israeli flag and its Star of David flying from the Dome of the Rock (incidentally, the moment that he heard of this, the Minister of Defence, Moshe Dayan, ordered that it should be taken down)[31].There were two particular Arab reactions in East Jerusalem itself to the defeat. The first was one of relief. As Abba Eban put it: 'In many places Arab populations had believed that Israelis would do to them what Arab armies would certainly have done to Israelis, had the fortune of battle gone the other way. They now knew that they were safe. But many who had feared the worst had concluded that prudence and safety lay across the Jordan.'[32] As in 1948, Arab propaganda had been blood-curdling, partly in order to stimulate Arab martial ardour and partly in the hope of frightening their enemies (in fact, it had the opposite effect: Israelis fought all the harder knowing that they were liable to be butchered if they fell into Arab hands). The East Jerusalemites now found that the Israelis were not devils with horns and tails, but quite ordinary people. Relief dominated in the first weeks after the war was over and found its chief expression in the ready intermingling of Jews and Arabs in the streets of both parts of Jerusalem.

But relief soon gave way to anger and shame. Israel, in Eban's evocative words, had 'committed the dark sin of survival',[33] which meant that it was 'transformed from David to Goliath overnight'. To the Arabs, this was unforgivable, for it destroyed the stereotype of the Jew as a 'dhimmi' and member of a subject race. Lest it be thought that this concept was transient, one should note that in February 1980 the Ayatollah Khomeini, the latest exponent of Islamic dogma, published a 'Little Green Book' in which he classified Jews with dogs and pigs as 'impure', and laid down that it was 'shameful' for any self-respecting Muslim to take orders from a Jewish foreman.[34] This was racism personified. In June 1967 the 67,000 inhabitants of East Jerusalem were among a million Arabs who suddenly had to take orders from uniformed Israeli conquerors. Their anger and shame, as Ben-Gurion rightly prophesied, would have repercussions.

For Israelis – indeed for most Jews, wherever they lived – the capture of East Jerusalem, and above all of the Western Wall, was a miracle, a gift from God. The following eye-witness account speaks for itself:

> I for one had never seen the Western Wall. But this was true of almost all the others who were with me today [June 7]. We dashed in through St Stephen's Gate and began to run, no one said where, but we all knew – to the Temple Mount and the Wall. We didn't know the way and we dashed around like blind people. I was suddenly afraid that I wouldn't find it. But then we did.
>
> Some of the soldiers simply caressed the stones. Some kneeled, some cried. They cried and then embraced and hugged each other. They were at a loss over what to do next. Strange sounds began to issue from one soldier's mouth; another began to stammer: 'We're in the Old City, we! Do you understand? The Wall! The Wall!' He looked round and everyone understood. 'Jerusalem is ours!' another soldier cried out, as if what we had before was not Jerusalem.[35]

Moshe Dayan was the first Cabinet Minister to reach the Wall. He said, 'We have returned to all that is holy in our land. We have returned never to be parted from it again.'[36] Menahem Begin, later to become Prime Minister, recited a prayer when he arrived at the Wall, thanking God in his mercy for restoring to the Jewish people what had for ever been their own and expressing the hope that 'the Temple may be speedily rebuilt in our days'.[37] Israel's Chief of Staff and another future Prime Minister, Itzhak Rabin, was 'breathless ... I felt truly shaken and stood there murmuring a prayer for peace. Motta Gur's paratroopers were struggling to reach the Wall and touch it. We stood among a tangle of rugged, battle-weary men who were unable to believe their eyes or restrain their emotions. Their eyes were moist with tears, their speech incoherent. The overwhelming desire was to cling to the Wall, to hold on to that great moment as long as possible.'[38]

One should remember that these were hard-bitten fighting men. So was their commander, Uzi Narkiss. His description: 'The Wall was before us. I trembled. There it was as I had known it – immense, mighty, in all its splendour ... overcome, I bowed my head in silence.'[39] Ezer Weizman, later to become Minister of Defence, was an air-ace – in 1980 he was still flying his own private Spitfire. He came to the Wall from the north, across the Temple Mount:

> The city was suddenly in our hands, but the air was still heavy with the stench of war. It's a unique smell, which the nostrils detect hours after battle subsides ... It was the first time my feet ever stepped freely on the Temple Mount. When I was seventeen, and entry into the area was strictly forbidden, I had put on the uniform of a British officer and entered the Mosque of Omar [Dome of the Rock], scared stiff that the disguise would be uncovered. Now I was here in triumph, a Jew in the uniform of an Israeli General. Bullets still whistled in the vicinity ... from the Temple Mount we went down to the Wall. We were getting closer, and I felt my heart and blood and breath revving up – faster and faster. I couldn't control it; I was breathing in thousands of years of my people's history.[40]

All these statements tell the same story. St Paul wrote: 'The Greeks seek after wisdom', but 'The Jews require a sign'.[41] The reunification of Jerusalem seemed to be such a sign, and the Chief Rabbi of the armed forces, Shlomo Goren, put it into ecstatic words: 'We have taken the City of God. We are entering the messianic era for the Jewish people.'[42] For the man in the street reunification was almost as dramatic; only one West Jerusalemite in five could recall the Old City at all clearly.

At the Western Wall Dayan offered, as far as he could, magnanimity, in a brief statement: 'To our Arab neighbours we extend, especially at this hour, the hand of peace. To members of the other religions, Christians and Muslims, I hereby promise faithfully that their full freedom and all their religious rights will be preserved. We did not come to Jerusalem to conquer the Holy Places of others.'[43] Man of action that he was, Dayan gave instant orders for all barriers which had marked the division of Jerusalem to be removed:

> The orders called for the demoliton of anti-sniping walls, clearance of minefields and disposal of the barbed-wire fences which had been a constant reminder of the partition of the city. I wanted the unity of Jerusalem to be given full practical expression, and I wanted it done quickly … I was regaled with howls of protest. There were urgent pleas from the Minister of the Interior and from Teddy Kollek, the mayor of Jewish Jerusalem. [But,] I heard them out, brushed aside their highly-coloured predictions and told them I saw no reason to change the orders. My reading of the situation and of the mood of the people, Arab and Jew, suggested that nothing untoward would occur, and if it did it could be handled. Free movement in both directions would be permitted forthwith, without hindrance, without checkposts, without special permits. We had to act immediately in accordance with the new reality.[44]

Dayan read the situation correctly. Later on, indeed, two-way movement in the reunified city became so great that the 'only thing the police had to do was try to unsnarl the traffic jams'. Kollek, with typical generosity, paid tribute to him: 'In one radiant day, Dayan proved right'.[45] For his part, Kollek repulsed a more serious challenge to commonsense. Ben-Gurion, allegedly, demanded that the walls of the Old City should be torn down, and Kollek's laconic rejection of such a step was: 'No sense of beauty'. The walls survived.[46]

There were some initial mistakes. The Arab Mayor, Rouhi al-Khatib, was treated somewhat roughly; he was sent for, not invited to sit down and interrupted when he began to make complaints.[47] Arab shanty dwellings in front of the Western Wall were demolished with dispatch; twenty-seven families were moved out of their homes and given temporary accommodation elsewhere, and around sixty buildings of one kind and another swept away. This clearance was completed by 12 June, and the reason for it was obvious: access to the Wall had been restricted to an alley-way; now a big square of open ground gave it space and dignity. Perhaps there could have been more effort to explain to the outside world what was being done, and why. There was a temporary curfew, but perhaps that too was unavoidable. There were still armed Jordanians taking refuge in the Old City.

On 14 June free movement throughout Jerusalem was instituted. In four days 350,000 people walked to the Western Wall. On 15 June all normal municipal services in East Jerusalem were restored, and the business began of linking them with those of West Jerusalem, to their mutual benefit. On 24 June more than 1,500 Israeli Muslims visited the El Aqsa Mosque, the first time they had been allowed to do so since 1948. On 26 June it was the turn of the Israeli Christians to visit the Church of the Holy Sepulchre. On 29 June the last restricted areas – restricted mainly in order to clear mines and unexploded shells – were opened up, and the last military check-points inside the city boundaries removed. Check-points remained only along the eastern outskirts of Jerusalem. West Bank Arabs were already enjoying free access to Jerusalem again, and in mid-July this was made possible for the 400,000 Arabs of the Gaza Strip – again, for the first time since 1948.

Jerusalem was formally declared a single, reunified city on 28 June and the Arab Municipal Council of East Jerusalem was officially abolished on 29 June. Its members found this undignified and unnecessary, for their council had automatically ceased to function the day before.[48] They had been ready to co-operate with the Israeli authorities in getting essential services working again, but they were not prepared to serve in the administration of Jerusalem under Israeli rule. This was understandable; their pride had been bitterly hurt, and they had no desire to be denounced as quislings by the rest of the Arab world.

In the meantime, several important steps had been taken, on 27 June, to clarify the administrative and religious questions relating to Jerusalem. The Knesset passed three pieces of administrative legislation. Under the first, the Government was empowered to apply Israeli law to any part of Palestine. Under the second, freedom of access to all holy places was guaranteed and they were placed under the Government's protection. Acts of desecration would be punished, with up to seven years' imprisonment. The third law enabled the Government to extend the municipal boundaries of Jerusalem and appoint whatever new municipal councillors might be needed. In a supplementary statement the Prime Minister, Levi Eshkol, declared that, 'It is our intention to place the internal management and arrangements for the Holy Places in the hands of religious leaders of the communities to which these places belong'. Eshkol met forty Muslim and Christian leaders on the same day, and told them that they would be consulted on all matters of religious importance. 'From the horrors of a war openly launched to obliterate the state of Israel', he told them, 'a situation has emerged that is full of hope and of almost unlimited possibilities for the people of our region – given the will on all sides to cast away the rancours of the past and start building together for a better future.'[49]

Basing its action on the laws of 27 June, Israel's Government quietly extended the borders of the Jerusalem Municipality to north and south on the day following. The Jordanian Government had, in fact, proposed an even greater enlargement of East Jerusalem in May 1967. There had been no time to carry it out.[50] The Israeli measures seem to have had three principal purposes. In the south, the new boundaries included rising ground at Gilo dominating Bethlehem and neighbouring Beit Jalla. In the north, the terrain of two former Jewish settlements, Neve Yaakov and Atarot, which had been lost in the 1948 fighting, was included. So was sufficient land for the Kalandia air-strip, running due north and south and only a short way from Ramallah.

In a period of barely three weeks, then, the situation of Jerusalem was transformed. It had been unified, by the simple enactment of declaring a single municipality. Interestingly, no act of annexation was promulgated, but this might be regarded as a matter of semantics. The Municipality had been enlarged to include a population of 263,000, nearly 196,000 of them Jews. Its area was about 250,000 acres, against the 100,000 acres of pre-1967 West Jerusalem. In the United Nations Abba Eban made a long statement on 29 June, claiming that Israel's administrative legislation contained 'no new political statement'. He was provoked by the Soviet delegate, Mr Federenko, and replied: 'It is easy to sneer at Israel's traditional concept of body and head, Israel the body and Jerusalem the head. This is a concept which lies beyond and above, before and after, all political considerations ... Israel will continue to pray, yearn and work for Jerusalem's unity and for Jerusalem's peace.'

The Jewish people are famous for their ability to evolve conflicting views. But on the subject of Jerusalem, the people of Israel were virtually totally united; they believed that Jerusalem, which had only been divided for nineteen years during its 3,000 years' existence, should not be divided ever again. It was equally fundamental that Jerusalem was the capital of Israel and should remain so. Here were the seeds of fresh conflict, for it was almost inconceivable that the Arab world would accept the loss of its third most holy city, the symbol of the dominance which it considered to be its right to assert over Christianity and Judaism throughout the whole of the Middle East. A new dimension was added to the Arab–Israeli conflict.

REFERENCES

1. Abraham Rabinovich, *Jerusalem Post*, 1 June 1973.
2. Ibid.
3. H. Eugene Bovis, *The Jerusalem Question*, Hoover Institution Press, Stanford University, Stanford, Calif., 1971.
4. *Rebuttals of Jordanian Misstatements about Israel's Administration of Jerusalem*, Israel Foreign Ministry publication, October 1972.
5. Martin Gilbert, *Jerusalem: Illustrated History Atlas*, Macmillan, New York, 1977.
6. Terence Prittie, *Israel: Miracle in the Desert*, Praeger, New York, 1967.
7. Ibid.
8. Maurice Samuel, in *Chaim Weizmann. A Biography by Several Hands*, ed. by Meyer Weisgal & Joel Carmichael, Atheneum, New York, 1963.
9. Teddy Kollek, *For Jerusalem*, Weidenfeld, London, 1978.
10. Meron Benvenisti, *Jerusalem: The Torn City*, Istratypeset, Jerusalem, 1976.
11. Teddy Kollek, op. cit.
12. Ibid.
13. Terence Prittie, op. cit.
14. Teddy Kollek, op. cit.
15. President Nasser of Egypt, on Radio Cairo, 22 May 1967.
16. Ian McIntyre, *The Proud Doers*, BBC Publications, London, 1968.
17. Teddy Kollek, op. cit.
18. A. L. Tibawi, *Jerusalem: Its Place in Islam and Arab History*, Institute of Palestine Studies, Beirut, 1969.
19. Uzi Narkiss *La Bataille pour Jérusalem*, Hachette, Paris, 1978.
20. King Hussein of Jordan, *My War with Israel*, London, 1969.
21. King Hussein of Jordan, interview with *Der Spiegel*, 4 September 1967.
22. Abba Eban, *An Autobiography*, Weidenfeld, London, 1978.
23. Ibid.
24. Ibid.
25. Uzi Narkiss, in personal conversation with the author.
26. Teddy Kollek, op. cit.
27. Uzi Narkiss, in personal conversation with the author.
28. Abba Eban, op. cit.
29. Teddy Kollek, op. cit.
30. Ibid.
31. Moshe Dayan, *The Story of my Life*, Weidenfeld, London, 1976.
32. Abba Eban, op. cit.
33. Ibid.

34. *The Times*, from Our Own Correspondent, New York, 26 February 1980.
35. Yosef Bar-Yosef, in *Bahamane* (Israel Defence Forces Weekly), 12 June 1967.
36. Ibid.
37. Harry Hurwitz, *Menahem Begin*, Excelsior, Johannesburg, 1977.
38. Yitzhak Rabin, *The Rabin Memoirs*, Weidenfeld, London, 1979.
39. Uzi Narkiss, op. cit.
40. Ezer Weizman, *On Eagles' Wings*, Weidenfeld, London, 1976.
41. St Paul, Corinthians, 1:22.
42. Charles Gulston, *Jerusalem: The Tragedy and the Triumph*, Zondervan, Grand Rapids, Mich., 1978.
43. Meron Benvenisti, op. cit.
44. Moshe Dayan, op. cit.
45. Teddy Kollek, op. cit.
46. Saul Bellow, *To Jerusalem and Back*, Secker & Warburg, London, 1976.
47. Meron Benvenisti, op. cit.
48. Ibid.
49. Walter Zander, *Israel and the Holy Places of Christendom*, Weidenfeld, London, 1971.
50. Meron Benvenisti, op. cit.

CHAPTER SIX

Trustees for Three World Religions

Many years before Jerusalem was reunified, the American Secretary of State, John Foster Dulles, stated what was then a commonly held view among deeply religious Christians. He wrote:

> Jerusalem is divided into armed camps split between Israel and the Arab nation of Jordan. The atmosphere is heavy with hate. As I gazed on the Mount of Olives, I felt anew that Jerusalem is, above all, the holy place of the Christian, Moslem and Jewish faiths. This has been repeatedly emphasized by the United Nations. This does not necessarily exclude some political status in Jerusalem for Israel and Jordan. But the world religious community has claims in Jerusalem which take precedence over the political claims of any particular nation.[1]

Apart from the phrase 'world religious community' – for no such thing exists – Mr Dulles's message was plain: the religious element in Jerusalem is, to many people, paramount. Most Israelis would see it rather differently: to them the historical, the political and the religious are all intimately interlinked in Jerusalem, and they would accord no priority for one or the other element. They realized keenly, at all events, that world interest has been focused on Jerusalem for thousands of years. Where religious rights and interests were concerned, the State of Israel had been left with a unique responsibility as a result of

Jordan bringing war to the Holy City and leaving it in Israel's keeping.

Three statements by Israel's Foreign Minister, Abba Eban, make it clear that Israel's Government understood this very well, when it came into this unsought yet priceless inheritance. On 10 July 1967, he wrote to the UN Secretary General:

> The measures taken by my Government to secure the protection of the Holy Places are only a part of its effort to ensure respect for universal interests in Jerusalem ... The international interest in Jerusalem has always been understood to derive from the presence of the Holy Places. Israel does not doubt her own will and capacity to secure the respect of universal and spiritual interests. It has forthwith ensured that the Holy Places of Judaism, Christianity and Islam be administered under the responsibility of the religions which hold them sacred. In addition, in a spirit of concern for historic and spiritual traditions, my Government has taken steps with a view to reaching arrangements to assure the universal character of the Holy Places. In pursuance of this objective, the Government of Israel has now embarked on a constructive and detailed dialogue with representatives of universal religious interests.[2]

In another letter to the Secretary General, of 30 April 1968, Eban elaborated further on Israel's policy towards the Holy Places:

> While I have spoken of Jerusalem's special and unique place in Israel's history, we are deeply aware of the universal interests which are concentrated in the city: the equal protection of the Holy Places and houses of worship; the assurance of free access to them; the daily intermingling of Jerusalem's population in peaceful contact; the removal of the old military barriers; the care of ancient sites; the reverent desire to replace the old squalor and turmoil by a harmonious beauty – all these changes enable Jerusalem to awaken from the nightmare of the past two decades and to move towards a destiny worthy of its lineage. I reaffirm Israel's willingness, in addition to the steps already taken for the immunity of the Holy Places, to work for formal settlements which will give satisfaction to Christian, Moslem and Jewish spiritual concerns ... Accordingly, we are willing to work out arrangements with those traditionally

concerned, which will ensure the universal character of the Christian and Moslem Holy Places and thus enable this ancient and historic metropolis to thrive in peace, unity and spiritual elevation.[3]

And on 19 September 1969, Eban told the UN General Assembly that:

Israel does not claim exclusive or unilateral jurisdiction in the Holy Places of Christianity and Islam in Jerusalem and is willing to discuss this principle with those traditionally concerned. There is a versatile range of possibilities for working out a status for the Holy Places in such a manner as to promote Middle East peace and ecumenical harmony. In the meantime, our policy is that the Moslem and Christian Holy Places should always be under the responsibility of those who hold them sacred. This principle has been in practical effect since 1967.[4]

The sincerity of Eban's statements was reflected in the immediacy with which Muslim and Christian leaders were reassured. As Minister of Defence, Moshe Dayan undertook to talk personally to the Muslim religious leaders, and visited them at the El Aqsa Mosque. Their faces, he would recount later, wore expressions of mourning and fear, and they made it plain that they would prefer not to talk to him at all. With typical sense of occasion, Dayan sat down on the carpet and folded his legs 'Arab fashion'; so 'they felt it necessary to do the same, and inevitably we engaged in talk'.[5] Dayan promised them full control of their own Holy Places, undertook to abolish the Jordanian practice of pre-censorship of sermons, and banned the holding of Jewish religious services in the whole area of the Temple Mount. He made one proviso, that Jews and Christians alike would be free to visit the Temple Mount and the two great mosques within its precinct.

General Chaim Herzog, newly-appointed Governor of the West Bank (which the Israeli Government henceforward referred to as Judaea and Samaria) was given the task of talking to the Christian leadership. He convened a meeting attended by the Greek, Latin and Armenian Patriarchs, the Apostolic Delegate of the Vatican, the Lutheran Bishop, and the leaders of the Syrian, Ethiopian and Coptic congregations, and told them how proud he was to inform them that his Government could guarantee them absolute freedom of worship, conscience and access to all holy places – in a manner which Jerusalem had not enjoyed for 2,000 years. 'When I had finished, the Greek Patriarch expressed the gratitude of all those assembled for Israel's humane approach and policy. And the Anglican Archbishop rose to place on historical record the general appreciation ... that the Israeli command consciously endangered the lives of its own soldiers in order not to direct fire against the Holy Places and to effect as little damage as possible to the Holy City of Jerusalem.'[6]

One does not need to take the word only of these two highly articulate spokesmen of Israel's policies in order to accept the fact of Christian and, to a minor degree, Muslim gratitude for Israel's manifest intention of discharging its obligations in a fair and enlightened spirit. The following statements by leaders of Christian Churches speak for themselves:

Early in July 1967 the Patriarch of the Ethiopian Church, His Beatitude Tehophilos, wrote to the Israeli authorities in these terms:

> The Patriarchate of the Ethiopian Orthodox Church would like to express its appreciation to the Israeli Government for the proper care with which it handled the sanctuaries in the Holy Land in general and the Ethiopian convent in particular. We also extend our thanks to the Israeli authorities for having granted unhindered ... movement to our clergy in Jerusalem during the war and after.[7]

On 14 July 1967, a group of Dutch Catholic and Protestant churchmen made the following statement in Amsterdam:

> Catholic and Protestant theologians ... feel themselves called upon to issue the following statement on Jerusalem, which they hope may offer for Jewish and Islamic theologians an acceptable point of departure for common thinking on the future of Jerusalem.
>
> The Jewish people, the Promised Land and the City of Jerusalem are, through Bible and history, linked with one another in a unique way. To separate by thought or deed the Jewish people from the land or from Jerusalem is tantamount to challenging Jewish identity.
>
> The autonomous existence of the Jewish people in its own country, with Jerusalem as its capital, is felt by the overwhelming majority of the Jewish people throughout the world as a vital condition for its existence. Recognition of the international character of the Holy Places cannot imply any

denial of the above-mentioned biblical and historical links binding the Jewish people with undivided Jerusalem.[8]

In the *New York Times* a group of American theologians declared:

During the past twenty years the City of David has experienced an artificial division. This has resulted in a denial of access to their Holy Places for all Jews and for Israeli Arabs of the Muslim faith. It has also severely limited accessibility to Christian shrines for Israeli Christians. This injustice, we must confess, did not elicit significant protest on the part of the religious leaders of the world. We see no justification in proposals which seek once again to destroy the unity which has been restored to Jerusalem. This unity is the natural condition of the Holy City.[9]

Les Filles de la Charité de l'Hospice St Vincent de Paul of Jerusalem wrote on 6 October 1967, on the subject of false accusations made against the Israelis since the Six Day War. These are extracts:

Within the charity of Christ we love both Jew and Arab. But we owe it to the truth to put on record that our work here has been made especially happy and its path smoothed by the goodwill of the Israeli authorities – in peace and in war alike – smoothed, that is, not only for ourselves, but more important, for the Arabs in our care ... War is war, and the Jews prosecuted theirs with the sole object of preserving their existence, while saving every single human life that they possibly could.[10]

On 8 April 1968, the Armenian Patriarch sent this message to the Israeli authorities:

I have to thank you ... for the genuine regard shown by the Israeli authorities for the Holy Places. I also present my deep thanks for your willingness to render us every help in order to restore our Monastery of the Holy Saviour and cemetery, situated on the front line for twenty years. I am confident that the Israeli authorities have always been animated by a spirit of justice and equity and that the great consideration and respect they have shown for the Holy Places will continue.[11]

Four days later, the Greek Orthodox Patriarch of Jerusalem, Benedictos, said:

It is true, and we would like to stress it again, that the Holy
Places in general, monasteries and churches were given full
respect and protection by the Israelis before the war, during
the war and afterwards, and we hope that in the future they
will be respected as well and the status quo which existed will
be safeguarded.[12]

The Latin Custos of the Holy Land reported on 27 April 1968
that pilgrimages to the Christian shrines were increasing day by
day, that services in Christian churches were proceeding
normally and that Easter was marked by extreme orderliness,
while only minor damage had resulted from the war.[13] American
Christians resident in Bethlehem wrote a letter to the *Jerusalem
Post*, in which they explained that: 'after the victorious army had
occupied our city for one month, residents felt that they had
been liberated ... The Jews have desecrated nothing that is holy
to another religion, either Christian or Moslem. They have
cleared away rubble and filth which have accumulated for
years.'[14]

Another American Christian who had something apposite to
say was Dr Douglas Young, the President of the Institute of Holy
Land Studies in Jerusalem. The Institute, evangelical in
background, had been active in Jerusalem for ten years prior to
the Six Day War. Dr Young pointed out that there had been a
Jewish majority in Jerusalem for many years, and that to 'unify a
Jewish majority city after twenty years of it being divided by
others is surely no cause for antagonism'. He praised the Israeli
authorities highly; they were providing funds for repairing the
damage done in the war to church buildings, they were
protecting the Holy Places by stringent legislation, and 'We feel
at peace and at ease in our united city as Christians, with actually
less fear of personal assault than in other cities in which we have
lived abroad, such is the force of Israeli law and order'.[15]

Christian expressions of appreciation and gratitude to the
Israeli authorities continued thereafter. Thus the Dominican
priest Father Marcel Dubois complimented the Israelis for
having faithfully preserved the Christian element in Jerusalem,[16]
and the President of the Roman Catholic charitable organization
'Caritas', Father Raymond Tournay, denied that Israeli
authorities interfered with the work of his mission. The
Protestant Archbishop in Jerusalem, Dr George Appleton,
speaking in Rome, noted that full freedom of access to all holy
places was being maintained, that there was no pressure on

Christian communities, and that the situation could be regarded as satisfactory.[17] For saying this he was, absurdly, denounced by the former Arab Mayor of East Jerusalem, Rouhi al-Khatib, as being 'linked to Zionism'. The ex-Mayor went on to say that the Archbishop had proposed internationalizing the Old City within its walls, under a supervisory council which would be 40 per cent Jewish, 40 per cent Muslim and 20 per cent Christian.[18] This statement, indeed, destroyed his case, for it directly conflicted with the accusation that Dr Appleton was 'linked to Zionism'. In reality, Dr Appleton's reputation for even-handedness and objectivity was unassailable.

One leading Arab religious leader, Tawfiq Mahmoud Asaliya, the former Qadi of Jaffa and Jerusalem, had two things to say about Israeli administration of Muslim Holy Places. Shortly after the reunification of Jerusalem he prayed for peace in the El Aqsa Mosque, afterwards thanking the Israelis for keeping holy places guarded, and adding: 'Let it be known to every Moslem in the world that religious freedom, which we have enjoyed since the establishment of the State of Israel, will continue forever'.[19] And in January 1970 he declared that it 'would be good, if those who have heard unfounded rumours of desecration and interference could come to witness the peace and tranquillity which prevail in this Holy Place during the prayers that are regularly held there'.[20]

Another Arab, the Mayor of Nazareth, Mussa Khatili, addressed himself to Arab governments, when he said: 'The Arab States have tried war and brought upon themselves ruin and destruction. Let them put aside the deceptive dreams of destroying Israel and come to the peace table.'[21] King Hussein of Jordan had doubtless been thinking along similar lines when he told British journalists in a confidential briefing in London just after the 1967 war that the Arab states would have to think out their policies towards Israel completely anew. He made no secret of his belief that these policies had been sadly wrong in the past.[22] But there were obvious reasons why it was harder for Muslim authorities in Jerusalem, than it was for Christian, to give Israel any praise. They were afraid of being looked upon as quislings. They were not, like the Christians, 'neutral' in the struggle for secular control of Jerusalem, and Israeli dominance was bound to cause feelings of resentment and sadness. And they had some grounds for complaint – more about these later, but first the obviously positive aspects of Israeli relations with the Christian Churches should be analysed.

One of Israel's first actions after the conquest of East

Jerusalem was to allocate six million Israeli pounds (at that time, the equivalent of about £170,000) for repairing damage done to church buildings during the Six Day War. This grant-in-aid was made irrespective of the fact that the Israeli troops were not responsible for most of the damage that was done, but it was in keeping with the subsequent Israeli policy of giving all possible financial help to Christian religious institutions. Thus the Armenian Patriarchate was helped to reorganize its fine library of manuscripts, and to restore its church on Mount Zion; the Maronite Christians were given a grant for their new centre in the Old City; when the Ethiopians and Copts were unable to agree as to which of them owned the roof of the Chapel of St Helena in the Church of the Holy Sepulchre, the repair costs were taken over by the State of Israel; money was made available for a Roman Catholic church and community centre in the suburb of Beit Hanina; more help was forthcoming for the Tantur Ecumenical Institute for Advanced Theological Study; and aid went to such varied institutions as the Ecce Homo Convent, the White Sisters (Franciscans), the Knights of Malta, the Romanian Orthodox Church near the site of the Mandelbaum Gate, the Evangelical Lutheran Church at Beit Jalla, the Notre Dame de Sion Convent at Ein Karem. By 1980 the Municipality had been looking after the cemetery of the Greek Catholic Patriarchate for over twenty years, and in 1967 it undertook to help find it a new burial site. A new road was laid to the St Pierre en Gallicante church of the Assumptionist Fathers. These were merely a few among many examples of direct Israeli aid to the Christian Churches.

The Mayor, Teddy Kollek, showed a keen personal interest in all of this work. He guaranteed the absolute rights of the churches in controlling their own schools and determining their curricula, and he established an advisory staff for organizing discussion of all Christian problems on a regular basis. He personally made sure that the Church of St Mary of the Germans was preserved when it came to light in the work of restoration being carried out in the Old City – yet the church was historically an unwanted reminder of the Crusaders who built it, and through its name, of the Germany which persecuted the Jews in the Nazi era.[23] The churches were given exemption from tax on church building, and tax rebates on certain imported goods. Kollek readily made himself available as a mediator in church disputes, which have flourished over the centuries, while another practical contribution of his was to sponsor trips abroad of

Christian travel agents, to promote pilgrimages. The Municipality also helped over the planning of gardens and the planting
of trees by church bodies.

All of this was on the credit side, but there were inevitably
problems too. An isolated but troublesome one was the affair of
the Greek Melkite (Catholic) Archbishop, Hilarion Capucci. An
Arab, he had been active in protests against Israeli occupation of
East Jerusalem, and in August 1974 he was arrested for
smuggling arms and explosives from Lebanon. He was, in fact,
gun-running for the Palestine Liberation Organization,
following meetings with leaders like Abu Jihad and other
militants.

Capucci gave conflicting evidence, offering two versions of his
escapade, that he had relied on his clerical immunity to smuggle
the arms,[24] and alternatively that he never knew that the arms
were in the boot of his car. He was tried and in December was
sentenced to twelve years' imprisonment. After delicate negotiations he was released and left the country, subsequently
carrying out propaganda work for the PLO. In retrospect, the
Israelis would probably agree that they would have done better
to have deported him, rather than give him the chance of posing
as a martyr to the Palestinian national cause.

Of much more fundamental importance was the question of
Israel's relations with the Vatican, the principal supporter of the
status for Jerusalem of 'corpus separatum', entailing some form
of internationalization. Early in 1968 the Vatican still held openly
to this view, although there were hints that a change of mind was
on the way.[25] A formula which was aired in May was that of 'an
internationally guaranteed agreement' on Jerusalem.[26] A
discreet visit was paid to Rome by Yaacov Herzog, the personal
adviser of the Prime Minister. The proposals which he allegedly
brought were that the Roman Catholic Church should be
accorded senior status among the Christian Churches in
Jerusalem, that the Holy Places should be given diplomatic
status, and that the Pope should be recognized in Jerusalem as
the chief representative of all Christianity. But Pope Paul VI
wanted no concordat with Israel – presumably he felt that such a
thing would endanger Catholic congregations in the Arab world
– and offered only to give his blessing to an Israeli declaration
according senior status to the Roman Catholic Church.[27] Israel
was, in fact, offered the possibility of antagonizing other
Christian Churches, while getting nothing in return.

Herzog, however, undoubtedly made a real impression on

Vatican thinking. In 1969 the Foreign Minister, Abba Eban, was received by the Pope and, significantly, all Vatican statements on internationalization ended thereafter. Another discreet Israeli offer was made in 1971, but was again refused; any agreement with Israel would have entailed Vatican recognition of the State of Israel and this was withheld on the dubious grounds that no state could be recognized until its frontiers were finally fixed. One critic has pointed out that the corollary given by Vatican spokesmen was that the non-delimitation of frontiers implied that a country was still at war.[28] All the countries of the Arab League, however, were in a declared state of war with Israel, while the Republic of Ireland maintains a permanent territorial claim to the six northern counties. This has not impaired relations between the Republic and the Vatican. At least Israel's Prime Minister, Mrs Golda Meir, was received by the Pope, and in July 1974 the United States Secretary of State, Henry Kissinger, was assured by the Vatican that it favoured only 'a special status for the Holy City, accompanied by international assurances'.[29] A degree of flexibility in relations with Rome had been gained, but Israel had reluctantly to turn down a proposal of a concordat from the Greek Orthodox Church! The Christian 'jungle' was still a confusing place into which to venture.

One man who was reasonably satisfied was Yaacov Herzog. He wrote: 'In the area of Jerusalem, with the Christian world, I would say that one of the miracles since June 1967 has been the silence – I would not say acquiescence – of the Catholic world. Those who remember the clash between Rome and Jerusalem in 1948 and 1953 ... will wonder today that Rome keeps its silence.[30]

Over relations with the Jews the Vatican would continue to drag its feet. According to one writer it had hesitated for ten years before issuing the guidelines for the encyclical *Nostra Aetate*, which should have offered real reconciliation with the Jews.'[31] This was what Pope John XXIII wanted, but opposition from the Catholic Arab Bishops and Catholic antisemites resulted in *Nostra Aetate* being watered down and lumping Jews together with Muslims, Buddhists and others. This failed to take account of the Jewish contribution to Christianity, and the central role which the Land of Israel plays in Jewish thought was ignored. The same writer came to the sad conclusion that 'The majority of Catholics – at least in Britain and America – are still, overtly or subconsciously, anti-Jewish'.[32]

Once again, Jewish susceptibilities were offended when Pope John Paul II spoke to the United Nations General Assembly on 2

October 1979. The Pope made several references to the Middle East and Jerusalem, asking for a 'just settlement of the Palestinian question' and for a 'special statute' which would 'respect the particular nature of Jerusalem'. He pointedly refrained from mentioning Israel by name, and as one commentator put it, left Israel 'unblessed'.[33] More than that, he put 'his enormous prestige and moral authority behind shopworn and, in current circumstances, mischievous political ideas', suggesting Papal backing for the Palestinian hope that Israel would 'somehow disappear'. There will, for sure, be further stutters along the road to eventual reconciliation and understanding between Israel and the Vatican.

The Pope's obvious sympathy for the Palestinians elicited a typically incongrous rejoinder from the PLO leader, Yassir Arafat. He sent the Pope a Christmas message of greeting, in which he stated that the Palestinians were the descendants of the earliest Christian saints and monks, and asked the Pope to stop the Israelis from expelling all Christians and Muslims from Jerusalem.

There were difficulties, too, with the Protestant Churches. In August 1969 the Central Committee of the World Council of Churches, venturing boldly into the political maelstrom, demanded at its Canterbury conference that the injustice done to the Palestinian Arabs should be redressed. In the autumn of the same year, the World Council of Churches convened a special meeting in Cyprus to examine the Palestinian refugee problem. Cyprus was ill-chosen; it was, after all, the place of detention to which Jewish refugees from Nazi-tormented Europe were sent by the British authorities of Mandatory Palestine. The delegates called for 'an adequate response to the injustice and misery' suffered by Palestinian refugees. This was unexceptionable. But they added that relief programmes could not satisfy Palestinian 'aspirations for self-determination and nationhood', thus obliquely endorsing the callousness of the Arab world in leaving their refugees in wretched living conditions, as political pawns. The World Council, finally, offered a really crazy explanation of how the Palestinian refugee problem had come into being – it was because of the 'Great Powers' who had supported 'the establishment of a Jewish state without recognizing the right of the Palestinians to self-determination'.[34]

The reality was that the 'Great Powers' had not been responsible for 'the establishment of a Jewish state'. It had been established by a vote of all of the members of the United Nations.

Those same members had sought to recognize the 'right of the Palestinians to self-determination'; they had indeed proposed the setting up of a Palestinian Arab state. It had been accepted by the Jews, but rejected by the Arabs themselves.

Protestant thinking on the Middle East dispute was stirred by appeals of this kind. One very important Protestant who was affected was the Archbishop of Canterbury, Dr Michael Ramsey. On 16 December 1971, he made a statement to the press in which he called Jerusalem 'a tragedy'. The statement, thereafter, fell perhaps a little flat. The Israelis were, indeed, commended for giving free access, to all people, to their holy places in Jerusalem. But the Archbishop then complained (and with some reason) about Israeli building programmes in Jerusalem. But he went on to denounce 'an insensitive attempt to proclaim as an Israeli city one which can never be other than the city of the three great religions and their peoples'. He called, therefore, for 'a halt to the building programme'.[35]

The Archbishop was invited by the Israeli Ministry for Religious Affairs to come to Jerusalem, and see for himself what went on there. Israelis, at the time, were a bit bewildered by the Archbishop's '*démarche*'. Had it concerned the Israeli trusteeship of Christian Holy Places, it would have been better understood. The weird situation arose of the Israeli Minister for Religious Affairs, Dr Zerah Wahrhaftig, briefing, by letter, the Archbishop of Canterbury, on the nature of the new buildings in Jerusalem. Never before can the thought of the blind leading the blind have been given more apt expression! The proper authority in Jerusalem as to what was being done was the Mayor – and the Archbishop had never seen the sites about which he was complaining.

In the event, a meeting was desirable between Dr Ramsey and the Mayor, Teddy Kollek. In June 1972 they met at Lambeth Palace, and their discussion was long, cordial and entirely satisfactory. The Archbishop satisfied himself that Kollek was doing his level best to look after the whole community in Jerusalem, Arabs and Jews alike. No further *démarche* came from Canterbury thereafter, but Anglican influence in Jerusalem has almost certainly suffered as a result of the Archbishopric being downgraded to a Bishopric and the practice discontinued of sending the head of the Anglican Church in Jerusalem out from Britain. Anglican Bishops in Jerusalem, from 1974 onwards, would be Arabs. One outcome would be the future inability of the Bishop to follow in the steps of Archbishop Appleton in bringing Christians, Jews and Muslims together and playing a special role in the ecumenical field.[36] Another was an inevitable loss of prestige. Arab Protestants must have felt, too, that an element of external 'protection' was being withdrawn.

A minor storm in the teacup was caused by the passing of a law by the Knesset in 1977 making it illegal to promise, give or receive material benefits in return for religious conversion. As a non-proselytizing religion, Judaism looks with much disfavour on any attempt to convert Jews – carried on, in centuries gone by, by means of torture and burning at the stake. The Christian communities in Jerusalem feared that the law, if rigorously interpreted, could constrict them in their task of preaching their faith to all who would listen. Some Christian charitable organizations did, in fact, reduce the scale of their activities in case they should be misunderstood. There was a fear that the new law could have an adverse effect on pilgrimage to the Holy Places, which had increased by roughly 40 per cent in a decade. These fears were not borne out by events; the law, as framed and applied, was unexceptionable, and the Israeli Ministry of Justice gave a firm undertaking that its working would not be allowed to interfere with religious liberties in any way.[37] The only possible sufferers were fringe groups offering inducements for conversion, or looking for some sort of synthesis between Christianity and Judaism – one such group's members remained Jews but were baptized in the Dead Sea, or the Jordan, as a token of their belief in the teachings of the Jewish Christ.

Since 1967 there were periodic complaints against Israeli citizens, usually young people, for alleged 'unseemly' behaviour in Christian places of worship – making too much noise, being too casually dressed, eating food on church premises or bringing in transistor radios (the Israelis are inveterate listeners to every possible news-programme). There were occasional cases of slogans and graffiti being chalked up on the Christian buildings. Accusations that cemeteries and churches were systematically profaned were, however, sharply denied by the Christian churches themselves. These stories included bringing dogs into churches, damaging the tombs of the Armenian Patriarchs and monuments in both the Latin and Greek Orthodox cemeteries, and thefts of icons and even 'mosaics'[38] – thus it was falsely claimed that an entire Byzantine mosaic was removed from Mount Zion. The truth is that there have been, and always will be, occasional acts of vandalism, in all countries. One informed Christian view was:

We have no particular problems which we did not have
before 1967 – we had vandalism by religious hooligans then
too. Christian cemeteries have been desecrated periodically
ever since I moved to Israel, seventeen years ago; that is
nothing new. Sometimes headstones with crosses have been
broken; the Government has always and carefully restored
the damage. The plastering of Mount Zion with graffiti by
Israeli soldiers is an unadulterated fabrication. I moved our
Institute there in 1966 and saw none of it then or later. Mayor
Kollek has been an outstanding example of fairness and
correctness in dealing with every religious segment of
Jerusalem's population.[39]

Perhaps the most serious rash of 'incidents' did, however,
occur at the end of 1979 and early in 1980. Thus at Christmas
1979, the secretary of the Russian Orthodox Church received
threatening letters, and a youth wearing a skull-cap broke into
the Christian Information Office at the Jaffa Gate and began
destroying its literature.[40] There were minor attacks on the
Dormition Abbey and the Baptist House. There were several
cases of priests being cursed and spat at in the streets. The walls
of the Bible Society's headquarters were daubed with slogans and
swastikas, with such injunctions as 'Pigs and Nazis, go home'. In
January 1980 the modest Bible-shop of a Mr Charles Cope in the
centre of the city was ransacked,[41] and an assessment of the
municipal authorities of damage done to church property so far
was quoted as more than 30,000 dollars.[42] On 11 February,
Charles Cope's shop was attacked for a second time and an
attempt was made to set it on fire.[43]

Christian leaders made a formal protest to the Prime Minister,
Mr Begin, on 1 February. Meanwhile, the municipal authorities
did two things – they undertook to carry out all necessary repairs
to damaged church property, and they launched their own
inquiries into the origins of this wave of vandalism. These
showed that the attacks were the work of a tiny minority of
Jewish religious extremists, in particular members of Rabbi Meir
Kahane's 'Kach' group.[44] The municipal authorities undertook
to bring vandals to book, and Mr Begin – somewhat late in the
day – promised to play his part on 4 February. The Kach group
openly admitted their depredations on Christian 'graven
images', and another organization, calling itself 'Yad Leachim',
distributed leaflets proclaiming 'war on missionaries' but
dissociating itself from attacks on property.[45] A police drive was

mounted to round up offenders, and a senior police officer specially appointed to be in charge of it.

A by-product of the wave of vandalism was the drawing-up and discreet circulation of a six-page document, whose authors were evidently Roman Catholic and Protestant clergy in Jerusalem, calling for new international guarantees for the Christian Churches in Israel.[46] The document, which stressed the uncertainty and insecurity of the Christian situation in Jerusalem, drew a sharp rejoinder from Israel's Foreign Ministry, which accused the clergy of 'trying to climb on the vandalism bandwagon'. The Foreign Ministry reiterated its already well-known view that a special statute for religious institutions in Jerusalem was perfectly feasible, but not a statute which applied to the whole city. An uncomfortable feeling persisted that the troubles of the Christian Churches, although relatively superficial, were not transient.

They owed something, for sure, to an overall growth of religious fervour in the Jewish community. Two particular battles were going on, coterminously with anti-Christian vandalism, which were on a much bigger scale and equally worrying for the Mayor. The first was over the building of a new road connecting the suburb of Ramot with the city. Ramot contained only a few religious zealots, but the road ran past Kiryat Zanz, a solidly religious housing settlement. Its tenants objected furiously to wheeled vehicles using the road on the Sabbath and began turning out in force to stop them. This led to pitched battles, and the 'secularists' responded by organizing 'flying columns' to quell the 'Shabbat-shouting' and stone-throwing. One of the secularists told a reporter: 'I served in a crack unit in war and my friends were paratroopers. We're going to show these people, who skip army service, that if it comes to violence, we're better at it.'[47] The religious Jews have never lagged behind in denunciation of the secularists, and even as great a patriot as David Ben-Gurion came under fire. In his book *The Rift in Israel*, S. Clement Leslie quotes an orthodox rabbi, Adin Steinsalz, as saying that 'for Mr Ben-Gurion we are a chosen people – chosen by a God he doesn't believe in, for reasons he denies, in a Book he doesn't accept'.

Even earlier, a 'stadium war' had broken out, over the building of a new football stadium at Shuafat, which was unluckily close to the religious quarters of Matersdorf, Itri and Sanhedria Murchevet. Since the Israelis work a six-day week, football matches would inevitably take place generally on the

Sabbath. Different religious groups objected, in differing degree. The most extreme sect, of the Neturei Karta, whose members do not believe in the State of Israel but only in biblical prophecy, was ready to go to any physical lengths to stop the stadium being built. The Agudat Israel party was equally determined, but preferred more peaceful means of persuasion. Its involvement, nevertheless, was acutely worrying to Kollek, for it played a role in municipal affairs and had served in his administration.

Jerusalem had always been short of sports facilities, and Kollek knew that, over the proposed stadium, he had the backing of at least 80 per cent of his constituents. Still, he looked for alternative sites for the football ground, but could not find one. The religious groups thereupon demanded that the Shuafat site should be used for the construction of flats for their members. Kollek secured a temporary compromise in January 1980. There would be a freeze on the building of the stadium, but the area would be used as a green belt until building could be finished. No flats would be built there in the meantime.[48] At least there had been no resort to physical violence in Shuafat, but Agudat Israel and the Neturei Karta now went to war on their own exclusive ground, the Mea Shearim religious quarter. According to one report,[49] one prominent rabbi was left with a head wound requiring forty stitches, and another had his telephone rung at the start of the Sabbath – which meant he had to leave it ringing, under religious law, for twenty-four hours!

As Mayor of Jerusalem, Teddy Kollek clearly had complex religious problems to deal with. Much more important than the internecine feuds of Jewish religious groups was the question of relations with the Muslim community, numbering more than five times the Christian community in 1967 and nearly ten times larger by 1980. Even their numbers were less important than their attitudes and inhibitions. Theirs had been the ruling faith in Jerusalem. To them, the Dome of the Rock was 'the hub of the universe, in the very centre of the fourth climatic zone, the central region in the world where civilized life develops'.[50] They had been humbled and many of them, to their shame, had panicked: 'On the day the city was united, about 20,000 Arabs left in fear that they might be slaughtered; most of them came back after three or four days when it turned out that not a single person was touched.'[51] Shame is liable to breed the most lasting resentment of all.

Two Arab statements give some idea of how deep-seated this resentment was. In 1970 King Hussein made recordings of his

thoughts about the Arab–Israeli dispute. By then, he had passed
the stage of looking for a total re-think of policy towards Israel,
and was much more concerned with keeping his dynasty afloat
in Jordan. His recordings went out on discs to Christian leaders,
and on one of them he complained that 'the religious
sensibilities of seven hundred million Muslims' were violated by
Israeli control of the Haram and its two great mosques.
Monsignor John Oesterreicher pointed out, in an 'open letter' to
Jordan, that Hussein was undermining the Arab position – if it
were insufferable that the Haram should be in an Israeli-
administered area, how could Christians and Jews be expected in
their turn to let their own holy places ever again fall into Muslim
hands?[52]

Even more negative was a statement by the late King Feisal of
Saudi Arabia. He went so far as to maintain that 'The Jews have
no connection whatsoever with Jerusalem and have no
sacraments there. They claim that the Temple of Solomon is
there ... The Temple of Solomon does not exist in Jerusalem;
when the Romans occupied Jerusalem, they took the Temple
with them. Therefore the Jews have no connection, or right to
have any presence in Jerusalem, or any authority there.' The
King added that the Jews deserted the teachings of Moses, tried to
murder Jesus Christ, and opposed God's directives.[53]

In face of such fanatical and totally uncompromising attitudes,
the Israelis might have been excused if they had simply set out to
suppress Muslim opposition and ignore Muslim complaints. In
fact, they did their best to establish reasonable co-existence. With
the Christians, they had to deal with a bewildering diversity of
interests and opinions. With the Muslims, they were confronting
a monolithic attitude, a banding together of Arabs whose basic
belief in any case is that they are all members of one large family.

Moshe Dayan had handed the Haram over to the Muslim
authorities on 17 June 1967. Any delay, he thought, would
encourage all sorts of people and authorities to have their say,
and a movement to secure Jewish equality of tenure of the
Temple Mount might easily have been the result. Instead, he
forbade Jews to hold organized prayers on the Temple Mount,
and instructed them to remove their shoes if they entered the
mosques. Teddy Kollek had his own views about the Muslims
and Jerusalem, summed up in one sentence: 'I believe that the
Jerusalem mosques are holy places to them; I do not believe that
Jerusalem is a holy city for them.'[54] He was insistent that nothing
should be done on the Temple Mount to antagonize the

Muslims, and circulated instructions that any Jews who wanted to pray privately there should do so with the greatest discretion.

Non-religious himself, Kollek well knew that deeply-religious and strictly-orthodox Jews must regard the Temple Mount as forbidden ground, for they are entitled to tread it again only on the coming of the Messiah, when the Temple will be rebuilt. He passed off the problem with dry wit: 'We are on easy street. The Temple cannot be rebuilt by us; it will come down from Heaven in its appropriate place. Of course, the Messiah may arrive at any moment – that is a risk we shall always have to take!'[55]

The Haram, the Temple Mount, was bound to cause controversy. To the Muslims these forty-five acres of ground constituted a sacred enclosure; the word 'enclosure' implied that it was forbidden to people of other faiths. Ownership of the area was vested in the 'waqf', the property-owning religious foundation, and administration was in the hands of the Supreme 'Shari'a' Council. This was 'a government within the Government', and one of the Council's first actions after the 1967 war was to declare that it could not recognize any annexation of Jerusalem and would continue to operate according to Jordanian law. Next came a memorandum signed by twenty-two religious leaders, rejecting all interference with internal Muslim affairs. They constituted themselves as the 'Muslim Council for the West Bank, including Jerusalem', evidently intending to act as the secular arm and ally of the 'Shari'a'.

The Israeli authorities arrested four of the signatories – surely a tactical blunder – and exiled them from Jerusalem. At the same time, responsibility for looking after Muslim affairs was transferred from the Ministry for Religious Affairs to Military Government. Trouble now threatened from another quarter; the Chief Rabbi of the Israeli Army, Shlomo Goren, demanded the right to hold prayer meetings, and to blow the 'shofar', the ram's horn, on the Temple Mount, and talked of building a synagogue in the esplanade of the El Aqsa Mosque. A half-hearted effort was made to hold one meeting, but the Army Commander in Jerusalem, Uzi Narkiss, had it dispersed and warned that Goren and his followers would be removed by force if there were any further provocation.

Next came a tactless statement by the Minister for Religious Affairs, Zerah Wahrhaftig. Doubtless trying to placate the Goren group, he said that the Temple Mount had 'been purchased with Jewish blood', that Jewish rights took precedence there over

JERUSALEM FROM ANCIENT TIMES
TO THE DESTRUCTION OF THE SECOND TEMPLE IN 70 AD

Jerusalem was an inhabited city in the early bronze age, well before 2500 BC. Later it was a Jebusite fortress. Conquered by the Jews under David, it became, from 1000 BC, the political and religious capital of the Jews. Here Solomon built the first Temple, and here the Jews were sovereign for more than 600 years, until the Babylonian conquest in 587 BC, when many Jews were slaughtered, and others sent to exile. Returning under the patronage of Persia fifty years later, the Jews, under Nehemiah, rebuilt their Temple, and restored the authority of Jerusalem as their religious centre.

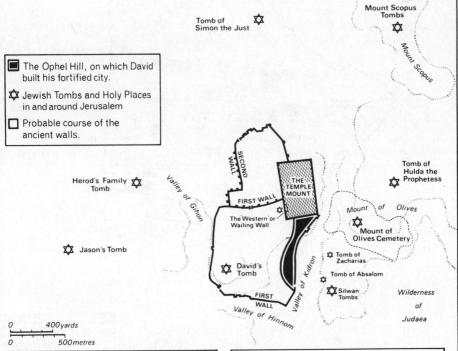

■ The Ophel Hill, on which David built his fortified city.

✡ Jewish Tombs and Holy Places in and around Jerusalem

▢ Probable course of the ancient walls.

Sanhedria Tombs

Tomb of Simon the Just

Mount Scopus Tombs

Mount Scopus

SECOND WALL

THE TEMPLE MOUNT

Tomb of Hulda the Prophetess

Herod's Family Tomb

Valley of Gihon

FIRST WALL

The Western or Wailing Wall

Mount of Olives

Mount of Olives Cemetery

Jason's Tomb

David's Tomb

Tomb of Zacharias

Tomb of Absalom

Silwan Tombs

FIRST WALL

Valley of Kidron

Wilderness of Judaea

Valley of Hinnom

0   400 yards

0   500 metres

332 BC Alexander of Macedon conquers the City, and confirms the Jewish privileges granted by the Persians.

301 BC The Ptolemys of Egypt grant the Jews autonomy in domestic matters. Jewish social and religious life flourishes.

198 BC The Seleucid conquerors grant the Jews the right to live by 'the laws of their fathers'.

167 BC Antiochus IV suppresses Jewish religious practices, desecrates the Temple, confiscates its treasures, and converts it into a Greek shrine.

141 BC Jerusalem captured by the Jewish Hasmoneans, remaining their capital for 78 years. Jewish religious and commercial life flourished.

63 BC The Roman conquest. 12,000 Jews massacred in Jerusalem. The priests, who refused to halt the service, were killed while still praying at the Altar.

66 AD The revolt of the Jewish 'Zealots', who held Jerusalem for 4 years.

70 AD Romans reoccupy Jerusalem. The Temple destroyed and the city laid waste. Many Jews taken as captives to Rome.

CRUSADER JERUSALEM

Once Jerusalem had been conquered by the Crusaders, as many as 10,000 Christian pilgrims made the journey every year, some from as far away as Scandinavia, Muscovy and Portugal; and each year a small number of these pilgrims decided to remain permanently in the city.

Following the Crusader entry into Jerusalem in 1099, all the Jews in the City were either murdered, sold into slavery in Europe, or ransomed to the Jewish community of Egypt. The Crusaders then brought Christian Arab tribes from east of the river Jordan, and settled them in the former Jewish Quarter, between St. Stephen's Gate and the Gate of Jehoshafat.

■■ Principal Crusader buildings.

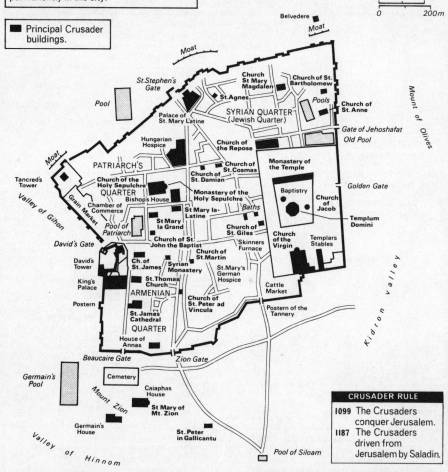

0   200 yards
0   200m

Belvedere

Moat

Moat

Mount of Olives

St. Stephen's Gate

Pool

Church St Mary Magdalen

Church of St. Bartholomew

St. Agnes

SYRIAN QUARTER (Jewish Quarter)

Pools

Church of St. Anne

Palace of St. Mary Latine

Gate of Jehoshafat

Old Pool

Hungarian Hospice

Church of the Repose

Church of St. Cosmas

Monastery of the Temple

PATRIARCH'S QUARTER

Church of St. Damian

Baptistry

Golden Gate

Church of the Holy Sepulchre

Bishops House

Monastery of the Holy Sepulchre

Church of Jacob

Tancred's Tower

Valley of Gihon

Moat

Chamber of Commerce

Grain Market

St Mary la-Latine

Baths

Templum Domini

Pool of Patriarch

St Mary la Grand

Church of St. Giles

Church of the Virgin

Templars Stables

David's Gate

Church of St. John the Baptist

Skinners Furnace

Church of St. Martin

David's Tower

Ch. of St. James

Syrian Monastery

St Mary's German Hospice

King's Palace

St. Thomas Church

ARMENIAN

Cattle Market

Postern

Church of St. Peter ad Vincula

Postern of the Tannery

St. James Cathedral QUARTER

Kidron valley

House of Annas

Beaucaire Gate

Zion Gate

Germain's Pool

Cemetery

Mount Zion

Caiaphas House

St Mary of Mt. Zion

Germain's House

St. Peter in Gallicantu

Pool of Siloam

Valley of Hinnom

CRUSADER RULE

1099 The Crusaders conquer Jerusalem.

1187 The Crusaders driven from Jerusalem by Saladin.

Even Crusader rule did not deter one Jew from trying to settle in Jerusalem, for in 1140 the Spanish-born poet and philosopher Judah Halevi set out for Jerusalem via Cairo. According to legend, he was approaching the City Walls when an Arab horseman, leaving by one of the Gates, trampled him to death. As he lay dying he is said to have recited one of his own poems: "Zion, shall I not seek thee".

'Beautiful heights, joy of the world, city of a great king. For you my soul yearns from the lands of the west.
My pity collects and is roused when I remember the past. Your story in exile, and your Temple destroyed....
I shall cherish your stones and kiss them. And your earth will be sweeter than honey to my taste'.

JUDAH HALEVI
c. 1140

© Martin Gilbert 1977

ORIENS.

ASIA

INDI
MEDEN
PERSIA
ARMENIA
Ragus 149
P. ropolis
Niliae 174
MESOPO
Susa 330
TAMIA
Babilon 770.
CHALDEA
SYRIA   Haran 110
Viga.
Antiochia 154.
ARABIA
Damasco.
Seba 312.

SEPTENTRIO.

SVECIA

DANIA

ANGLICA

EVROPA
Saxonia.
GALLIA
Germania
Russia
Bohemia   Polonia
Muscuia.
Lothuingia
Vngaria   Turcia
Hispania
Grecia.
Mediolani
ITALIA
Romã 358.

MARE RVBRVM

AFRICA
Meroe 240
AETHIOPIA
REGNVM
MELINDE.
Ptus
Alexandria 72.
LYBIA
CAPVT BONAE
Cyrene 104.
SPEI,

MERIDIEN

MARE MEDITERRA
NEVM.

AMERICA
TERRA NOVA.

OCCIDENS.

Mediéval maps like this often showed Jerusalem at the centre of the world.

JERUSALEM 1830-1850

1831 Jerusalem captured by Mohammed Ali of Egypt.
1836 Ibrahim Pasha allows the Jews to repair their four main synagogues.
1840 Ottoman Turkish rule restored, but many Muslims from Egypt settle permanently in the City.
1842 The London Society for Promoting Christianity among the Jews sends a physician.
1843 A Jewish physician arrives, to relieve Jews of dependence upon the London Society physician.

'A large number of houses in Jerusalem are in a dilapidated and ruinous state. Nobody seems to make repairs so long as his dwelling does not absolutely refuse him shelter and safety. If one room tumbles about his ears, he removes into another, and permits rubbish and vermin to accumulate as they will in the deserted halls'.
DR. JOHN KITTO
'MODERN JERUSALEM' 1847

MUSLIM QUARTER

'in the N.E. the whole slope within the city walls is occupied by gardens, fields, and olive yards, with comparatively few houses or ruined dwellings; the whole being more the aspect of a village in the country than of a quarter in a city'.
E. ROBINSON AND E. SMITH,
'BIBLICAL RESEARCHES' 1838

0 ——— 300 yards
0 ——— 300 metres

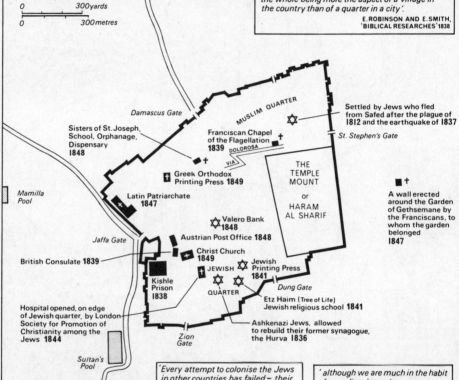

Damascus Gate

MUSLIM QUARTER

Sisters of St. Joseph, School, Orphanage, Dispensary 1848

Franciscan Chapel of the Flagellation 1839
VIA DOLOROSA

Settled by Jews who fled from Safed after the plague of 1812 and the earthquake of 1837

St. Stephen's Gate

Greek Orthodox Printing Press 1849

THE TEMPLE MOUNT or HARAM AL SHARIF

Mamilla Pool

Latin Patriarchate 1847

A wall erected around the Garden of Gethsemane by the Franciscans, to whom the garden belonged 1847

Valero Bank 1848
Austrian Post Office 1848

Jaffa Gate

Christ Church 1849

British Consulate 1839

JEWISH
Jewish Printing Press 1841

QUARTER

Kishle Prison 1838

Dung Gate

Etz Haim (Tree of Life) Jewish religious school 1841

Hospital opened, on edge of Jewish quarter, by London Society for Promotion of Christianity among the Jews 1844

Zion Gate

Ashkenazi Jews, allowed to rebuild their former synagogue, the Hurva 1836

Sultan's Pool

'Every attempt to colonise the Jews in other countries has failed – their eye has steadily rested on their beloved Jerusalem'.
JUDGE NOAH 'VOICE OF JACOB' OCTOBER 1844

' although we are much in the habit of regarding Jerusalem as a Moslem city, the Moslems do not actually constitute more than one-third of the entire population'.
DR. JOHN KITTO
'MODERN JERUSALEM' 1847

JEWISH QUARTER

' what a painful change has passed over the circumstances and condition of the poor Jew that in his own city, and close by where his temple stood, he has to suffer oppression and persecution. In Jerusalem his case is a very hard one, for if he should have a little of this world's goods in his possession, he is oppressed and robbed by the Turks in a most unmerciful manner; in short, for him there is neither law nor justice'.
JOHN LOTHIAN
4 DECEMBER 1843

'The influx of Jews has been very considerable of late. A fortnight since 150 arrived here from Algiers. There is now a large number of Jews here from the coast of Africa, who are about to form themselves into a separate congregation'.
REV. F.C. EWALD
LETTER FOR 'JEWISH INTELLIGENCE' 30 NOVEMBER 1843

POPULATION ESTIMATE, 1845 OF DR. SCHULTZE, PRUSSIAN CONSUL

Jews	7,120
Muslims	5,000
Christians	3,390
Turkish Soldiers	800
Europeans	100
TOTAL POPULATION	**16,410**

© Martin Gilbert 1977

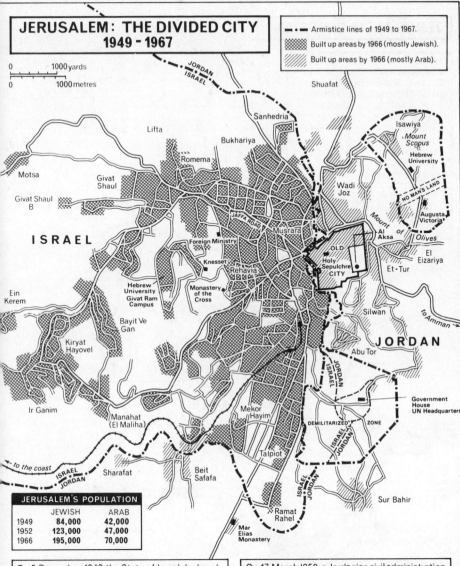

JERUSALEM: THE DIVIDED CITY 1949-1967

- —·—·— Armistice lines of 1949 to 1967.
- ▨▨▨ Built up areas by 1966 (mostly Jewish).
- ⫽⫽⫽ Built up areas by 1966 (mostly Arab).

0 ——— 1000 yards
0 ——— 1000 metres

JORDAN
ISRAEL

Shuafat

Sanhedria

Lifta

Bukhariya

Isawiya

Mount Scopus

Hebrew University

Romema

Motsa

Givat Shaul

Wadi Joz

NO MAN'S LAND

Givat Shaul B

Augusta Victoria

JAFFA ROAD

ISRAEL

Foreign Ministry

Musrara

Mount of Olives

Al Aksa

El Eizariya

Knesset

OLD CITY

Holy Sepulchre

Et-Tur

Rehavia

Ein Kerem

Hebrew University Givat Ram Campus

Monastery of the Cross

Silwan

to Amman

Bayit Ve Gan

JORDAN

JORDAN ISRAEL

Kiryat Hayovel

Abu Tor

Ir Ganim

Mekor Hayim

Government House UN Headquarters

DEMILITARIZED ZONE

Manahat (El Maliha)

ISRAEL JORDAN

to the coast

ISRAEL JORDAN

Sharafat

Beit Safafa

Talpiot

ISRAEL JORDAN

Sur Bahir

JERUSALEM'S POPULATION

	JEWISH	ARAB
1949	84,000	42,000
1952	123,000	47,000
1966	195,000	70,000

Ramat Rahel

Mar Elias Monastery

On 5 December 1949 the State of Israel declared west Jerusalem its capital. On 23 January 1950 the Israeli Parliament, meeting in the City, proclaimed that "Jerusalem was and had always been the capital of Israel". On 12 July 1953 the Israeli Foreign Ministry transferred from Tel Aviv to Jerusalem, despite earlier protests from the United States, Britain, France, Italy, Turkey and Australia, each of which refused to move its Embassy to Jerusalem.   By 1967 however, 40% of all diplomatic missions (but not the USA, USSR or Britain) were located in the city.

On 17 March 1950, a Jordanian civil administration was set up in east Jerusalem, and on 24 April 1950, the Jordanian Parliament in Amman ratified the annexation of east Jerusalem, with Amman as capital of the enlarged State. Only two States recognised this annexation – Britain and Pakistan. On 27 July 1953 King Hussein declared east Jerusalem to be "the alternative capital of the Hashemite Kingdom" and an "integral and inseparable part" of Jordan, but his Government discouraged economic development in east Jerusalem, and refused to set up an Arab University there.

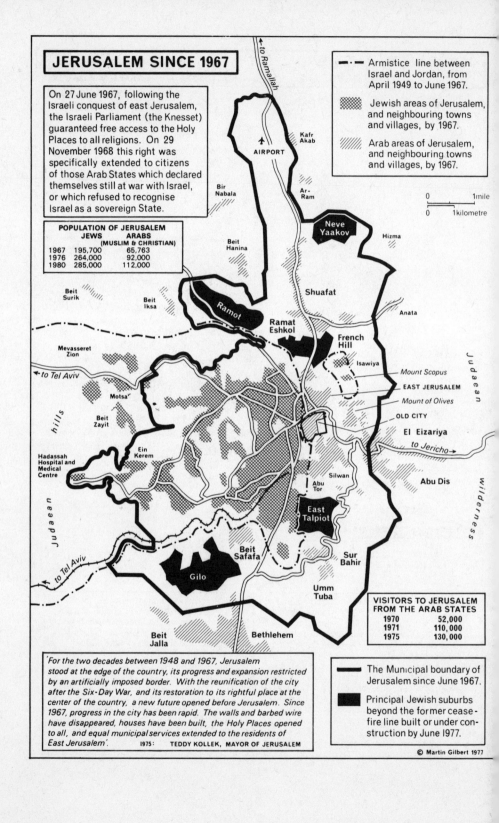

JERUSALEM SINCE 1967

On 27 June 1967, following the Israeli conquest of east Jerusalem, the Israeli Parliament (the Knesset) guaranteed free access to the Holy Places to all religions. On 29 November 1968 this right was specifically extended to citizens of those Arab States which declared themselves still at war with Israel, or which refused to recognise Israel as a sovereign State.

POPULATION OF JERUSALEM

	JEWS	ARABS (MUSLIM & CHRISTIAN)
1967	195,700	65,763
1976	264,000	92,000
1980	285,000	112,000

Legend:

– · – Armistice line between Israel and Jordan, from April 1949 to June 1967.

▒ Jewish areas of Jerusalem, and neighbouring towns and villages, by 1967.

╱ Arab areas of Jerusalem, and neighbouring towns and villages, by 1967.

0 ___ 1mile
0 ___ 1kilometre

to Ramallah

AIRPORT

Kafr Akab

Bir Nabala

Ar-Ram

Neve Yaakov

Hizma

Beit Hanina

Shuafat

Anata

Beit Surik

Beit Iksa

Ramot

Ramat Eshkol

French Hill

Mevasseret Zion

Isawiya

← to Tel Aviv

Mount Scopus

EAST JERUSALEM

Motsa

Mount of Olives

Beit Zayit

OLD CITY

El Eizariya

to Jericho →

Hadassah Hospital and Medical Centre

Ein Kerem

Silwan

Abu Tor

Abu Dis

hills

East Talpiot

Judaean

Judaean

wilderness

Beit Safafa

Sur Bahir

Gilo

Umm Tuba

VISITORS TO JERUSALEM FROM THE ARAB STATES

1970	52,000
1971	110,000
1975	130,000

to Tel Aviv

Beit Jalla

Bethlehem

─── The Municipal boundary of Jerusalem since June 1967.

▉ Principal Jewish suburbs beyond the former cease-fire line built or under construction by June 1977.

'For the two decades between 1948 and 1967, Jerusalem stood at the edge of the country, its progress and expansion restricted by an artificially imposed border. With the reunification of the city after the Six-Day War, and its restoration to its rightful place at the center of the country, a new future opened before Jerusalem. Since 1967, progress in the city has been rapid. The walls and barbed wire have disappeared, houses have been built, the Holy Places opened to all, and equal municipal services extended to the residents of East Jerusalem'. 1975: TEDDY KOLLEK, MAYOR OF JERUSALEM

© Martin Gilbert 1977

Left: For religious Jews there was in 1967 especial bitterness when returning, for the first time in 19 years, to the Jewish Quarter of the Old City. They found it utterly devastated.

Below left: Jewish tombstones from the desecrated, age-old cemetery on the Mount of Olives, were used by the Arabs – in this case – to pave a path to a Jordanian Army latrine.

Below right: Here, a mundane usage of Jewish tombstones, in a low wall enclosing a humble pasturage. Doubtless, no offence was intended; the stone in question was large, and useful.

The El Wad road through the heart of the Old City was, under Jordanian administration, reduced to a desolate alley-way. Since it led into the Jewish Quarter, it was not maintained.

The El Wad road, after restoration. This end of it has been integrated with the neatly and compactly rebuilt Jewish Quarter.

The German Lutheran Church was reduced to this state of ruin under Jordanian rule. This was a Christian place of worship, but Christian churches often fared badly between 1948 and 1967.

Since 1967, under Israeli rule, Christian monuments have been lovingly restored, often with the help of financial grants from Israel's Government. The Lutheran Church is a case in point. The mosque in the background has been carefully preserved.

Right: By the end of Jordanian rule, the Jewish Rabbinical High Court in the Old City was a shell, surrounded with ruined buildings and piles of rubble. Goats grazed around it, and paved streets were reduced to pitted paths.

Below: The Batei Mahaseh Square contained some of the administrative offices of the Jewish Quarter up to 1948. They were reduced to rubble under Jordanian rule.

Left: Restoration of the Rabbinical High Court under Israeli rule has been totally successful. The streets have been cleaned up and a nearby Arab mosque has been scrupulously preserved.

Below: Batei Mahaseh Square has now been carefully restored and houses the offices of the Quarter's Chief Architect.

The Eliahu Anavi synagogue was one of a group of four, all standing close together and all systematically wrecked after the Jordanian capture of the Old City in 1948. Everything of value in the four synagogues was destroyed or stolen. In two of the four, Arab families were found living in utter destitution when the Israelis recaptured the Jewish Quarter which had been theirs from time immemorial. Of all the four, the Eliahu Anavi had been most ravaged.

After restoration, the Eliahu Anavi synagogue is once again in full use. So are the other three of the 'group of four', the Ben Zakkai, Istanbul and Central synagogues. Only the biggest of all the synagogues in the Jewish Quarter, the Hurva, has still not been restored; its ruins were used under Jordanian rule as a donkey-park and goat-pen.

Right: Up to 1967 the Notre Dame
Hospital stood on the border between
East and West Jerusalem, in no Man's
Land, an area of ruins.

Below: Ramat Rahel used to be on the
southern border of Jewish Jerusalem, a
fortified outpost. Its population
farmed this land, under fire, for more
than two decades and fought a fine
defensive action against Jordanian
and Egyptian regular troops in 1948.

Left: Under Israeli rule this area has been transformed into a trim, tidy corner of the city, with a main thoroughfare running through it down to the Damascus Gate of the Old City. There used to be a miniature 'Berlin Wall' across the road.

Below: Today the barbed wire has been cleared from Ramat Rahel. It is now a flourishing agricultural community, on the edge of the city.

The Hadassah Hospital has become, in effect, a 'regional medical centre' for much of the almost entirely Arab West Bank. Services are free of charge, and freely given. There is a generally friendly and easy atmosphere and, on the Arab side, a keen awareness that the Hospital's medical services are of a high standard which they did not experience prior to the 1967 war. Good medical facilities are not a substitute for the political aspirations of the West Bank Arabs, but these pictures are a reminder that they really do help in the daily existence of the Arab population. Arab and Jewish patients are treated on a basis of equality. Israel is justly proud of its medical achievements, which have increased life expectancy and reduced infant mortality among the Arab population. This record of compassion and care is the true answer to accusations of a covert Israeli policy of genocide.

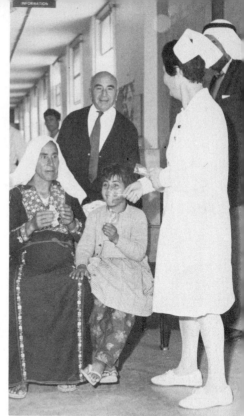

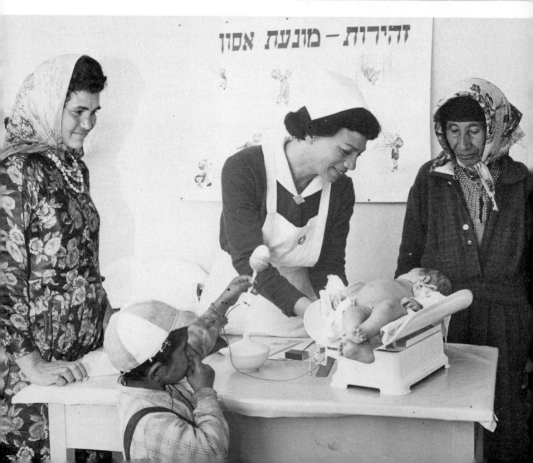

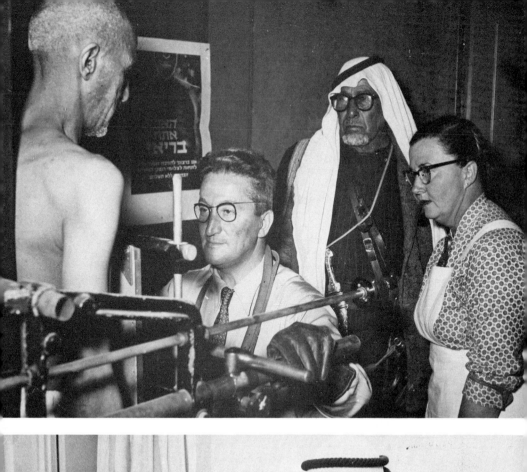

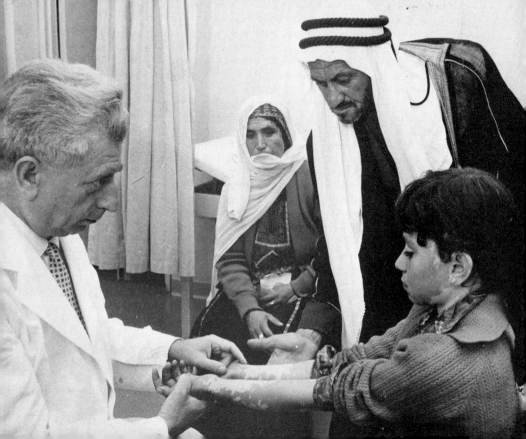

Right: The Jewish and Arab
communities in Jerusalem still
remain, to a large extent, apart. But
there is a useful degree of coexistence,
with more than a mere hint of
compassion and understanding. Here,
an Israeli soldier guides a blind Arab
down steps in the Old City.

Below: Jewish and Arab 'get-
togethers' are becoming less rare all
the time; given peace, they would be
everyday affairs. Here young Jews and
Arabs are watching a display by Jewish
jugglers.

Left: Two veterans, Jewish and Arab,
wait for a bus with the same look of
philosophical patience on their faces.

Below: Children leaving on their way
home from a 'mixed' cultural centre.
Children, if left to themselves, have no
political inhibitions.

Above: The Israelis have been accused of tasteless and, often, high-rise building in Jerusalem. Ramat Eshkol is a building settlement created with care and discretion. Most of its houses are built in stone which will weather and mellow. It was named after Levi Eshkol, the Prime Minister who tried his utmost to avert the 1967 war.

Right: A view of a corner of the Jewish Quarter of the Old City, which lay in ruins from 1948 to 1967. Every effort has been made to utilize the limited space available. Old and modern styles have been blended with an elegance which is the antithesis of the ghetto-like conditions which existed here before.

Muslim, but that Israel would not insist on destroying the mosques although undoubtedly having the right to do so.[56] This caused intense alarm among Muslim leaders, for ever since 1921 it had been a main plank in Arab propaganda that the Jews would try to seize the Haram. The situation was temporarily restored by the Chief Rabbinate ruling against prayers on the Temple Mount and forbidding religious Israelis to set foot upon it, since they might by so doing be desecrating the Holy of Holies of the Temple. But on 17 August 1969, a number of members of the 'Betar' National Youth Group held a ceremonial meeting near the Dome of the Rock and called for the rebuilding of the Temple. They were dispersed by Arab members of the Israeli police force, who now looked after the security of the area.

For the moment, the controversy slumbered. But on 21 August, only four days later, a mentally unstable young Christian, Dennis Michael Rohan, from Sydney, Australia, deliberately set the El Aqsa Mosque on fire. He was a fundamentalist, who believed that the second coming of Christ was at hand, and that the mosque had to be removed so that the Temple could be rebuilt. He had previously paid more than twenty visits to the Temple Mount, had distributed money freely to the Arab policemen on duty there, and had been allowed by one of them to enter the mosque at a time when it was closed to tourists.[57]

The Israeli authorities did everything they could to help. They called out fire brigades from West Jerusalem, Ramat Gan, Bnei Brak and Beth Shemesh, for the East Jerusalem fire brigade could not get the fire at once under control. The vitally important ladder, which enabled firemen to climb onto the dome of the mosque and fight the fire from above, came from West Jerusalem.[58] Their work was rendered very difficult by a hysterical mob of Arabs, which poured up onto the Temple Mount, pelted firemen with stones and later accused them of spraying petrol on the flames.[59] Nor was the matter over when the fire had been put out; there were riots in East Jerusalem and a storm of accusations in the outside world. The Jordanian Government, which controlled the mosque's purse-strings, refused to give the Jerusalem Arabs money for restoration work. The Israeli Government lost no time in appointing a commission of inquiry. Its report found that there had been negligence on the part of the Waqf and its employees, that the fire brigades and police had done their duty, and that better arrangements for guarding the Haram were urgently needed. Two of the five members of the commission were Arabs, the Mayor of Nazareth and the Judge of the Nazareth District Court. There was no question that its inquiry was impartial.

The question of prayer meetings on the Temple Mount nagged on. There were several more attempts to hold prayers there and in October 1970 the Israeli High Court ruled against the practice, on two grounds: it was contrary to a British Order in Council of 1924, and it was liable to cause a breach of the peace. In 1976 came a test case. Once again, it was a group of Betar youths who held a meeting in the Haram precinct, in May 1975. Once again they were charged, but this time a magistrate found in their favour in January 1976, because there was 'an inherent Jewish right' to pray there.[60] Once again there were Arab riots in East Jerusalem, and this time several people were killed, including an Arab boy of ten. Opinion in both parts of Jerusalem was critical of the magistrate's findings, in East Jerusalem because they implied a change in the status quo and questioned Muslim rights in the Haram, in West Jerusalem, because they encouraged further trouble. Fortunately, the High Court nullified the magistrate's findings on 30 June, and the Temple Mount became a much quieter place thereafter. Teddy Kollek drew solace from the affair with the thought that it 'was proof that there is a possibility of living together'.[61]

Yet the Temple Mount, and areas adjacent to it, continued to be a focus of Muslim distrust and complaint. The archaeological excavations beyond the Southern Wall of the Old City, brilliantly conceived and executed, were held to endanger the actual structure of the Haram. The demolition of the 'Moghrabi Quarter' abutting on the Western Wall – extolled by Arab writers as a dignified survival from the eighth century,[62] and depicted by the Israeli authorities as a 'decrepit slum'[63] – was alleged to be a first step in a creeping assault on the Haram. Tunnelling carried out to reveal a northwards extension of the Western Wall was denounced as a plan to bring the Dome of the Rock crashing down in ruins. The Jerusalem correspondent of *The Times*, not noted for personal friendliness towards Israel, admitted that this Arab fear 'proved unfounded'.[64]

The former Arab Mayor of East Jerusalem, Rouhi Al-Khatib, has claimed that the excavations 'were not meant to uncover Jewish history, but to cause cracks and the eventual collapse of various buildings', and that they were motivated by 'bigotry, prejudices, bitterness and hatred'. He claimed to have discovered a 'plot' to drive 18,000 Muslim Arabs out of the Old City (in fact, about 80 per cent of the Muslim Arab inhabitants there). The burning of the El Aqsa Mosque had been 'a link in the chain of the Israeli schemes for the Judaization of Jerusalem', and the trial of the Australian arsonist was 'fictitious, and evidence of his madness was devised'. The ex-Mayor even alleged that, with the fire raging in the mosque, the Israelis cut off the water-supply![65]

The wildness of such allegations should blind nobody to the depth of Muslim feeling about the Haram, the Temple Mount. Any Israeli move in its neighbourhood is regarded as a threat. Any interference with Muslim administration of it is a desecration. Muslim veneration of its great and beautiful shrines is sincere and deep rooted. It would probably be true to say that if the Dome of the Rock and the El Aqsa Mosque did not exist, Muslim attachment to Jerusalem would fade. This was just another reason why imagined threats to them caused such emotion; the Arab imagination is fertile and vivid.

After thirteen years in possession of all of Jerusalem's Holy Places, Israel's record could in 1980 be summed up in simple terms. Generally good, often excellent, relations were established with the Christian Churches. With the Muslim authorities there was, in the main, a state of uneasy truce – but nothing better than this could possibly have been expected. As trustees for the three great monotheisms of the world, the Israelis certainly tried hard to be just and made only a few mistakes. The dignity of the three faiths has, on the whole, been preserved – least successfully, perhaps, in the Jewish community where internal disputes were in danger of becoming as acute as those of competing Christians in the past. What the Israelis could claim, incontestably, is that they scrupulously maintained freedom of worship, the rights of the different religious communities to manage their own affairs and administer their own institutions, and complete freedom of access to all Holy Places. Could anyone else have done better? The Jordanians, from 1948 to 1967, certainly did not do nearly so well.

Both the Jordanian and Saudi Arabian dynasties might lay claim to a hereditary or historical right to be guardians of the Arab Holy Places of Jerusalem. The Saudi claim, at least, is unworthy of consideration; its rulers are already guardians of Mecca and Medina, and Jerusalem has never been theirs. Nor did the multitudinous members of the Saudi royal family show the slightest interest in the great mosques when free to visit them at a time when they were under Arab control.

The Jordanian Hashemites are, of course, direct descendants of the Prophet. Should that reinforce their claim to a share in the control of Jerusalem? In his open letter to King Hussein, Monsignor Oesterreicher summed up as follows:

> The Jerusalem of today is not a city in 'captivity'. It is free, as it has never been before. Whoever has walked its streets during these last four years, must have felt as I did that he was privileged to breathe the air of holiness, of God's special presence. He must have perceived that it was a city in search of peace, not one given to strife and hate … No, I cannot agree with the King [Hussein] that Jordan or the Arab world is the City's 'rightful owner'. Biblically speaking, Jerusalem is God's city, as the land is God's land. Men are but tenants.[66]

REFERENCES

1.   John Foster Dulles, reporting to the US Government as Secretary of State, 1 June 1953.
2.   UN Document A/6753, 10 July 1967.
3.   Letter to UN Secretary-General, 30 April 1968.
4.   UN General Assembly official records, 24th Plenary Session.
5.   Moshe Dayan, *Story of my Life*, Weidenfeld, London, 1976.
6.   Chaim Herzog, *Who Stands Accused?*, Weidenfeld, London, 1978.
7.   Yosef Tekoah, *Barbed Wire shall not return to Jerusalem*, Israel Information Services publication, New York, 1968.
8.   Ibid.
9.   Letter in *New York Times*, 12 July 1967.
10.   Yosef Tekoah, op. cit.
11.   Ibid.
12.   Ibid.
13.   Ibid.
14.   *Jerusalem Post*, 30 April 1968.
15.   *Jerusalem Post*, 9 December 1968.
16.   *L'Espresso* (Italian weekly), 12 September 1971.
17.   Reported in Arab paper *Al Anba*, 12 December 1971.
18.   *Jerusalem Post*, 7 January 1972.
19.   Yosef Tekoah, op. cit.
20.   Statement on Temple Mount, quoted by Chaim Herzog, as above.
21.   Yosef Tekoah, op. cit.
22.   Briefing in Royal Jordanian Embassy, Summer 1967.
23.   Teddy Kollek, *For Jerusalem*, Weidenfeld, London, 1978.
24.   Meron Benvenisti, *Jerusalem: The Torn City*, Isratypeset, Jerusalem, 1976.
25.   Thus in the *Tablet*, 4 May 1974. The paper suggested that Pope Paul VI would prefer the Arabs and Israelis to reach agreement on Jerusalem by themselves.
26.   Walter Zander, *Jerusalem and the Holy Places of Christendom*, Weidenfeld, London, 1971.

27. Meron Benvenisti, op. cit.
28. Gerard Noel, *The Anatomy of the Catholic Church*, Hodder & Stoughton, London, 1980.
29. Meron Benvenisti, op. cit.
30. Yaacov Herzog, *A People that dwells alone*, Weidenfeld, London, 1975.
31. Gerard Noel, op. cit.
32. Ibid.
33. Stephen S. Rosenfeld, *Washington Post*, 5 October 1979.
34. Michael Adams, *The Churches and Palestine*, pamphlet of the Council for the Advancement of Arab–British Relations (undated).
35. The Archbishop of Canterbury, *Canterbury Diocesan Notes*, January 1972.
36. Venerable Carlyle Witton-Davies, *Church Times*, 9 May 1975.
37. Geoffrey Wigoder, *Jewish Chronicle*, 21 December 1979.
38. A. M. Goichon, *Jérusalem. Fin de la Ville Universelle?*, Masonneuve & Larose, Paris, 1976.
39. Dr Douglas Young, in letter to the author.
40. Robert Rozenberg, *Jerusalem Post*, 24 January 1980.
41. Christopher Walker, *The Times*, 25 January 1980.
42. Dial Torgerson, *New York Herald Tribune*, 29 January 1980.
43. *Jerusalem Post*, 13 February 1980.
44. *The Times*, 2 February 1980.
45. *Jewish Chronicle News Service*, 12 February 1980.
46. Christopher Walker, *The Times*, 6 February 1980.
47. Jewish Telegraphic Agency, 4 December 1979.
48. *Jerusalem Post*, 2 February 1980.
49. Christopher Walker, *The Times*, 23 November 1979.
50. Eliyahu Ashtor, 'Jerusalem in Muslim Thought', from *Jerusalem*, Israel Pocket Library, Keter, 1973.
51. Teddy Kollek, *Jerusalem Perspectives*, ed. by Peter Schneider & Geoffrey Wigoder, Furnival Press, London, 1976.
52. Mgr John Oesterreicher, *Jerusalem the Free*, Anglo–Israel Association pamphlet, London, April 1963.
53. King Feisal of Saudi Arabia, on Radio Riyadh, 30 December 1973.
54. Teddy Kollek, op. cit.
55. Ibid.
56. Meron Benvenisti, op. cit.
57. Moshe Brilliant, *The Times*, 1 September 1969.
58. Report of the Commission of Inquiry into the Circumstances of the Fire at the Aqsa Mosque, September 1969.
59. Ibid.
60. Teddy Kollek, *Foreign Affairs*, July 1977.
61. Ibid.
62. A. L. Tibawi, *The Islamic Pious Foundations in Jerusalem*, Baskerville Press, London, 1978.
63. Professor David Amiran, Institute of Jerusalem Studies, in letter to the author.
64. Eric Marsden, *The Times*, 9 December 1976.
65. Rouhi al-Khatib, *The Judaization of Jerusalem*, Amman, 1979.
66. Mgr John Oesterreicher, op. cit.

CHAPTER SEVEN

To Build,
or Not to Build

In September 1971 the Israeli Foreign Minister, Abba Eban, responded to a telegram from the UN Secretary-General, U Thant, which called upon Israel, in conformity with UN Resolution 298, 'to rescind all previous measures and actions and to take no further steps in the occupied sector of Jerusalem which may change the status of the city, or prejudice the rights of the inhabitants'. Eban's answer was full of calculated irony.

He pointed out that a restoration of what had been the 'status' of Jerusalem before June 1967 'would involve the restoration of a military demarcation line and other barriers cutting through the centre of the city; the cancellation of free access to their holy places for Jews and Israeli Moslems ... and the reimposition of a ban on residence or visit of anyone of Jewish faith in the Old City'. Israel, moreover, 'would have to demolish the synagogues and other sites destroyed by the Jordan authorities and restored since then, and to close the cultural, humanitarian and educational institutions on Mount Scopus which have been reopened since June 1967. Thus the restoration of the previous status would involve rescinding the unity, peace and sanctity of Jerusalem today in order to restore the divisions, conflict and sacrilege which made the period 1948-67 one of the darkest ages in Jerusalem's long history.'[1]

Eban proceeded to give U Thant an account of Israel's stewardship in the reunified Jerusalem since June 1967. The Holy Places had been safeguarded. The disastrous decline of the

Christian community had been halted, and its population had risen from 10,800 to 11,500. Universal suffrage had been introduced for municipal elections, whereas Jordanian rule had restricted the vote to property-owners and appointed the Mayor from Amman. Proper municipal services had been organized for the whole community; they had been 'non-existent or inadequate during the nineteen years of illegal Jordanian military occupation'. Israel had introduced compulsory education into East Jerusalem, created a kindergarten system where none existed before, expanded vocational training, organized free medical services for mothers and babies, created parks, public libraries and youth clubs, and put all existing Israeli offices at the disposal of the people of East Jerusalem – for instance, a Labour Exchange and a Trade Union Federation.

Eban said little about housing, which had become perhaps the most controversial issue of all in Jerusalem. He referred only to 'low-cost public housing and generous mortgage opportunities provided by the Municipality to Arab residents'. There were all too many reasons why the housing question should be controversial.

The capture of East Jerusalem by Israel in 1967 had not been planned; it was a totally unexpected bonus. As Mayor of West Jerusalem, Teddy Kollek already had his hands very full; now he was landed with responsibilities far beyond anything he had envisaged and fraught with immensely important potential consequences. He adjusted himself with typical aplomb, but made no secret of his difficulties. In a speech made just two years after the 1967 war, he outlined some of them.[2]

Jerusalem had one of the most heterogenous populations in the world to administer; its 20 per cent of Arabs came from many different groups, but its Jews from no less than one hundred different countries. Jerusalem's Jews had a birth rate of twenty-six per thousand, or roughly twice that of Tel Aviv or Haifa, but the Arabs' birth-rate, at over forty per thousand, was one of the highest in the world. Jerusalem had the highest proportion of children in the country, but also the highest proportion of old-age pensioners, many of whom had come from all over the world to end their days in their holy city. East Jerusalem's standard of living had to be brought into line with that of West Jerusalem, and this problem was exacerbated by the fact that 'the Arabs consider us an occupation force'. 'I think', Kollek went on, 'we have a better chance to overcome our problems more quickly than ... in other mixed cities in the world.' But, 'I am not talking about weeks, months or even years; it is a question of decades'.

Kollek knew that Jerusalem was burdened by social and economic problems which could only be overcome by rapid development, that it was now once again the natural centre of a whole region and that all sorts of demands would be made upon it, and that it had the worst problems of overcrowding of any Israeli city. It was, further, a relatively poor city, with little industry, heavily dependent on tourism, which had been badly hit by the Six Day War. The city had to expand in order to live, and expansion would mean a major housing problem, for Jerusalem was already over-burdened with slums.

Here, Kollek was up against a school of thought which was, at the least, conservative, even obscurantist. Its protagonists believed that Jerusalem should be 'preserved', as it had been in Ottoman days, as a kind of beautiful village in the hills, a relic. Otherwise it would assuredly be 'spoilt', or even profaned. Some of these ultra-conservatives were writers, historians, archaeologists, diplomats, and sometimes ageing Peter Pans who wanted everything to remain as it always had been. Jerusalem's enemies, as they saw it, were wheeled vehicles (except for those put at their personal disposal), good roads, modern plumbing and, of course, building of any kind. They would agree that, under the British Mandate, a number of concrete plans had been put forward, dealing with Jerusalem's future, but these had seemed innocuous, or even designed to preserve the fossilized Jerusalem which they desired.

Thus, there had been a 'Maclean Plan' in 1918, which proposed inner and outer 'protective rings' round the walled Old City. In 1922 there was the 'Ashbee and Geddes Plan', which accepted the Maclean Plan's objectives and related them to topography and land-ownership. The 'Holliday Plan' came in 1934. It was of a more practical nature; the 'green belt' round the walls of the Old City would be reduced in size, and there were even proposals for the creation of a West Jerusalem 'commercial centre' – a horrific thought for the purists – along the axis of the Jaffa Road. Only the 'Kendall Plan' of 1944 departed from altruistic motivation, drastically reducing the projected green belt and allowing for shops and banks to be built almost up to the Jaffa Gate of the Old City. Possibly, the Kendall Plan swung too far towards a utilitarian modern approach to Jerusalem's problems.[3]

Kollek always regarded Jerusalem as a 'living city', not a

melting-pot but a 'mosaic' of differing communities.[4] His actions
during the first six months after Jerusalem's reunification speak
for themselves.[5] Nearly fourteen miles of roadway were either
built or repaired within the city's boundaries; street lamps
everywhere were repaired or installed, and street signs in the Old
City put up in Hebrew as well as Arabic; 6,000 trees were
planted; nine miles of water-pipes were laid and water
consumption increased by 50 per cent; twenty-eight school
buildings were repaired and six youth clubs and sports
associations formed; 2,000 families were registered with the
welfare department, and a census was held. All this was done in
Arab East Jerusalem, yet accusations that this part of the city was
neglected continued. In addition, the sewage system of the Old
City was overhauled, and a water purification plant planned.
Instructions were given to householders not to use sewage water
for growing their vegetables – this had caused outbreaks of
cholera in the past and would cause yet one more in 1970.

Moshe Dayan had laid down the maxim that the way to go
about things in East Jerusalem was to 'create facts' first and
argue about them later on.[6] Kollek and his advisers had no doubt
as to what the building priorities were. They were the rebuilding
of the Jewish Quarter of the Old City, the reactivation of the
Hadassah Hospital and Hebrew University on Mount Scopus,
and the creation of new housing settlements between the
Sanhedria Quarter of West Jerusalem and Mount Scopus.[7] In this
way, what had previously been an isolated enclave on Mount
Scopus would be directly linked with the rest of Jewish Jerusalem.
This was not a dark plot; the Israelis went boldly and openly
ahead with their plans. A decisive part was played by the Prime
Minister, Levi Eshkol, with the encouragement of his
predecessor, David Ben Gurion. The immediate aim was to build
7,000 homes for Jews in North Jerusalem.

Where the Jewish Quarter was concerned, opinion was
unanimous that it should be fully restored and a Jewish
population brought back there. Under Jordanian rule it was left
largely in ruins, the result of the 1948 war, of looting, subsequent
deliberate destruction and a long period of total neglect. A
UNESCO mission which visited the Quarter in 1960 found it a
ruinous slum.[8] By a law passed on 18 April 1968, virtually the
whole area of the Quarter, only around 30 acres, was purchased
or taken over. The Israeli authorities left intact and in Arab
hands two mosques, a Muslim library and a number of Arab-
owned shops along the dividing line between the Jewish and

Muslim Quarters. Arabs living in the Jewish Quarter were almost entirely squatters, but the Municipality undertook to find alternative accommodation for them.* One Arab complaint was that the Quarter was only 20 per cent Jewish-owned; the true figure was around 40 per cent, but many of the other buildings were state property rented by Jewish tenants. According to one authority,[9] no property belonging to the Muslim property administrators, the Waqf, was either seized or destroyed – Kollek, indeed, told him that no Waqf property was for sale anywhere in Jerusalem, when he tried to buy land for his Christian religious foundation in 1967.

Absurdly, one writer has claimed that 12,500 Arabs were driven out of the Jewish Quarter.[10] It is possible that, at one stage, about 6,000 Arabs were living, mainly as squatters, in the Quarter, in cramped and generally miserable conditions, in corners of ruined and plundered synagogues, in cellars and mere holes in the ground. Most of them fled during the fighting. The Israeli authorities set about the work of slowly, carefully and with infinite love and patience, restoring the whole of the Quarter. After thirteen years of work, four synagogues had been fully rebuilt and 400 families, a total of about 2,000 people, had moved in. The final target was 650 families and just over 3,000 people, and all but about fifty families were scheduled to have moved in by the end of 1982. The plans allowed for about 750 of the Jewish inhabitants of the Quarter to be students at the 'yeshiva' or religious schools.

There were at once far more applicants for homes in the Quarter than available housing units; preference was given to families who had lived in the Quarter before 1948. Planning was perfectionist; every building had to be approved by the Chief Architect, and the utmost ingenuity was shown in securing maximum space and light – for the whole Quarter would fit within the precinct of the two great mosques. Storeys of houses were set back in echelon, floors were recessed, roofs opened up

---

* In his book *For Jerusalem*, Teddy Kollek claimed that almost all of the Arabs 'camping' in the Jewish Quarter were glad to leave, so long as they were given either compensation or far better alternative housing. He added, 'The truth is that we have evacuated many more Jews than Arabs in the course of our town-planning activities'. In a statement made to the *Jerusalem Post* (24 January 1977), Kollek said that thirty Arab families living on the southern side of the Street of Chains, which was just within the area of the Jewish Quarter, would be left undisturbed. So would about a hundred Arab shopowners, on the same side of the same street. The whole street would remain virtually entirely Arab in character.

to provide penthouse rooms and gardens, and intervals allowed wherever possible between buildings to give as many as possible wonderful views of the Old City, Mount Scopus and more distant horizons.

While new foundations were being laid, numerous archaeological 'finds' were uncovered – relics of Herodian Jerusalem, a key section of the pre-Christian outer wall at its north-western 'turn', mosaics, and a section of the Roman 'Cardo' road of the second century AD, 22 metres broad and planned to be opened up as a historic monument-cum-shopping arcade. The scrupulous preservation of everything of archaeological interest cost a lot of money and put up the prices of apartments – by 1980 a four-room apartment was priced at $70,000 to $80,000. Special designs were sought for building directly opposite the piazza in front of the Western Wall; the empty corner of the Quarter there could eventually be terraced and offered fascinating possibilities for Jerusalem's town-planners. The Quarter was to be kept as quiet as possible, as a place of contemplation and dignified repose, but by 1980 a number of small workshops and restaurants had been built. Cars could come only as far as one corner of the Quarter, although the construction of a single underground garage was still being considered.

Mayor Kollek explained overall building plans on many occasions and the following extracts from one article written by him give a picture of his thinking.[11] Jerusalem's 'ancient glory' would be restored, it would be no 'parochial city'. The quality of life would be improved; this had meant building museums, a theatre, art-centres and a green belt round the Old City: 'Jerusalem is, I believe, the only city in modern times to create, by purchase, a large central green area such as was preserved by the Boston Common, New York's Central Park, London's Hyde Park and the Bois de Boulogne'. Advice was sought, in particular by establishing a 'Jerusalem Committee' of sixty eminent people from all over the world, and their criticisms were welcomed. There had, Kollek admitted, been controversies, especially over the building of homes for Israeli citizens outside the walls of the Old City. 'This dispute was hardly justified since we did not infringe on Arab housing. We built mainly on rocky ground newly incorporated into the city. We used no wooded land or land that was employed for agriculture. We removed nothing of value. Our plans call for no further land expropriation in the future.'

The amount of building that was envisaged called for detailed planning. The municipal authorities carried out careful studies of the various British plans of the Mandatory era. The ruling Labour Alignment appointed its own committee of seven, who produced a draft plan by 10 July 1967. Early in 1968 a 'Master Plan' had been drawn up by a team led by architects Avia Hasimshoni and Yosef Schweid. It provided for an 'outer edge' to the city, surrounded by a green belt, and there would be a smaller green belt round the inner, Old City.[12] It foresaw an immensely increased functional capacity for Jerusalem and, in order to meet this, 'imposed an unnatural unity ... at the expense of many aesthetic and environmental qualities'.[13] It proposed building major roads through the heart of the city, something which might be acceptable in rebuilt modern cities like Berlin and Düsseldorf, but was hardly suitable in Jerusalem. Finally, it provoked a stringent, perhaps over-harsh criticism: 'A new way of thinking about Jerusalem has sprung up: the city is a resource to be exploited, its spiritual and visual qualities are commodities to be bought and sold'.[14]

The Master Plan was, of course, subject to revision, for there were a number of people with views to voice and a say in the matter. The Ministry of Finance may indeed have seen the city as a 'resource', for it had as far as possible to pay for itself and this could only be done by expanding tourism, increasing the population and encouraging trade and industry. The Ministry of Housing was more concerned with straight resettlement and, to save money, fitting in as many people as possible into as small a space as possible. This led to a bias in favour of high-rise building. The Mayor was intent on preserving the beauty of the Holy City as well as making its unified whole a worthy capital of Israel. Even two years after the Master Plan was drawn up, it was still a matter of fierce controversy.

Kollek looked for outside advice, and the sort of advice which would support his own reasoned and enlightened approach. Accordingly he secured the formation of the 'Jerusalem Committee', which met for the first time in Jerusalem in July 1969. The names of just a few of its members are indicative of its quality: the British sculptor Henry Moore, the American writer Lewis Mumford, the Austrian painter Oskar Kokoschka, the German writer Heinrich Böll, the former Australian Prime Minister Sir Robert Menzies, the heads of King's College London and St Antony's College Oxford, Lord Annan and Professor Raymond Carr.

The Jerusalem Committee was purely complimentary at its first meeting, finding 'a devotion to work and a fervour which gave us courage and hope'. But when its town-planning subcommittee met in December 1970 it called for radical revision of the Master Plan; all the emphasis of its recommendations was directed towards preserving the true character of the city. It was partly due to its criticisms that a British expert, Professor Nathaniel Lichfield, was appointed chief planning officer in 1971. Lichfield was keenly aware of the mistakes which had been made in the past, in fact before the 1967 war. Chief among them was the Intercontinental Hotel on the Mount of Olives and the 'three sore thumbs' which began to appear on the opposite, western ridge running along the Jaffa Road – the Hilton and Plaza Hotels and the Omaria tower block, all three approved before Kollek became Mayor.[15] These decisions, sadly, could not be reversed. Paradoxically, although most complaints thereafter were directed against building in East Jerusalem, the skyline which suffered worst was in Jewish West Jerusalem.

The full plenary sessions of the Jerusalem Committee were to take place every three years. In 1973 the Committee achieved two successes. It condemned high-rise building anywhere near the Old City and it had its way. The principle was laid down, and firmly pursued ever since, that no new high-rise building should 'obtrude' upon the Old City. Oddly enough, King Hussein of Jordan's brother, Crown Prince Hassan bin Talal, was still propagating the myth that huge apartment blocks were being constructed 'in the areas round the Old City', in 1980![16] This was demonstrably untrue. In addition, the Committee managed to have the building permits for one hotel, two office blocks and a department store rescinded. It recommended more careful conservation of gracious neighbourhoods, the cancellation of plans for obtrusive suburbs (as in Nebi Samwil), and improved siting of other new housing estates. The members of the Committee complimented the Mayor for his 'remarkable wisdom and foresight',[17] and on the work done in archaeological excavation and in the restoration of historic buildings. Kollek might well have reciprocated their kindly words and feelings, for both their aims and thoughts dovetailed.

In 1976 members of the Committee found a dozen achievements to praise. First was Kollek's enlightened supervision of archaeological work. Then, in less concrete terms, 'a sense of orderly growth and stability mindful of change' and 'a clear and definitive delineation of the boundaries of the City'.

There had been a welcome co-ordination of physical development and organic growth of population, and greater restriction of the height of buildings. Then the proposed 'super-highway system' had been rigorously curtailed, social planning had made great strides, and 1,100 buildings had been registered for special protection. Three special projects were singled out – the 'tastefully designed' Armenian Seminary, the 'archaeological garden' constructed along the South Wall of the Temple Mount, and the imaginative embellishment of the outer walls of the Old City, which had been restored to their 'former charm and splendour'. The Waqf was complimented on its restoration of Muslim holy places, and Teddy Kollek for placing contemporary works of art in the city and for the expansion and remarkable improvement of schools.[18]

Finally, the Committee's 1978 Report commended the Municipality for meeting three of its previous requests: a city engineer had been appointed (Professor Lichfield had returned to Britain in the meantime), excellent progress had been made in the creation of the green belt round the walls of the Old City, and no more high-rise building was taking place. The Committee asked that plans for building any sort of garage in the Old City should be re-examined, that traffic to service the Old City should be limited to 'a bare minimum', and that there should be an immediate traffic study covering such servicing and the location of parking areas outside the walls.[19] The Committee also regretted that it had not been possible to go ahead with plans to rebuild the 'Great', or Hurva Synagogue, and suggested an international competition for a new design. Other recommendations by the Committee included maintenance of the ban on high-rise building, step-by-step development of the proposed central business district close to the old border which had run through the city, the building of a new civic centre, and the development of individual character and necessary services for the new and still unbuilt suburbs.

These recommendations, too, were adopted and, as far as possible, put into practice between 1978 and 1980. The Committee's practical and aesthetic ideas acted both as inspiration and brake where planning was concerned. In 1967 the Municipality spent a mere £150,000 on planning, but by 1973 the planning budget had jumped to £700,000 and the full-time planning staff had risen to twenty-four.[20] Planning cost even more by 1980, but the budget may only be reduced when the suburbs under construction begin to reach completion and an improved city centre begins to take shape. There will always be major problems, although the first hectic pace of development is now over: the population of Jerusalem jumped from 195,000 in 1967 to 315,000 in 1973 and to about 400,000 in 1980, and everyone had to be housed. Even though the rate of increase of population had slowed down, there were expected to be over half a million people living in Greater Jerusalem by 1990.

In his struggle to maintain the beauty of Jerusalem and increase its efficiency, Kollek was harassed by two different forms of criticism. The first was aesthetic, the second political, and sometimes the two were interlinked. Aesthetic criticism was welcomed, if not always justified. Political criticism had very different connotations, based as it was on the deep resentment of the Arab world that East Jerusalem was in Israeli hands and on the sincerely-held Arab belief that Israel had no right to build there at all. Criticism on both aesthetic and political grounds was generally very fierce, often degenerating into diatribe. This was understandable; Jerusalem is a unique city, and its whole future was at stake.

First, then, aesthetic criticism. One of the early, trenchant critics was the Italian architect, Bruno Zevi. He expressed despair over 'chaotic' planning and called some of the new building 'lousy' (schifoso).[21] Two distinguished Britons, Professor Arnold Toynbee and Sir Geoffrey Furlonge, expressed their concern in *The Times*.[22] They believed that the Israelis were turning Jerusalem into 'a kind of Los Angeles' and called the building programmes 'vandalism' and 'desecration'. They followed this up with a second letter to the same newspaper; Jerusalem's appearance had 'been irreparably impaired. The bitterness and resentment of the Arabs had justifiably increased – and it is directed not only against the Israelis, who have committed this outrage, but also against the international community, which has done nothing to give effect to the formal and universal condemnation of Israeli policy in Jerusalem'. Israel was 'not only threatening the beauty of Jerusalem but also damaging the prospect of a lasting settlement in the Middle East'.[23]

The objections of the Arabs and their friends were summed up by Michael Adams, for many years the key member of the Council for the Advancement of Arab–British Understanding in London. He wrote[24] that five major building projects in Jerusalem would 'encircle the Arab sector with a ring of housing blocks for Jewish settlers, 100,000 of them, who will then outnumber the whole Arab population of the city'. He deplored the French Hill project, with its six-storey houses and 'air of menace', and he claimed that the Israelis were building with 'a frantic speed' in the belief that 'so long as we keep Jerusalem Jewish, it doesn't matter if we ruin it in the process'. He did not go as far as Toynbee and Furlonge in stating that all was already lost, but 'if the Israeli building programme continues, the beauty of the city will soon be irreparably damaged and the tenuous hope of peace in the Middle East will be gone beyond recall'. His refrain was the same as theirs.

There was plenty of criticism in the same vein, but some of it came from Israel's friends as well, although in much more moderate terms. Thus Saul Bellow agreed that 'There are hideous new buildings in Jerusalem, it is true. Kollek is, I think, humiliated by them. The Wolfson Condominium is most unattractive. The multitudinous windows of the new Hilton look to me like the heavy-lidded eyes of insomnia sufferers, aching for rest.'[25] A member of the 'Jerusalem Committee' found 'nothing new or in construction which is objectionable', with two exceptions: 'The constructions on Mount Scopus are very ugly indeed, destroying the beautiful line of the Mount Scopus ridge. But I always found the Augusta Victoria (Hospital) a ghastly mistake, the Jordanian hospital a barbarism, the Intercontinental Hotel and now the Greek Orthodox Church in the Kidron Valley profanation by Christians.' Then 'the Wolfson Tower, facing the Parliament across the valley is an ugly and brutal realization'.[26] The same critic deplored the projects for a high-rise twenty-two storey annexe for the King David Hotel, and a fourteen-storey tower close to it. But these projects were, in fact, scrapped. So was the twenty-four storey Hyatt Hotel, planned to be built on the slopes of Mount Scopus.[27]

A cry of woe came from the former British Labour Party Minister, Richard Crossman.[28] Admirable work had been done in conserving buildings and parks, but, 'The more I saw of the half-dozen skyscrapers which already tower over the western sector of the town, the more shocked I was ... the two Wolfson blocks which dwarf the graceful Knesset, and the even higher Hilton now under construction are eyesores which ruin the skyline of Old Jerusalem ... Anything over eight storeys should be vetoed in this area without any concession to developers'. For, if the developers had their way, 'the peace of the old city will be threatened and much of old Jerusalem will degenerate into a slum'. It would at least have been a consolation for Mr Crossman – had he lived – to know that, seven years afterwards, only two more high-rise buildings had been added on the western ridge, and no more were likely to be built.

One of the most persistent and objective critics of high-rise defacement of Jerusalem was the Israeli architect, Art Kutcher, who had worked for a time for the Municipality. In an interview with Eric Silver of the *Guardian*[29] he explained his thinking. The growth of tourism had led to damage being done in Jerusalem before the 1967 war; it had brought the building of new hotels, massively constructed because this was cheapest. Modern technology had been misapplied, in the mistaken belief that a technological age must 'express itself', and that the contrast between new and old would 'create a new kind of beauty which will heighten Jerusalem's special quality'.

Kutcher wanted a 'qualitative' rather than quantitive approach. Rather more hazily, he wanted tourism 'controlled'. In 1973 he published a book about Jerusalem's town-planning, which set out his views fully.[30] In a nutshell, the 'choice' lay between 'building the New Jerusalem according to the principles of Baron Haussmann, or according to the principles of the Prophet Isaiah. The one is a city manipulated to achieve certain political and economic ends, the other is a city as an affirmation of human values, and the promise of a spiritual reality.' But he did not want Jerusalem preserved as a 'quaint and semi-pastoral relic'; rather, he wanted conservation of its panoramas, its mosaic of diverse communities, its visual harmony, its open spaces, its architectural features and its overall landscape. His three chief objections to what was being done were that high-rise building had been encouraged by allowing one or two projects to go ahead – knowing that this would be used as an argument for others – that too many roads were being built – 'There is nothing like a really good road to make politicians and their constituents happy' – and that some of Jerusalem's planners, knowing that they could never rival Manhattan, had set their sights a bit lower, on a 'sort of copy of Kansas City'.

Kutcher took particular exception to the major building project on French Hill. This lay astride the road to Ramallah, and linked the Ramat Eshkol settlement – itself in East Jerusalem – with the complex of Hebrew University buildings, already standing or planned, on Mount Scopus. There could be no mistaking the strategic purpose of this long, left-hook all the way from the Sanhedria quarter of Jewish West Jerusalem; it turned the Scopus enclave into an integral part of Jewish Jerusalem. The military importance of Mount Scopus has already been explained, and it was seized upon by Israel's critics as the pretext for the location and nature of the French Hill project. Kutcher advanced his own case against French Hill with solid arguments, but mistakenly circulated a trick photograph first published in *The Times*[31] and subsequently in many other papers. The photograph had been bought from the German paper, *Stern*, which had recently gone over to an anti-Israeli political line. It was ostensibly taken from Government House, and two strips of ground – between Government House and the Old City, and between Mount Scopus and the outer edge of the part of Arab Jerusalem opposite – had been 'eliminated'. One result was that the photographer would seem to have been standing directly overlooking the Temple Mount area. More relevantly, the French Hill and Scopus buildings, of five to eight storeys, towered above the whole of the Old City.

Publication of this faked photograph caused a storm of criticism – understandably, for it produced a frightening effect of the splendours of the Old City being dwarfed by gigantic constructions at least four times as high as what had actually been built. One critic called them 'frigid monsters',[32] and when newly built they certainly looked bare and unprepossessing. One complaint was that they had no balconies, and small windows which suggested they were designed as fortresses. The truth was that the buildings were grouped facing south towards the city, and residents would feel the full force of the hot, 'hamsin' wind which blows all the way from the Arabian Desert in summer. Kollek himself was not dissatisfied with the project; his view was that the buildings would mellow and blend with the landscape, that they commanded wonderful views over the city and did not damage the skyline, and that they were purposefully and strongly constructed.[33] One leading Israeli journalist defended French Hill unhesitatingly; he found it 'a simple, pleasing composition', with buildings well-grouped and terraced.[34] It might not be 'great architecture', but he preferred it to the Intercontinental Hotel, and to the Augusta Victoria Hospital 'and other ungainly structures dating from before World War I'.

French Hill would have looked better had its buildings been restricted to five storeys only. But Kollek's judgement would in time be largely vindicated; the buildings seemed far less obtrusive in 1980 than nearly a decade earlier. Their stone had mellowed and the trees which had been planted round them had grown. The people who lived in them were happy there, and other Jerusalemites grew used to them. The controversy was probably salutary, for Kollek needed all the support which he could get to combat far more damaging projects. He could not stop the Plaza Hotel being built sixteen storeys high – he called it the ugliest building in Jerusalem[35] – and even in 1980 he was being confronted with unseemly proposals. They included a group of buildings rising to a peak in a thirty-five storey tower, near the Government buildings in West Jerusalem, and a 'luxury suburb' near Government House complete with hotels and towers. Kollek called the first of these 'megalomania',[36] and demanded extensive modification of the second.[37] The track-record, fortunately, shows that he should get his way.

Whatever the views about his successes or failures, nobody would ever deny that Kollek did his level best with an immensely difficult task on his hands, and worked incredibly hard – his working day often ran from 6.30 a.m. to 10 or 11 at night. Sometimes he was a little resentful over the lack of credit given to his staff and himself. He once remarked that 'perhaps the municipality itself is at fault for not having told its story properly'.[38] At least, whatever anyone may say about buildings, nobody can deny that he made Jerusalem the greenest city in Israel, with 424 parks and gardens, with 4,700 park benches, and 940 school and small children's playgrounds.[39] He was a magnificent fund-raiser for Jerusalem; one of the offspring of his enthusiasm was the 'Jerusalem Foundation', established in 1966 in the USA, and its involvement in communal welfare in Jerusalem became phenomenal. The Foundation raised funds for 104 parks, gardens and playgrounds, 35 synagogues and 7 mosques, 22 community centres and 20 dental clinics, 17 libraries and 16 sports grounds. Its activities have covered the whole of Jerusalem, whether Jewish or Arab.

Kollek's love of 'his' city was exemplified in an incident in 1979, when an American lady from a batch of guided tourists picked a flower from one of the strips of garden along the outer wall of the Old City. A car drew up at that moment, and an irate Kollek descended from it and berated her. Did she understand, he asked, that if every tourist picked a flower as she had done, there wouldn't be a flower left in Jerusalem? Allegedly, she asked: 'Who's this crazy fat man?' The party were told it was the Mayor, and one of them took a ten-dollar bill from his wallet and handed it to Kollek, with the thought that if flowers were that valuable in Jerusalem, perhaps this would cover the cost. As usual, Kollek collected a handsome profit for his beloved Jerusalem.

Kollek claimed, more than once, that 'We are building a beautiful city'.[40] There was no question that he believed it and that, where aesthetics were concerned, he expected to get a far better deal for Jerusalem than anyone else could have done. But building had a political side too, and there Kollek could never act unilaterally and had very often to co-ordinate his views with those of Government Ministers. Between 1967 and 1980 there were a great many Arab complaints about housing which had to do with politics. They covered such fields as those of expropriation of Arab householders and landholders, deportations of Arabs, the subject of compensation for Arabs who lost homes or land, and archaeological excavations which were held to endanger Arab property. Arabs held that all of these subjects, in one way and another, were connected with the Israeli attempt to make Jerusalem a Jewish city for ever, and in the course of doing so, to diminish or eliminate the Arab stake and presence.

First, the expropriations. Part of the Arab case was that all expropriations were illegal, and that the Israeli authorities had no right to settle Jews on Arab land. The question of legal rights will be dealt with later (see Chapter 8), but the mingled irritation and sense of helplessness felt by the Arabs can be appreciated. The Israeli case was that the end of the British Mandate, and the subsequent war, had left nobody in legal political ownership of East Jerusalem. Private rights were another matter; there, the Israeli case was that much of the land used for new buildings was not privately owned, that only bare and rocky ground was used, and that fair compensation was offered, wherever required. The Arabs retorted that valuable land was taken and fair compensation was not offered. In fact, the Israeli authorities sought the advice of the Greater London Council on the procedures and ethics of compulsory land purchase, and only dispensed with that advice in September 1971.[41] Teddy Kollek wanted to be quite sure that everything should be done with scrupulous correctness. Whether the GLC advised on the terms of compensation, too, has never been made clear.

All sorts of figures of the expropriation of householders, the demolition of Arab homes, and the expropriation of Arab landholders have been given. A categorical denial that hundreds of Arab homes had been dynamited was given by Kollek's Deputy Mayor, Meron Benvenisti.[42] Eighty Arab families lost their homes in the Moghrabi Quarter close to the Western Wall in 1967. This was regarded by the Israelis as slum clearance.

Otherwise only nine houses, some belonging to proven murderers, were demolished, and eleven more seized because saboteurs and terrorists had been sheltered in them. Kollek quickly interposed his objections to the blowing up of houses as an act of reprisal or warning; he regarded this as senseless destruction. One Arab authority gives the total figure of Arabs who lost their homes in 1967 at 650, who were in 135 houses.[43] But he claimed that the religious foundation of the Waqf lost 595 buildings, including 434 shops. Only, his account does not make clear whether some of these were lost in the 1967 war.

According to Benvenisti, the two major expropriations of Arab land which took place in the early years after the 1967 war were of 840 acres early in 1969 and 4,200 acres in 1970.[44] The latter expropriation drew a dignified protest from the Arabic paper *Al Kuds*: 'Respect for private property is a humane law, which should be implemented everywhere … even if the land is occupied territory. What kind of a peace will there be if land is expropriated in the Holy City? It is possible to understand the expropriation of a small plot for some public purpose, but the expropriation of thousands of acres, for the purpose of building houses for people who do not own the land, is incomprehensible.'[45]

Another authority[46] listed three major expropriations; of 840 acres, 220 acres and 3,070 acres in 1968–70. A third estimate was 3,750 acres up to April 1972.[47] On the whole, Benvenisti's figures, which happen to be the highest, are likely to be the most accurate; he was, after all, working in the Municipality's office.

Arab landholders, to a man, would claim that the Israeli authorities had no right to take their land, whatever legislation covered this or whatever compensation was offered under the terms of compulsory purchase. Generally, Arabs refused to accept compensation, on the grounds that they would be conniving in an illegal act, and in the hope that their land would one day – perhaps after yet another war – be restored to them. According to one critic of the Israelis, 'little of the land' which had been taken could be worth less than £12,000 an acre (he based this on his own assertion that land in the middle of the city was worth ten times as much).[48] Here, another paradox; for Israel's critics were opposed to any building on much, if not most of the land which was expropriated. Most of it was fit only to graze goats, and if not built on, worthless. An informed Israeli view was that rocky ground on the outskirts of the city might be worth up to £900 an acre only, since there would be no infrastructural development there prior to purchase.[49] But the question of the scale of compensation remained academic, as long as Arab landowners did not lodge claims for compensation.

The Israeli authorities had another vexed question in the field of compensation. This was that, after the reunification of Jerusalem, many East Jerusalemites who had owned property in West Jerusalem up to the 1948 war were listed under Israeli law as 'absentees'. This had to end, as they were now citizens of the united Jerusalem and subject to normal Israeli law. An 'Absentee Property Compensation Bill' was accordingly passed by the Knesset in July 1971.[50] Compensation would be paid at the full value of the property in 1947, plus 25 per cent, but it would be paid, not in cash but in Israel Government bonds, redeemable over twenty years in equal annual instalments. One Arab businessman claimed that he would get about £6,000 in twenty-year bonds for property which by 1980 would fetch perhaps £450,000.[51] The Israeli Ministry of Justice argued that former owners had had no hand in developing property left in West Jerusalem during the previous twenty-five years, and that compensation would cost Israel $100 million.[52]

In November 1971 the Ministry of Justice submitted an amendment to the compensation bill, making 1956 the key date for valuation of property.[53] In June 1972 there were reports that the Israeli offer would be increased by 100 per cent.[54] An amendment passed in 1973 laid down that, from 1975, claimants of compensation would receive the first 10,000 Israeli pounds in cash, not in bonds.[55] This would cost, initially, about 800 million Israeli pounds. These amendments showed, at least, some Israeli goodwill, but the Arab view remained adamant, that compensation was inadequate and inequitable and that all householders and landholders would do well to reserve their claims to the return of their land and their property.

There were three ulterior reasons for Israeli readiness to pay only limited compensation to the pre-1948 Arab property-holders. The first was the purely mundane one that Israeli governments were perennially short of money. The second was that really generous compensation could establish a precedent for the 600,000 or so Palestinians who left their homes in what became Israel in 1948, as refugees; Israel could, in fact, be inundated with gigantic claims for compensation. Finally, there was a strongly-held view that the question of compensation for refugees should be treated as a whole and should take in the 700,000 or so Jews who left their homes in Arab countries and sought refuge in Israel. Almost all of them arrived in Israel penniless. Yet there had been highly prosperous Jewish communities in many parts of the Arab world, especially in Cairo, Alexandria and Baghdad. In terms of wealth, the Jews of Arab lands probably lost more than their Palestinian counterparts who fled or were driven from Israel. The Palestinian refugees received $985 million of aid from the outside world up to 1974.[56] By 1980 the figure was around $1,200 million. The Jews from Arab countries received nothing.*

The expropriation and compensation of Arab land in Jerusalem were bound to remain subjects of bitter controversy. One argument that Arabs would not accept was that Jews, as well as Arabs, have been expropriated: they lost roughly 350 acres through compulsory purchase in the early years after the 1967 war. To Arab landowners, this was beside the point, for their land was being used by other Jews and they themselves needed to have no inhibitions about accepting compensation and could well be able to seek legal help to claim more. The issue of expropriation festered on. By contrast, Arab complaints about Israeli archaeological excavations in Jerusalem were of relatively little importance. Yet they led to one political setback for Israel; in November 1974 the General Conference of UNESCO in Paris censured Israel for carrying out excavations which could endanger historic monuments. This led to Israel being excluded from the European group of UNESCO. It had already been refused entry into the Asian group.

UNESCO had never complained when Dame Kathleen Kenyon started excavating round the Temple Mount in 1961, and when

---

* The value of land and property left behind by the emigrated Jews of Egypt has been estimated at over £500 million (*Ha'aretz*, 13 August, 1971). In 1980 only 140 out of 40,000 Egyptian Jews who had once lived there remained in Alexandria (*Times*, 31 March, 1980). Their property was valued at £4 million, clear evidence of the wealth of that once prosperous and cultured community. The figure given by *Ha'aretz* would, moreover, have more than doubled between 1971 and 1980.

Property held by the Government Custodian in Iraq was worth an estimated £250 million (*Jewish Chronicle*, 23 December, 1977), and in Libya £260 million (*Jewish Chronicle*, 14 September, 1979). There were rich Jewish communities in many other places, like Tunis, Casablanca, Tangier, Aden, Algiers, Aleppo and Damascus – where a single Jewish family left property behind worth an estimated £2 million (*Jewish Tribune*, 16 March 1973). It is, of course, impossible to calculate, with any degree of accuracy, the total losses sustained by Jewish refugees from the Arab world or, more recently, from Iran. Even without Iran, they may total between £3,000 million and £4,000 million.

Professor William Stinespring worked in the same area in 1966[57] This was presumably because no objections came from Israel, even though some of the work was done close to the Western Wall. Dame Kathleen Kenyon, interestingly, was one of the first to accuse the Israelis of dangerous and even 'disastrous' effects of tunnelling close to the Temple Mount, in a letter to *The Times*.[58] She maintained that cracks were appearing in a number of buildings, that some of them were among the finest Muslim structures in the Middle East, and that tunnelling was an outdated method of excavation and, in this case, 'criminal'.

From this initiative it was but one step to raise the matter in UNESCO, and, with the usual 'block' vote of the anti-Israel lobby, to secure condemnation of Israel. Yet UNESCO's own advisers, Professor Raymond Lemaire and Professor G. de Angelis d'Ossat, had stated that the work being carried out under Israel's Professor Benjamin Mazar was thoroughly professional and caused no danger to any historic building.[59] Israel's archaeologists claimed that cracks reported by Arab houseowners had been there before and that the only building which might have been endangered was carefully restored and its foundations strengthened. An independent observer reported that 'I have reasons to believe that Jerusalem's Moslems are fully aware that the digging does not violate the sanctity of the Temple Mount, involves no bores into it, presents adequate guarantees against danger to the streets and populations above'.[60]

In the *Guardian* Eric Silver had pointed out, long before, that the single building which had been threatened was a 'dilapidated three-storey house abutting the Western Wall'.[61] It had been rescued by the Israeli authorities, at a cost of £20,000, after it had become 'demonstrably dangerous'. It was an early Mameluke structure, but had fallen upon evil days: 'As the rich Arabs for whom the house was intended moved to more salubrious quarter, tenants have become poorer, rents lower, and less has been spent upon maintenance'. The Jerusalem Committee rejected UNESCO's condemnation of Israel and urged that digs which were bringing Muslim and Christian, as well as Jewish buildings to light, should go on.[62] As it happened, excavations round the Temple Mount came to an end in December 1976, and Israel's archaeologists turned their attentions to the City of David, farther to the south. *The Times* was one of a number of papers noting that 'Arab fears that the excavations were undermining the foundations of Muslim shrines have proved unfounded'.[63]

Teddy Kollek's comment was equally succinct: 'The excavations are the best thing that has happened in Jerusalem in a long time. They have, of course, been going on since Wilson and Warren and Robinson, who came from Britain in 1860 to start excavations and brought Scottish and Welsh miners to drive shafts along the Wailing Wall and various other places ... Nobody said a word until we did it.'[64]

There were plenty of other irresponsible accusations against Israeli policies in East Jerusalem. One was that 'The real life of venerated Jerusalem, unique in the world, is to be destroyed', and be replaced by 'a Jerusalem of night-clubs'.[65] The night-club theme was given considerable exposure in the Jordanian press, along with the accusation that the Israelis had instituted a 'red-light quarter' in East Jerusalem. The Israelis took this so seriously that an official inquiry was conducted. This showed that there had been seventeen night-clubs in East Jerusalem up to 1967, and not a single new one had opened since. As for brothels, a number were 'found in brisk business when the Israel Defence forces entered the Old City: they were closed down forthwith'. The addresses of the now defunct Jordanian/Palestinian brothels were listed, with the endearing instruction to Israeli information offices 'not to be drawn into any argument, or offer any gratuitous information, on this unsavoury subject'.[66] On a more fantastic note, the wife of a British knight declared that Israeli planes were 'buzzing' the sacred Muslim precincts of the Dome of the Rock and the El Aqsa Mosque to produce vibrations which would knock them down. And at an Islamic Conference in London at the end of 1979 an executive member of the PLO, Khalid al-Hassan, said that Jews were trying to 'practise sex' in the El Aqsa Mosque.

Of more importance was the Jordanian accusation that the Mamillah cemetery, unpropitiously sited not far from where East and West Jerusalem met from 1948 to 1967 – mainly in park and waste land – had been subjected to 'one of the most massive and sinful programmes of desecration that the world has ever known'. The Jordanian statement claimed that this cemetery was at least a thousand years old, and had been turned into a public park 'for man or beast'.[67]

The true history of the Mamillah cemetery is revealing. In 1932 leading members of the Muslim community denounced the Supreme Muslim Council for allowing a certain Ibrahim al-Husseini – probably a member of the Grand Mufti's family – to open a quarry on top of the cemetery and demolish hundreds of graves.[68] The Council had built stables for horses and donkeys in the cemetery and authorized the building of the Palace Hotel there. It was also planned to build a headquarters for the Arab League there; they were switched to Cairo because of the termination of the British Mandate. By 1945 only about half of the cemetery's 840 graves were intact.

Cemeteries are not hallowed under Muslim law for more than thirty-three years after the last burial there. This, according to one source, had last taken place officially eleven centuries ago.[69] As it happened, the Grand Mufti himself had banned 'public' burials – meaning the occasional, haphazard private burial – in 1927. The 1948 war put an end, more effectively, to further burials there, since they were hardly practicable when the area was totally cut off from Arab East Jerusalem.

One Arab authority has accused the Israelis of having levelled the Mamillah cemetery to make way for a recreation ground and for public lavatories, where the pious were buried.[70] The Israelis, in fact, preserved the surviving part of the cemetery, which in 1980 could still be found intact at the corner of Agron Street and Princess Mar Street.[71] All surviving graves had been carefully repaired, and a fiat of permission to turn a further part of the cemetery into a section of well-tended and flowered park-land was issued in 1952 by the Muslim authorities of Jaffa and Nazareth.[72] The Israelis did a tidying-up job, removing debris and dung. By 1975 the Municipality was committed to further development nearby, with a park, piazza and shopping district replacing the unkempt waste ground straggling over the approaches to the outer wall of the Old City.

There were many other wild and unfounded Arab misstatements, but Arab susceptibilities deserve some sympathy. Helplessly, they had to watch Jerusalem expand under Israeli control, and their suspicions, even when groundless, were understandable. To many Arabs there seemed to be nothing patently fantastic about stories that Israeli planes were buzzing their holy places, that Israeli tunnellers were undermining them, and that Jewish 'desecrators' were taking part in sex orgies within their walls. They did not see these things happening with their own eyes, but what their own eyes told them seemed sinister enough. To the north, Arab Jerusalem had been outflanked by the new buildings which curved round to Mount Scopus. To the east, only the Jericho road connected Arab Jerusalem with the Arab West Bank. Even this corridor was almost blocked; for the Israelis were building suburbs in a wide defensive ring which looked anything like defensive to the nearly encircled Arabs of East Jerusalem.

An unwittingly chilling description of these new suburbs came from the Director of the Graduate School of Geography at Clark University in Massachusetts.[73] These are extracts:

> In the north the new housing estates of Ramot and Neve Yaacov dominate Ramallah and its Muslim twin town Bira, by reaching to within three to five kilometers of these Arab centers and thereby dominating all of the Beth El Mountains region ... The Ramot development commands a number of Arab villages northwest of Jerusalem, and ... overlooks a very ancient ridge road that presents an alternative route through the West Bank to the coastal plain ... The development also commands a Jerusalem by-pass route that leads south-westward to the Tel-Aviv–Jerusalem highway. To the south new Israeli suburbs dominate Bethlehem and the Hebron Mountains region, and thus the rest of Judaea. The south-eastern development of Armon HaNatziv overlooks the major Arab villages east of Jerusalem (Abu Dis, Sur Bahir), and dominates the eastern suburbs of Bethlehem. The south-western development of Gilo is on the municipal boundary of Bethlehem and adjoins Beit Jala, the latter a commanding height from which Jordanian artillery once were trained on Jerusalem ... These northern and southern suburban outgrowths are major projections which impose the Israeli presence on the key Arab urban centers of Judaea and Samaria.

The author did not write all this in a spirit critical of Israel; on the contrary, he believed that these strategically-sited suburbs made good sense from Israel's point of view. Israeli preoccupation with security is a fact. His diction could hardly have reassured Arabs – 'overlooks', 'dominates', 'commands' are words suggestive of military thinking and planning. Nor did Israeli writers give a different impression. In the *Jerusalem Post*, Abraham Rabinovitch described the new suburbs as 'a political sword and a military shield'.[74] They already contained 50,000 people, and this number would double by 1985. Another reporter of the same paper wrote, even more disturbingly for the Arabs, that Israel was building an outer ring of settlements too, and that the Housing Minister David Levy 'last week laid a cornerstone for a town which will help complete the Jewish encirclement of Arab East Jerusalem'.[75] This was at Maale Adunim, sitting on the one 'escape route', the road to Jericho.

This outer ring would include Efrat and Tekoa to the south, Baal Hatzor to the north-east, and Givon and Jebel Mukatem to the north-west. That, at least, seemed to be the plan in 1976–7. But there were solid objections against the creation of an outer ring. With the future of the West Bank in doubt, its settlements could become hostages to fortune. It was in any case preferable to firm-up the existing suburbs within the boundaries of Jerusalem. For his part, Teddy Kollek made it plain that he was utterly opposed to a dissipation of effort; large sections of inner Jerusalem needed developing and it seemed senseless to him to leave these sections derelict while building dormitory towns far beyond the city limits.

Maale Adunim was, perhaps, a different matter. A small settlement was already there in 1979; the cornerstone laid by the Housing Minister was of a second and larger one. The site was strategically important; it commands the road from Jericho to Jerusalem and a stretch of road from Jericho to Amman, with a magnificent view over the Dead Sea to the Mountains of Moab. There was not a single Arab building in the vicinity and none of the land used had any agricultural value; there was nothing there beyond some limited grazing in spring and early summer for the Bedouin herds of goats. Maale Adunim would be an ideal artillery post for repelling an army advancing on Jerusalem from the east, and the best imaginable site for an early-warning system. Uzi Narkiss, the general who captured the Old City in 1967, called the place 'the military key to Jerusalem'.

To build, where to build, and how to build, remained persisting and immensely difficult problems for the Mayor of Jerusalem. In 1980 there was not, of course, any end to them in sight: Jerusalem is an organically developing entity. Nor has its growth lessened differences between Jews and Arabs, probably the reverse. The most basic Arab complaint was that Jews were settling at all in East Jerusalem; but of almost equal importance was their claim that far too little was being done for them. Kollek denied this; he pointed to the installation of electricity and running water, to the overhauling of the entire sewage system of East Jerusalem, to the building of good roads – an Arab quarter like Silwan, for instance, had only dusty tracks through it up to 1967. At times, Kollek complained of Arab ingratitude, in one statement maintaining that 4,000 Arab families had been helped through mortgage loans to build new homes or improve existing ones, and that the necessary finance had come from the Israeli taxpayer.[76]

Arab building in East Jerusalem certainly did not keep pace with Jewish building in the whole city. Building starts averaged about 3,500 a year in the city as a whole, and only about one-eighth of these were Arab homes. The Arabs necessarily made a slow start after 1967, for there was political uncertainty for them, their funds were frozen through the closure of Arab banks or because they themselves were in Amman, and Arab labour was drifting into West Jerusalem. In 1975 about one-third of the Arabs of East Jerusalem suffered from inadequate housing conditions; by 1980 this had dropped only to about a quarter of them. Increasing prosperity brought more building to the private sector, but the Arabs claimed that they did not have a fair share of publicly-built housing. There was a pilot scheme in Wadi Joz in 1971, another in Al Azariyah two years later.

Deputy Mayor Benvenisti noted the sad paradox of Arab building-workers erecting homes for Jewish immigrants on Arab land, but not building homes for their own next generation.[77] He estimated that only 100 apartments had been built out of public funds for Arab families by 1971, but that building loans enabled four times as many to be constructed privately. He sensed an element of demographic competition.[78] By 1980 the situation had improved marginally; in two years, over 200 Arab families received building loans totalling over nine million Israeli pounds, and a 'Build your own home' scheme had been launched in East Jerusalem with a total of 1,500 units envisaged. This would meet the needs of about 40 per cent of the Arabs of Jerusalem in urgent need of better housing.

By 1980, a balance could be struck. In thirteen years of Israeli rule, 1,400 building permits had been granted to Arabs in East Jerusalem. Of these, 400 new homes were given government financial backing. In addition, 3,000 other Arab applicants were given low-interest loans and mortgages for new homes. New housing, in fact, was built during these thirteen years for about 20,000 to 25,000 Arabs in Jerusalem. In addition, an ever-increasing number of successful Arab traders built homes outside the boundaries of the city. This building achievement, admittedly, cannot be compared with what was done for Jews in Jerusalem, with government financial help covering at least half of the new housing. But it may help to explain the very steady growth of the Arab population in Jerusalem – up from 66,000 in 1967 to close on 120,000 in mid-1980. Here, at least, was a fitting answer to critics who claimed that the Jews were driving the Arabs out of their holy city.[79]

Ahead lay one hideously difficult problem to solve; the cramped, confined Old City had a population of about 24,000 and almost 60 per cent of the space available was occupied by mosques, churches and other religious or public institutions. The Muslim and Christian Quarters were by far the most crowded, but any overt attempt to thin out their populations would be certain to bring an outcry and the accusation that the Jews were trying to gain demographic control of the Old City.

As Mayor, Teddy Kollek had an immensely difficult task to discharge. He and the Municipality had no totality of control over housing, which was bound to be the most controversial issue of all in the field of Jewish–Arab communal relations. He had to wrestle with the Ministries of Housing, Finance, Tourism and Religious Affairs – with the Prime Minister, too, whenever necessary. The number of competing interests in Jerusalem was legion. Sometimes, an unsatisfactory compromise was struck by these competing authorities.

He sought, and accepted outside advice, from the 'Jerusalem Committee', the Greater London Council, and other organizations and individuals. His aim, as he said many times, was to build a beautiful city. And he won all sorts of unchronicled victories; thus he blocked plans to build a Jewish settlement round the mosque on the commanding heights of Nebi Samwil, got his way in granting financial aid to half a dozen pilot schemes for building Arab homes, and steadfastly resisted demands to build 'luxury suburbs' which would have offended sophisticated Jewish as well asArab opinion.[80] Even Israel's most baleful critics have paid tribute to him in a personal sense. This is indeed remarkable, considering the single-mindedness and periodic violence and virulence of the propaganda war which inevitably marked and accompanied the Arab–Israeli dispute. But whatever Kollek could have done – over high-rise building, the expropriation and compensation of Arab lands, building programmes in East and West Jerusalem, the preservation of historic buildings, the maintenance (or otherwise) of a 'demographic balance' – there would, at the end of the day, be one abiding certainty of adverse judgement. This would come from the Arab world.

Israeli occupation of the whole of Jerusalem was unacceptable. It was a disaster in the history of Islam. It had, in addition, properties which were startling in an ocular sense. They related to the erection of buildings in 'Arab East Jerusalem', which had not shown itself capable of independent development during its brief nineteen years of umbilical existence. Buildings have an ocular impact. Some of those erected in Jerusalem were aesthetically unfortunate into the bargain. If they happened to be in East Jerusalem, politics intruded. The apposite question which should, perhaps, be asked is not whether Israel's trusteeship of Jerusalem, from 1967 to 1980, was perfect, passable or a disaster, but whether anybody else could have done better. One of the most important cities in the world's history has to have a future. To build or not to build was hardly a valid question. Jerusalem had to be built; the alternative was stagnation.

REFERENCES

1. Abba Eban, Letter to UN Secretary General, U Thant, published in *Jerusalem Post*, 20 September 1971.
2. Teddy Kollek, speech to the 'Jerusalem Committee', Jerusalem, 1 July 1969.
3. Art Kutcher, *The New Jerusalem*, Thames & Hudson, London, 1973.
4. Teddy Kollek, *For Jerusalem*, Weidenfeld, London, 1978.
5. Meron Benvenisti, *Jerusalem: The Torn City*, Isratypeset, Jerusalem, 1976.
6. Moshe Dayan, *Story of my Life*, Weidenfeld, London, 1976.
7. Meron Benvenisti, op cit.
8. Yosef Tekoah, *Barbed Wire shall not return to Jerusalem*, Israel Information Services, New York, 1968.
9. Dr Douglas Young, in letter to the author.
10. A. M. Goichon, *Jérusalem. Fin de la Ville universelle?*, Maisonneuve & Larose, Paris, 1976.
11. Teddy Kollek, 'Jerusalem', in *Foreign Affairs*, July 1977.
12. Art Kutcher, op cit.
13. Ibid.
14. Ibid.
15. Professor Nathaniel Lichfield, in personal converation with the author.
16. Crown Prince Hassan bin Talal, *A Study on Jerusalem*, Longmans, London, 1979.
17. *Report of the Jerusalem Committee, 1973*, Isratypeset, Jerusalem, 1975.
18. Monica Pidgeon of the Jerusalem Committee, Ribag, 1976.
19. *Report of the Jerusalem Committee, 1978*, Municipality publication, 1979.
20. Eric Silver, London *Observer*, 26 August 1973.
21. Bruno Zevi, *Oriente Moderno*, 8 December 1970.
22. *The Times*, 15 March 1971.
23. *The Times*, 2 October 1971.
24. *New Statesman*, 16 July 1971.
25. Saul Bellow, *To Jerusalem and Back*, Secker & Warburg, London, 1976.
26. Etienne Boegner, privately circulated memorandum, 11 April 1971.

27. Eric Silver, loc. cit.
28. Richard Crossman, *The Times*, 28 August 1973.
29. *Guardian*, 14 October 1972.
30. Art Kutcher, op. cit.
31. *The Times*, 4 June 1974.
32. Dr Aryeh Shimon, *Jerusalem Post*, 22 July 1973.
33. Teddy Kollek, in personal conversation with the author.
34. David Krivine, *Jerusalem Post*, 18 January 1972.
35. Abraham Rabinovitch, *Jerusalem Post*, 14 July 1975.
36. Eric Silver, *Observer*, 19 February 1978.
37. Robert Rosenberg, *Jerusalem Post*, 15 February 1980.
38. Teddy Kollek, *Jerusalem Post*, 7 January 1972.
39. Eva Baznizki, *News from Israel*, 1 June 1979.
40. Eric Marsden, *The Times*, 4 July 1971.
41. Eric Marsden, *The Times*, 8 September 1971.
42. Meron Benvenisti, op. cit.
43. A. L. Tibawi, *The Islamic Pious Foundations in Jerusalem*, Baskerville Press, London, 1978.
44. Meron Benvenisti, op. cit.
45. *Al Kuds*, Jerusalem, 21 August 1970.
46. Saul B. Cohen, *Jerusalem. Bridging the Four Walls*, Herzl Press, New York, 1977.
47. David Hirst, *Guardian*, 26 April 1972.
48. Ibid.
49. Professor David Amiran, of Institute for Jerusalem Studies, in letter to the author.
50. *Jerusalem Post*, 2 July 1971.
51. David Hirst, loc. cit.
52. Walter Schwarz, *Guardian*, 30 June 1971.
53. *Financial Times*, 24 November 1971.
54. Eric Silver, *Guardian*, 15 June 1972.
55. *Jerusalem Post*, 28 June 1973.
56. Martin Gilbert, *The Jews of Arab Lands. Their History in Maps*, Furnival Press, London, 1975.
57. Katherine Kuh, *Saturday Review*, 24 January 1976.
58. *The Times*, 17 August 1952.
59. Katherine Kuh, loc. cit.
60. Herbert Lottman, *Present Tense*, Autumn 1975.
61. Eric Silver, *Guardian*, 17 August 1972.
62. Abraham Rabinovitch, *Jerusalem Post*, 21 December 1975.
63. Eric Marsden, *The Times*, 12 December 1976.
64. Teddy Kollek, *Jerusalem Perspectives*, Furnival Press, London, 1976.
65. A. M. Goichon, op. cit.
66. Rebuttals of Jordanian Misstatements about Israel's Administration of Jerusalem, Israel Foreign Ministry, October 1972.
67. Ibid.
68. Ibid.
69. Walter Schwarz, *Guardian*, 9 May 1972.
70. A. L. Tibawi, op. cit.
71. Adam Kaye, in letter to the *Guardian*, 26 January 1980.
72. *Rebuttals of Jordanian Misstatements*.

73. Saul B. Cohen, *Midstream*, May 1975.
74. Abraham Rabinovitch, *Jerusalem Post*, 9 June 1979.
75. *Jerusalem Post*, 18 August 1979.
76. *Jerusalem Post*, 1 September 1975.
77. Meron Benvenisti, op. cit.
78. Ibid.
79. All figures supplied by Jerusalem Municipality to the author.
80. Teddy Kollek, 'For Jerusalem'.

CHAPTER EIGHT

Political Puzzle

General Chaim Herzog, who became Military Governor of the West Bank immediately after the 1967 war, has told a revealing story about one of his very first interviews with a leading Arab official. This was Anwar Al-Khatib, the Jordanian Governor of the Jerusalem district, who called on him to pay his respects. 'He began to talk to me', Herzog recounted, 'about the entry of our soldiers into Beit Hanina, his village outside Jerusalem. And as he talked about it he broke down and cried like a child.'

Herzog was worried and asked him what the Israeli soldiers had done. Al-Khatib's answer was: 'Nothing'.

'And then', Herzog wrote, 'I understood. I asked him, "You expected them to behave towards you as you would have behaved towards us?". He nodded his head in assent.'[1]

The story illustrates the deep psychological shock caused by shattering military defeat. The initial reaction of relief tinged with gratitude, quickly wore off. Increasingly, the Arabs of East Jerusalem withdrew as far as possible from contact with their conquerors, to nurse their pride and hide their shame. A mood of partially veiled, settled resentment developed. Al-Khatib had suggested to Herzog that an Arab Council should be set up to administer the West Bank. This went beyond the Military Governor's brief, and he had to turn the proposal down.[2] But when East Jerusalem's leading Arabs were asked in turn to serve on municipal committees, they agreed at first and then withdrew en bloc as a result of blood-curdling threats against them uttered

by Fatah Radio. This was a bad mistake; as one commentator
pointed out, Israeli municipal politics were highly divisive and
the Arabs would have gained real influence in municipal affairs,
had they participated in them.[3]

The same authority believed, however, that subsequent Arab
non-co-operation on the municipal level owed something at
least to the mistakes made by the Israelis. He listed the following:

The Law of Israel and Administrative Arrangements
regulating the status and rights of the inhabitants of East
Jerusalem was well conceived, but the Arabs were not consulted.
Of course, they might have refused to discuss the law, but at least
they would have been given the chance. Then Arab lawyers were
instructed that they would be members of Israel's Bar
Association. That was necessary to get the advantages required
to practise, but they considered that they had been forced to join.
Arab tradesmen were invited to register their businesses, but
held back out of a feeling of suspicion: the problem was solved
by all Arab businesses receiving licences and the Ministry of
Justice automatically registering them. This was just acceptable
to the Arabs, since they had not actually had to apply to be
registered.

There was a failure, too, to consult Arabs who had lost
property in West Jerusalem, before legislating on its future. Next
came a census, in which 57,996 Arabs were registered as resident
in Jerusalem. But thousands more were not given registration
slips to fill in. This led to many Arabs not being issued with
identity cards, which were needed for movement in or out of
Jerusalem. A second census uncovered another 9,681 Arab
residents, but Arabs were in the meantime being fired from their
jobs and even arrested. Others who had been out of Jerusalem
during the Six Day War had considerable difficulty in getting
permission to return home; others again found themselves
waiting endlessly for permits to study or visit abroad.[4]
Bureaucracy was already biting deep into Israeli administration
by 1967.

The Arabs had plenty of other grievances. Thus they had
suddenly to compete with a totally new tax structure. Jordan
collected only 8 per cent of its revenue from direct taxation, and
only 500 people in East Jerusalem were taxpayers, exceptionally
reluctant ones at that. Israel had high taxation, but offered very
comprehensive services in return; the Arabs were used to
neither. Nor were they pleased at having to pay what they must
have regarded as iniquitous contributions to national insurance.

Arab taxi-drivers had their own grievance; for a time they were not allowed to drive in West Jerusalem, whereas West Jerusalem drivers had the freedom of the city. More anger resulted when the Israeli Egged bus-service extended its activities into East Jerusalem, and real hardship was caused by the closure of all Arab banks; the Israeli offer to allow them to reopen and maintain their links with Amman, if they would merely respect Israeli laws and regulations, was turned down.

There were difficulties over electricity supply, for the Arab Electricity Corporation sought the right to remain independent of the Jewish Municipality and continue to serve its customers. This was perfectly reasonable, but trouble arose out of housing being built in East Jerusalem for Jewish families – some of the householders objected to having to accept 'Arab electricity'. The first reaction of the Israeli authorities was to give way to this somewhat inverted 'patriotism', then it was decided, wisely, that the Arab corporation should go on looking after East Jerusalem and should be allowed to 'buy electricity' from its West Jerusalem counterpart if it found difficulty in serving all of its customers. Israelis who settled in East Jerusalem were, on the whole, prepared to accept this decision without complaint.[5]

Education created special problems. The Israeli authorities called in all text-books for examination, and rejected about eighty out of something more than one hundred. They abolished the Jordanian school and examination curriculum, and introduced teaching programmes which paid far too little heed to the deep and sincere Arab interest in Arab history and the Arabic language. This was all the work of the Ministry of Education, operating in the honest but superfluous belief that Israeli education set higher standards, and in the knowledge that some Arab text-books had contained incitement to hatred of the State of Israel. The Arab reaction was instantaneous; teachers went on strike and refused to return unless both curriculum and text-books were reinstated. There were bitter complaints that education was being 'Judaized' and Palestinian spokesmen have maintained ever since that the schools in East Jerusalem were reopened 'by force' and that the 'great majority' of Arab teachers refused to co-operate and lost their jobs.[6]

Initially, a great many Arab families removed their children from the state schools; thus only 10 per cent of the pupils remained in the El Rashadiya secondary school.[7] But opposition to the Ministry of Education came from two other quarters – the Military Government and the Municipality. Military

Government on the West Bank – for the new regulations applied there as well as in East Jerusalem – conducted its own survey of text-books and appealed to the Ministry to set up a commission of inquiry. The result was that only two text-books were discarded, and twenty others were censored, on the whole quite mildly. Other sensible steps were taken: extra classes were organized, for eight to nine hours' teaching weekly of Arab subjects; new teachers were recruited; and kindergartens were introduced into East Jerusalem for the first time, with thirty-five classes dealing with five-year-olds.[8]

The result was that by the end of 1967 at least half of the former teachers were back at work, along with about 80 per cent of their pupils. Vocational schools were opened in East Jerusalem, and night-classes organized. By the end of the year, Arabic was being taught in over forty classes. The Jordanian Government continued, for political reasons, to pay teachers' salaries (it did the same for all Palestinians who had been in government service of any kind), and the Municipality insisted on the Jordanian as well as the Israeli curriculum being available. But the Ministry of Education continued to fight a rearguard action; it was only by 1976 that two separate study programmes were available for the upper six grades in the Arab schools – the Jordanian, with the addition of studies in the Hebrew language and in Israeli 'civics', and the 'mixed' curriculum available to the Arabs of pre-1967 Israel.[9] Private and ecclesiastical schools carried on normally throughout the entire controversy. There was no interference from the Ministry of Education, and a marked drift to the private sector took place, which was accentuated as living standards began to rise.

Education, then, was only one subject on the long list of those causing friction between the Israeli authorities and the Arabs of Jerusalem, but it was one which rankled particularly. The Palestinians are an intelligent people, valuing learning for its own sake but perhaps even more as one obvious means available to them to build themselves into a potentially more powerful and influential community. Their country was occupied and about half of their total population was dispersed and exiled, even though most of these were only just across the border with Lebanon, or living in Jordan which had originally been a part of the British Mandatory area. Education was a way of developing their sense of community and their national identity; it gave them a degree of independence from Israeli control and a valuable bond with the rest of the Arab world.

Teddy Kollek was entirely in favour of Arab schools having their own curriculum. He saw neither purpose nor prospect of turning the people of East Jerusalem into some sort of 'sub-Israelis'. This would have run counter to his belief in the need to maintain the 'mosaic' of different communities in the city, and to his philosophy on Jewish–Arab relations. 'Our most important task', he wrote, 'was still to develop a viable relationship with our Arab neighbours in Jerusalem. Everyone knew that building such relationships would take a long time.'[10] What he was discovering was that the Arabs would co-operate up to a point, but would not accept responsibility. Co-operation seemed to them justified, since it was directed towards helping to look after the Arab community and maintain its presence in Jerusalem. Acceptance of joint responsibility would have been regarded by the rest of the Arab world as equivalent to the treason of a Marshal Pétain or a Vidkund Quisling.

Kollek referred to Arab feelings in an account in April 1968 of his stewardship in the whole of Jerusalem.[11] He wrote:

> Of course, the 70,000 Arabs of East Jerusalem do not sing songs of praise. We do not claim that they do, nor do we expect them to. What we do claim is that we managed rapidly to restore their normal life and that, taking the picture as a whole, they are certainly not worse off than before in terms of municipal services. We are making efforts to make them feel at home with us together in this city, and I think the beginnings of success are evident. Inevitably, within the context of continued hostility of the Arab states towards Israel, this will be a slow and gradual process. [But] it is quite wrong to state that the atmosphere in East Jerusalem is taut; the opposite is true. Thousands and thousands of Jews and Arabs mingle freely in the streets and bazaars, every day, by day and by night. During all these months, almost a year now, there has not been a single communal clash.

Kollek turned to practical achievements. Tourism was now running at a rate 30 per cent higher than a year earlier, and 'the hotels are full to the last bed in *all* parts of the city'. Trading and human links between East Jerusalem, the West Bank and Jordan had been maintained by the 'open bridges' policy. Although the Arab banks had not reopened for business, the Municipality had eased the lack of credit by making long-term, low-interest loans to merchants and hotel-owners: Business had picked up as a result. More than 3,000 Jerusalem Arabs had found work in West

Jerusalem, which had reduced unemployment drastically. Welfare, available to just seventy-five Arabs under Jordanian rule, was now being given to over 3,000. All but a singleton of the almost 500 officials of the Jordanian municipality were incorporated into the unified city government. Regular consultations took place between the municipal authorities, and the 'mukhtars' or village elders, and other representatives of the Arabs. Kollek was careful not to make over-optimistic forecasts, but he was quietly confident.

One phrase which he used, however, had a special relevance: 'within the context of continued hostility of the Arab states towards Israel'. This continued hostility was bound to have an impact on the thought and actions of the Arabs of East Jerusalem. When the 1967 war was over, a great majority of Israelis thought that peace with neighbouring Arab states would be possible. They were strangely and naively unaware of the devastating shock of defeat to Arab dignity and pride. Forgotten, too, were some of the statements of President Nasser of Egypt, the acknowledged leader of the Arab world. Thus: 'It is utterly inconceivable that Egypt should ever consider peace with Israel', 'The Arab peoples will cleanse Palestine. Hold your tears in readiness, Israel, for the day of your annihilation', and 'We cannot but be in a state of war with Israel. This impels us to mobilize all Arab resources for its final liquidation.'[12]

Nasser's attitude after the 1967 war was predictable. If peace with Israel had previously been unacceptable, it was doubly so now. Nasser set out to prepare his people for yet another war with Israel, and it would be one of his most rational and moderate followers, Sadat, who would eventually launch it. Nasser was the architect of the 1967 Khartum Conference of the Arab states, which laid down three cardinal principles: no recognition of Israel, no negotiations with Israel, and no peace and normal relations with Israel. The 'Three Noes' of Khartum dictated the future attitude of every other Arab state towards Israel; obviously, it affected the Palestinian Arabs too, including the inhabitants of East Jerusalem. For Israel remained the openly-proclaimed enemy of the Arab world.

Two years after Khartum came the Palestine National Covenant of 1969, proclaimed by the Palestine Liberation Organization led by Yassir Arafat. The Covenant denied Israel's right of existence, in explicit terms repeated times over. It denied even the right to live in Palestine of the vast majority of the people of Israel.[13] It proclaimed the determination of the

Palestinians to regain total control of all of Palestine only through armed struggle, which was 'overall strategy, not merely a tactical phase'.[14] The Covenant laid down, expressly, that it would remain in force, unless amended in special session, convened for that purpose.[15] Up to 1980 no such special session had been convened; nor was there any discussion about the possibility of doing so. From 1969 onwards the Arabs of East Jerusalem had to regard themselves as the representatives of the only proclaimed Palestinian leadership group, the PLO.

Nothing that happened up to 1980 – with the single exception of the Camp David bilateral agreement between Egypt and Israel – gave the Arabs of East Jerusalem any new option. After another decade of unrelenting Arab hostility, another war in 1973, and a prolonged PLO terrorist campaign, Arab statements sounded as relentless as ever. Thus Crown Prince Fahd of Saudi Arabia said that his country was ready to join in a 'holy war' against Israel and was ready for 'martyrdom', if that were required to win it.[16] The PLO representative in London repeated that the Palestinian aim was to establish a secular Palestinian state in the whole of Palestine. He added that the 1974 decision to accept a state on the 'liberated' West Bank and Gaza Strip was 'transitional' only.[17] Crown Prince Hassan bin Talal of Jordan maintained that Israel had no legal title to West Jerusalem, let alone East.[18] As for the PLO leader Yassir Arafat, acclaimed in much of the western world as a 'moderate'; he made his position clear in the following terms:

> We do not mind dying. I have married a woman – her name is Palestine. Peace for us means the destruction of Israel. We are preparing for an all-out war, a war which will last for generations ... We shall not rest until the day when we return to our home, and until we destroy Israel ... The destruction of Israel is the goal in our struggle, and ... revolutionary violence is the only means for the liberation of the land of our fathers. This action will be one of long duration.

This statement, one might reasonably have assumed, could have dated from 1965 or a little later. In fact it was made on 11 February 1980.[19] Subsequently, Arafat claimed he had been misquoted, but he had said much the same thing before.

In whatever they did the Arabs of East Jerusalem had to take account of the Arab states and of the PLO. Any instinct which they might still have had towards quiet co-operation with the Israeli authorities was further discouraged by the United Nations.

On 4 July 1967, the General Assembly voted for three different resolutions on the Middle East situation. A Yugoslav resolution demanding the unconditional withdrawal of Israeli forces from occupied territories received 53 votes against 46, with 20 abstentions. A Latin American resolution, linking Israeli withdrawal with the termination of the state of belligerency, received 57 votes against 43, with the same number of 20 abstaining. But the third resolution, declaring all Israeli measures to change the status of Jerusalem invalid, was carried by 99 votes to none, with 20 abstentions. Ten days later, the UN General Assembly repeated its censure, deplored Israel's failure to 'implement' the earlier resolution, and called on its Government to refrain from all further action which could alter the status of Jerusalem.[20]

A whole string of UN resolutions ensued during the years that followed. The Security Council deplored Israel's failure to take heed of the General Assembly's demands on 21 May 1968, and ordered Israel to rescind all measures taken so far in Jerusalem.[21] On 3 July 1969 the Security Council declared all steps taken by Israel to be invalid and requested Israel to give information about its intention of implementing the provisions of this resolution.[22] As on each occasion before, Israel rejected the UN resolution. One leading British newspaper commented:

> It is not surprising that Israel rejected the resolution. Her objection that the United Nations attitude is one-sided is valid … Israel has no need and no wish to alter the situation which gave her the canal as her frontier with Egypt. The Egyptians, on the other hand, have every reason to want to change it. The opposite is true with regard to Jerusalem. Israel has every interest in integrating the Old City with the New. This is why the Jordanian sector was formally annexed immediately after the war, and why each succeeding month sees some new Israeli move to cement the forced union between the two halves of the city. If this is a provocation, and illegal, then so are the daily bombardments across the canal, and the United Nations should either condemn them both equally, or neither.[23]

But the paper thought that it would help if Israel showed 'a decent respect to the opinions of mankind', instead of causing offence by 'stridently claiming exclusive possession' of Jerusalem. And although it might be hopeless to expect Israel to allow the city to be partitioned again, 'by pushing forward with the annexation Israel is greatly reducing the chances of an early settlement'.

More than ten years later, and after other resolutions on the affairs of Jerusalem, the United Nations were still banging away at the subject. Thus on 1 March 1980, the Security Council voted unanimously in condemnation of Israel's alteration of Jerusalem's status. Surprisingly, the United States voted with the rest, but three days later President Carter admitted that this was a 'serious error' – the United States had abstained in a vote on a similar resolution a year earlier, and should have done so again.[24] All of this was small consolation for the Israelis; the United States had been alone in abstaining on the previous occasion. European countries which conventionally abstained when Israel was under attack at the UN had now joined the ranks of Israel's opponents. They had given other evidence of their hostility. The British Foreign Secretary, Lord Carrington, informed the Zionist Federation in London that East Jerusalem was a part of the Israeli 'territorial occupation' which ought to be ended.[25] At roughly the same time the Canadian Government, which had announced its intention of transferring its Embassy from Tel Aviv to Jerusalem – an indirect way of recognizing Israel's rights there – went back on its decision. There was trouble between Israel and the European Economic Community, which refused to establish its newly-appointed representative in Jerusalem (the result was that he remained grounded in Brussels).[26] Meanwhile the French Government was indicating, in repeated statements, that it was thoroughly sceptical about Israel's policies, especially with regard to Jerusalem.

The prompting of the PLO and outside Arab states, the critical attitude towards Israel in the United Nations, and the inevitable friction and disputes which arose in a Jerusalem totally controlled by Israel could have combined to create an explosive situation in the city. On the whole, however, it remained remarkably quiet over the years, in spite of periodic trouble. There were a number of strikes in August and September, 1967. They collapsed in face of firm Israeli action; Arab shopkeepers, it seemed, were not inclined to join in and opened their doors to customers as soon as there was a modest show of force by the Israelis in the shape of continuously patrolling soldiers. There were more strikes, usually of a few hours' duration only, and demonstrations, in April 1968, and then again in October and November. The demonstration of 1 October 1970, three days after the death of President Nasser of Egypt, was massive, orderly and impressive. In East Jerusalem, as in the rest of the Arab world, Nasser remained a hero.

Strike action was very rare after 1970, and never protracted. The Israeli technique was to allow the strike to run for a few hours and give it time to peter out; if it did not do so, then troops were sent to patrol the shopping areas. Shopkeepers thereupon reopened for trade; their instinct told them that there was nothing more to achieve – their protest had been made and registered and to prolong it would only damage their own business and cause inconvenience to their fellow Arabs. But there were more serious, if sporadic, attempts at sabotage and terrorist action. Thus there was a bomb explosion in the Fast Hotel in September 1967, and a bomb that would have caused considerable loss of life was placed in the Zion cinema in the following month, but was fortunately spotted in time. In June 1968, there was an explosion near the Ambassador Hotel; the only victim was one of two thirteen-year-old Arab boys who were carrying the bomb.

In November came the first serious bomb explosion. This took place in the Mahaneh Yehudah fruit and vegetable market, with twelve people killed and fifty-four wounded. In 1969 there were thirty terrorist incidents in Jerusalem, and they continued thereafter, reaching a peak in 1974 and 1975, with sixty-five casualties in the former and seventy-three in the latter year.[27] Bombs used were almost always small and deposited almost casually outside shops or other buildings. Very few deaths were caused, and the life of the city remained remarkably unaffected. Yet there were over 400 arrests between 1967 and 1975, and the former Mayor of East Jerusalem, Rouhi al-Khatib, was deported for his part in stimulating active resistance.[28] As in the West Bank, schoolchildren were used in the forefront of demonstrative resistance, and the Union of Palestinian Pupils on the West Bank was closed down by the Israeli authorities. In the West Bank, schoolchildren stoned Israeli military vehicles and built barricades across streets, but in Jerusalem itself they were less inclined to perpetrate acts of violence. The use of children in the 'front line' was reminiscent of Northern Ireland, and the Israeli police and soldiers were bitterly criticized for the occasional use of truncheons and tear-gas. In a propaganda sense, no 'battle' against children can be won.

Palestinian terrorist groups undoubtedly were responsible for whatever violence occurred. Fatah supporters were active in Jerusalem and, particularly after 1969, those of the more

extreme Popular Front for the Liberation of Palestine, led by Dr
George Habbash. Violence waxed and waned, to some extent
according to how the PLO was faring; there was a low point after
the PLO failure and ejection from Jordan in 1970, but there was
increased activity after the PLO was accepted at the 1974 Rabat
Arab 'Summit' Conference as the legitimate representatives of
the whole Palestinian people, and again after its leader, Arafat,
was received with acclamation in the UN General Assembly.

The Israeli authorities kept their nerve. They demolished a
very few houses, deported a very few people, but did not restrict
movement unduly and kept the bridges across the Jordan open,
although well aware that some Fatah and other terrorist agents
were bound to cross by them into Israel. By 1980 the internal
security situation in Jerusalem had not worsened. In Teddy
Kollek's view: 'The reason is not that the Arabs of Jerusalem love
us, or that they would like us to continue to rule the city, but
simply because they lead a reasonably tolerable life now'.[29]
Reasoning Arabs realized that their first duty was to maintain
their presence in Jerusalem; viable economic conditions made
this easier, and acts of terrorism were liable to defeat their own
ends by dislocating the life of the city and damaging its economy.

The relative lack of resistance to Israeli rule in Jerusalem –
compared with that in the West Bank – owed something, too, to
the anomalous civic status of the East Jerusalem Arabs.
Technically, they were still citizens of Jordan, for Jordan had
been the only Arab state automatically to offer citizenship to the
Palestinians inherited from the 1948 war. Yet they remained
citizens of East Jerusalem, and were entitled to vote in its
municipal elections. On the other hand, they could not vote in
Israel's national elections, unless they chose to accept the Israeli
citizenship which was offered to them. But to do that would seem
an act of betrayal of their Arab heritage, and it could well expose
them to reprisal of a violent kind. Jordan did not explicity seek
the re-division of the city and thus failed to underline their right
to Jordanian citizenship.[30]

Their anomalous position was further stressed by the juridical
situation of East Jerusalem. Israel's representative in the United
Nations, Abba Eban, had argued that it had never been annexed. 'The term annexation used by supporters of the [UN]
resolution is out of place. The measures adopted related to the
integration of Jerusalem in the administrative spheres, and
furnish a legal basis for the protection of the Holy Places in
Jerusalem'. One authority found this argumentation 'not legally

convincing'.[31] In his view, Israel's stake in East Jerusalem (and in the West Bank too) 'is limited to belligerent or, at best, trustee occupation, until the advent of a peace treaty establishing finally recognized borders'. Another authority, this time Israeli, largely concurred. He found that 'Israel cannot legally annex East Jerusalem, and in fact – contrary to the widely accepted myth – has never done so'.[32] Furthermore:

> In theory, Israel can gain title to East Jerusalem either through cession or prescription. Cession would necessarily be based on a peace treaty with Jordan ... should Israel derive benefits from a future peace treaty with Jordan, it is imperative to demonstrate that Israel was the victim of Jordanian aggression in June 1967. As for prescription, it is based on a 'continuous and peaceful display of State authority' over many years. Yet, in the past twelve years, Jordan has made sure through actual exchange of fire as well as Security Council resolutions, that Israeli prescription will not begin to run its course. In practice, if Israel desires to gain title to East Jerusalem, it must conclude a peace treaty with Jordan.

Such juridical considerations may not have played much part in the thoughts of the average East Jerusalem Arab. But he was aware, in addition to the anomalous nature of his personal status, of the peculiar forlornness of his position. The Arabs of Israel 'proper' had felt this forlornness too, but they could reasonably claim that, isolated as they were from the rest of the Arab world, they had no alternative but to accept Israeli citizenship and all that this implied. The Arabs of the West Bank also had cause for unhappiness under foreign occupation. But they had not been incorporated into Israel in any way, and they maintained direct contact with their Arab brethren across the bridges over the Jordan. It was a simple enough matter for them to show their distaste for Israeli military occupation without disturbing their daily existence: they could stone Israeli vehicles to their hearts' content. Only in one important instance did demonstrations lead to really hurtful retribution, when the West Bank's single university was temporarily closed down in 1979.

The Arabs of East Jerusalem faced a more difficult dilemma. Where the terms of their daily existence were concerned they needed to co-operate fully with the Israelis. Politically, they had to maintain their independence, and socially, their Arab identity. Something extra was expected of them by the rest of the Arab world, precisely because they were the ostensible 'guardians' of the two great mosques and the remainder of the Arab heritage in the city. Their frustration fed upon their physical helplessness, and the reverse. They were offered material inducements – improved living standards, municipal services, education and social benefits. They had to accept them, for to refuse them would have been pointless. Yet acceptance was a further reminder of their dependence on their conquerors.

In these circumstances, it was perhaps surprising that they took part so readily in the October 1969 municipal elections. Only 5,000 Arabs of East Jerusalem had been qualified to vote under Jordanian rule in the elections of 1963 and the Mayor, Rouhi Al-Khatib, was elected with just 1,163 votes. They had to be twenty-one years old, male, property-owners and ratepayers. In 1969 the Israeli authorities extended the suffrage to the whole adult population, roughly 35,000 people. The press of the Arab world believed that barely one thousand of them would vote. In fact, nearly 8,000 did, and 7,135 of their votes were validly cast. The Mayor believed that another 3,000 would have voted, if there had not been delays and difficulties over the registration of voters.[33] He was very well satisfied with the result, which was indeed surprising. For there were no Arab candidates in the field, nor was there an Arab party. The Arab vote was, according to analysts, almost solidly for Kollek, as a man who inspired trust and confidence.

The 1973 war brought a setback. The municipal elections were due in October and had to be postponed. In the event, the Arab vote was almost halved. But in 1978 it was back to well over 7,000, although admittedly the Arab electorate now numbered over 53,000. An Arab boycott had been predicted, in protest against the Camp David Agreements between Israel and Egypt, and there were reports of local intimidation, including warnings chalked up on the walls of Arab homes.[34] The result of the election was yet another landslide victory for Kollek.

Could it have been that the Arabs of East Jerusalem were, in an inconspicuous way, registering a degree of support for the Camp David Agreements? Or that material benefits were, after all, having some effect? One must recognize that there was absolutely no compulsion to vote and no obvious advantage to be gained from doing so. Of course, they could have been landed with someone far less desirable as mayor; but then Kollek's re-election was a certainty, and it had even been a surprise that anyone had been ready to run against him.

Material benefits should not be underestimated. In 1967 the Arabs of East Jerusalem were often living seven or eight to a room, and rooms tended to grow smaller as a result of the habit of building the 'room within the room' for newly-grown-up members of the family. The state of public services has already been mentioned; the Old City contained some of the dirtiest and most desolate streets in the whole of the Middle East. Two features of them, and of open spaces in front of every hotel, were the beggars and the shoe-shiners. The beggars included the small boys who were anxious to 'conduct' any stranger a hundred yards along the road he was already walking. No shame on either the beggars or the shoe-shiners: theirs was a normal part of day-to-day existence. No shame on householders and shopkeepers in the Old City, either, with gutters filled with filth flowing past their doors: these were the consequences of an antediluvian plumbing system and an inadequate water supply. It is a singular commentary on some friends of the Arabs that they have 'blamed' the Israelis for introducing modern sanitation into the city's dark alleys and robbing them of their supposed romance. One might prefer to regard the trebling of garbage-collection services as a useful step forward.

Some of the benefits conferred by Israeli administration have already been mentioned. These were others:

A free Arab press was created. In November 1968 two daily papers, *Al Anba* and *Al Quds*, began publishing, and the Editor of the latter stated that 'There is no doubt, and I must speak the truth – we now have freedom of the press, which, to my great regret, the Arab reader has never before enjoyed'.[35] The only limitation placed on these papers related to classified military information, but that applied to the Hebrew press too. Arab papers could, if they wished, publish Nasser's most inflammatory speeches in full, and sometimes did. Other Arab papers which began publishing included the daily *Al-Sha'ab*, the weekly *Al Fajar* and the monthly *Alwan*, a literary paper which catered especially for youth. One Arab commentator decided that Jerusalem was becoming an Arab cultural centre and that a real effort was being made to revive its publishing and newspaper industry.[36]

Public libraries were opened. In 1967 there was a single such library in East Jerusalem, in A-Zahra Street, with only 2,500 books. By mid-1969 there were four public libraries, with 32,000 books between them.[37] In 1967 the A-Zahra library had 34,000 readers, who took out 13,000 books. By 1979 readership had risen to 125,000, and 42,000 books were taken out. The library's stock of books rose during that period from 2,500 to 26,800.

In spite of understandable reticence on the Arab side, much was done in the field of youth activities. Arab football, basketball and table tennis teams were organized and played against Jewish teams. Hundreds of young Arabs went on excursions to Israel 'proper' and in particular to Arab centres like Nazareth. Regular school trips to the seaside followed – many of the East Jerusalem children had never seen the sea – and in 1968 500 young Arabs for the first time joined 2,000 young Jews in the annual Jerusalem 'Boys Town Camp'.[38] A mixed Arab–Jewish 'Youth Council' was formed at the end of the year. Hebrew and Arabic language classes were started, so that children could get to know each other's languages. All of this helped to bring down the high rate of juvenile delinquency in East Jerusalem; in two years it dropped to the average rate found among Israeli Arabs.[39]

There were other efforts to bring the young together, for their friendships could make the best foundation of all to Arab–Jewish understanding. Thus the French order of the Sisters of Zion organized joint classes and social occasions for young Arabs and Jews, and invited teachers and administrators from both sides to help. One participant, the Arab Director of St John's Ophthalmic Hospital in East Jerusalem, declared: 'For twenty years, since I was sixteen, I never saw a Jew. I sat, motionless, in a world of ignorance and hate. Am I still to sit, doing nothing? Someone must break out of this.'[40] By 1972 the Sisters of Zion had enrolled 400 students. A year earlier the First National Conference of Voluntary Arab–Jewish Organizations was formed under the auspices of the Hebrew University of Jerusalem and the American–Jewish Committee. Israeli women's groups, in which Moshe Dayan's first wife Ruth played a leading part, were formed to bring Arab and Jewish adults together.

Of particular interest was Neve Shalom (The Oasis of Peace), an interfaith centre formed by a Dominican priest, Father Bruno Hussar, of Isaiah House in Jerusalem. The centre brought Jews, Muslims and Christians together to pray, study and converse together. Later it opened its own miniature 'village' for prayer and discussion groups, just off the road from Jerusalem to Tel Aviv. In all, there were about twenty different organizations preaching and practising reconciliation of Arab and Jew.[41]

Yet these brave attempts to induce coexistence based on human understanding should not conceal for a moment that the two communities in Jerusalem, Arab and Jewish, remained for the most part separate and apart. Whatever was achieved in the field of inter-race human relations was, as one observer put it, 'limited, thin, vulnerable'.[42] In the minds of most of the Arabs of East Jerusalem lurked the deadly fear that Arab Jerusalem was in process of being lost, or had indeed been irretrievably lost already. This fear expressed itself in oblique forms, in songs, poems, allegorical stories in prose, endless meetings and conventions. All of this was part of the effort to maintain identity and to shake off the slur of behaving as a subject race. The literature of passive resistance was directed towards survival, in Jerusalem. The Arabic word in the hearts of the East Jerusalemites was 'jumud', meaning to 'hold out'.[43]

In their hearts too was the fear that they had been deserted by the rest of the Arab world, that the declamations made on their behalf by such different people as the King of Saudi Arabia and the leader of the PLO, Yassir Arafat, had no practical significance. A somewhat paradoxical view sometimes found was that, since no real trust could be placed in any existing Arab state, Palestinian Arabs might actually find it easier to co-operate with the Israelis than with other Arabs, if only the Israelis would first return what they sincerely believed to be their rights to them.[44] For what had the Arabs of Jerusalem to expect from semi-feudal Arab monarchs, Egyptian, Syrian and Iraqi regimes which were preoccupied with their own interests, or even a PLO which had provoked civil war in Jordan, acted as the catalyst of far worse civil war in Lebanon, and preyed ruthlessly on fellow Arabs in the Gaza Strip?

In a more material sense, Israeli administration brought very marked improvements in medical facilities. East Jerusalem had for a long time had a wide variety of church homes and clinics, but its only government hospital was overcrowded and poorly equipped – for instance, it had only one broken-down x-ray machine.[45] In 1968 the hospital was taken under the wing of the West Jerusalem Health Department, which increased its staff, raised nurses' rates of pay, and brought in new equipment. The disinclination of Arab doctors and dentists to register with the authorities was only gradually overcome, but the Municipality put its West Jerusalem hospitals and the Magen David Adom (Red Shield of David) emergency service at the disposal of the people of East Jerusalem. In particular the revived Hadassah Hospital on Mount Scopus, cut off from West Jerusalem and lying empty for nearly twenty years, was turned into the regional medical centre for East Jerusalem and the West Bank. Its

Director-General, Professor Kalman Mann, called this 'a bridge of health to peace'.[46] Incongruously, thousands of Arabs from countries officially at war with Israel began crossing the Jordan bridges to receive medical treatment at the bigger of the two Hadassah Hospitals, at Ein Karem, on Jerusalem's southern outskirts. In particular, it offered cancer treatment and free open-heart surgery.

Islamic culture was not neglected. Two Arab cultural centres were established by the Municipality, with the co-operation of the Jerusalem Foundation, at Beit David and Shuafat. At the Rockefeller Museum the Paley Centre was set up, supplying courses in art and archaeology for young Arabs. The Municipality provided the initiative for building an Arab theatre, and gave its blessing and help to the Islamic Museum which was opened in West Jerusalem. The fund-raising for this museum was carried out by Israelis. The point will always be made that much more has been done for Jewish Jerusalem and its Israeli citizens than for East Jerusalem and its more or less stateless Arabs. The Israeli authorities would argue that they did the best that they could, considering an everlasting lack of funds, for all the people of Jerusalem, in the cultural as in other fields.

In 1980, looking back over a period of thirteen years of a united Jerusalem, Teddy Kollek must have had real grounds for satisfaction.[47] He had eliminated unemployment, which stood at over 5,000 in 1967, with about 3,500 of these in East Jerusalem, or 20 per cent of its work-force. He had extended efficient social welfare to East Jerusalem – there had been just 78 recipients there before 1967. He had helped to build up light industries which by 1980 accounted for 12 per cent of the city's economic activity (still less than half the figure in Tel Aviv). He had boosted tourism, in spite of temporary slumps caused by the wars of 1967 and 1973. He had seen the city's population grow from about 260,000 to close on 400,000, yet had planned successfully to keep pace with its buoyantly expanding needs. He had successfully avoided damaging communal strife – an exceptional issue was the controversy which arose at the beginning of 1980 over the proposed take-over of the Arab-owned Jerusalem District Electric Company – and he had at least contained Arab terrorism. He would be the first to admit that there were mistakes during his stewardship, but he would certainly maintain that Israel has shown itself to be the best, probably the only feasible guardian of the interests of the Holy City, and of the orderly lives of its inhabitants.

REFERENCES

1. Chaim Herzog, *Who Stands Accused?*, Weidenfeld, London, 1978.
2. Meron Benvenisti, *Jerusalem: The Torn City*, Isratypeset, Jerusalem, 1976.
3. Ibid.
4. Ibid.
5. Yehosophat Harkabi, in personal conversation with the author. He added that he would not, personally, mind at all living in an Arab-administered borough.
6. Rouhi Al-Khatib, *The Judaization of Jerusalem*, Amman, 1979.
7. Diane Shalem & Giorga Shamis, *Jerusalem*. Jerusalem, 1970.
8. Ibid.
9. Meron Benvenisti, op. cit.
10. Teddy Kollek, *For Jerusalem*, Weidenfeld, London, 1978.
11. Teddy Kollek, reply to a World Council of Churches article by Hugh Samson, 'The Agony of Jerusalem', April 1968.
12. Elie Kedourie, *Diplomacy in the Near and Middle East*, Van Nostrand, Princeton, N.J., 1956.
13. Palestine National Covenant, Art. 6.
14. Ibid. Art. 9.
15. Ibid. Art. 33.
16. Crown Prince Fahd of Saudi Arabia, interview with *Al Hawadess*, London 18 May 1979.
17. Rashid Hamid, *What is the PLO?*, pamphlet distributed at the London International Conference on the Muslim World, December 1979.
18. Crown Prince Hassan bin Talal of Jordan, *A Study of Jerusalem*, Longmans, London, 1979.
19. Yassir Arafat, in Venezuelan paper *El Mundo*, 11 February 1980.
20. UN General Assembly Resolutions 2253 and 2254.
21. UN Security Council Resolution 252.
22. UN Security Council Resolution 267.
23. *The Times*, 5 July 1979.
24. Christopher Walker, in *The Times*, 28 February 1980.
25. *Jewish Chronicle*, 20 July 1979.
26. *The Times*, 2 April 1980.
27. Meron Benvenisti, op. cit.
28. Ibid.
29. Teddy Kollek, *For Jerusalem*.
30. Allan Gerson, *Israel, the West Bank and International Law*, Frank Cass, London, 1978.
31. Ibid.
32. Professor Yoram Dinstein, Dean of Faculty of Law, Tel Aviv University, in paper given to the author.
33. Teddy Kollek, *For Jerusalem*.
34. A. J. McIllroy, *Daily Telegraph*, 9 November 1978.
35. *Rebuttals of Jordanian Misstatements about Israel's Administration of Jerusalem*, Israel Foreign Ministry, Jerusalem, 1972.
36. Atallah Mansour, *Ha'aretz*, 15 June 1971.
37. Gideon Weigert, *Israel's Presence in East Jerusalem*, Jerusalem, 1973.
38. Ibid.
39. Ibid.
40. Alfred Friendly, *Washington Post*, 28 February 1970.

41. Father Edward H. Flannery, *America*, 27 May 1972.
42. Meron Benvenisti, op. cit.
43. Ibid.
44. A Palestinian Arab student to the author.
45. Gideon Weigert, *Keshet* (Hebrew weekly), Spring 1968.
46. Report of Hadassah 64th National Convention, 1977.
47. Teddy Kollek, *For Jerusalem*.

CHAPTER NINE

The Crux of the Middle East Dispute

The late Yaacov Herzog, personal adviser for many years in the office of the Prime Minister of Israel, might have been described as the most spiritual and idealistic, if not the official, spokesman of Zionism since 1948. A few of his thoughts bear this out.

Thus, in June 1968 he said:

> I believe that, from the political point of view, we may expect that the central struggle will be about Jerusalem, and it is only beginning to develop ... During the past year, Jerusalem has become a focal point for the Arabs. They had always regarded Jerusalem as an Islamic centre; today, it has become an Arab centre, as if its loss had irreparably degraded the Arab world and there can be no remedy for the degradation unless they regain the city. They speak of Jerusalem and there are tears in their eyes.[1]

And again: 'When access was opened to the Western Wall, when Jerusalem was reunified, we saw with our own eyes how a new kind of communication emerged among the Jews the world over. Assimilated aristocrats and millionaires, children of mixed marriages, came to that stone wall and shed tears, without rhyme or reason.'[2]

Later, he wrote: 'Jerusalem makes of the whole of Israel one great family, from one end of the world to the other.'[3] And he quoted the historian, Arnold Toynbee, as saying: 'When I heard your soldiers at the Western Wall on the radio, I began to grasp the nature of your bonds with this city of Jerusalem.'[4] In a broadcast 'confrontation' with Herzog, Toynbee had said that the Jewish people was a 'fossilized' relic of an obsolete culture, with no continuity and therefore with no right of existence. Toynbee thought that the only parallels to the Jewish people were the surviving Assyrians – almost all driven from their homes in Syria and Iraq – and the Zoroastrians of India. He compared the attitude of the Jews of Israel towards the Arabs of Palestine with that of Hitler towards the Jews.

Yaacov Herzog was statesman as well as philosopher. On the more restrictive religious plane, Martin Buber had equally little doubt about the centrality of Jerusalem to the existence and beliefs of the Jewish people. Zion, the holy city, could only be built in Palestine, 'because it is the structure hidden in the material of this Land, to the perfection of which this people can bring this Land ... Zion means a destiny of mutual perfecting'.[5] Jerusalem was the inevitable focus of Jewish aspiration and the symbol of the Land 'hallowed to God', and Buber quoted Zechariah on Jerusalem: 'For I, saith the Lord, will be unto her a wall of fire.'[6]

Spokesmen of the Arab cause have been equally positive, if usually in rather more mundane vein, about the importance of Jerusalem. One writer maintained that

> Jerusalem is clearly the critical factor. The return of the West Bank without Jerusalem would be unacceptable; it would mean that the Israelis gave back the body after cutting off the head, as one man put it. King Hussein could not present this to the rest of the Arab world as the basis for a reasonable settlement, nor would his own people agree to it. It would perpetuate the Arab sense of injustice and victimization, inflicting a terrible wound on Arab pride and religious sensibilities. It would also destroy the economy of Jordan.[7]

On this last point, clearly, he was mistaken. Rid of Jerusalem and the West Bank, which it had treated in the past as a troublesome burden, Jordan, with plenty of external aid, has prospered greatly since 1967.

'Any peace plan', according to an Arab historian, 'must be tested first in respect of Jerusalem, not Sinai, or Gaza, or the West Bank or the Golan. The sooner the Arabs and Muslims make Israel realize that a span of the hallowed land near the El Aqsa Mosque is worth more than all the miles of sand in Sinai, the more clearly they will discover whether there is any real chance of peace.'[8] And so: 'No Arab government could under any circumstances renounce Jerusalem as part of any remotely conceivable settlement; nor is there any power in the world which could force the Arabs to do so ... If Israel insists on retaining physical control of the Old City of Jerusalem, then peace in the Middle East is well out of anyone's reach.'[9]

As already indicated, the shared realization of the cardinal importance of Jerusalem has produced differing Israeli and Arab reactions. Almost all Israelis, and Jews in the outside world too, have come to regard Jerusalem as an inheritance and trust which cannot be forsaken, and which must be defended at any cost. There is no general desire to dramatize this; indeed the Israelis, as anybody who saw their young men marching off to war in 1967 and 1973 soberly and without any sort of display can bear witness, are little given to self-dramatization.

For the Arabs, nursing their sense of affront and injustice, the fate of Jerusalem has been a matter for declamation and occasional wild over-statement. Thus one Arab spokesman declared that Israel 'has stripped the Holy City of its universal character, obliterated much of its Islamic past, and depressed its Arab presence'.[10] Another accused the Israelis of devising 'measures aiming at the disfiguration, transformation and destruction of the famous, religious landmarks of Holy Jerusalem'.[11] The Israelis, in their excavations, uncovered new memorials to Jerusalem's Islamic past (Christian, too, for that matter), and preserved everything that was already there. Not a single religious landmark was disfigured or destroyed, while the Arab presence grew from 66,000 in 1967 to about 120,000 in 1980.

Arab propaganda has been understandably active over the Jerusalem Question, but sometimes erratic. Thus a broadsheet of the Free Palestine Information Office claimed that Jerusalem was the second Islamic holy city, after Mecca; it is the third only.[12] According to the same publication, Muslims were unable to 'pray freely' in Jerusalem; there is no restriction whatever on prayer. In another publication, Mecca and Medina were cited as places of visit in Muslim ritual, and Jerusalem as the place of pilgrimage. The exact opposite is true.[13] There is generally a fierce fervour in statements of Arab rights in Jerusalem. Yassir Arafat, so often depicted as a man of peace and moderation, put this fervour into words in a newspaper interview:

Question: 'What do you see as being the solution to the big problem of Jerusalem?'

Arafat: 'I don't see it as a big problem. Zionist propaganda portrays this as a big problem. Jerusalem is an Arab city; it was an Arab city and it will remain an Arab city. Its occupation will not last long.'

Question: 'Who is going to liberate it?'

Arafat: 'My armies. Sooner or later, together, we will enter Jerusalem.'[14]

One Christian churchman, the former Patriarch of Acre, Nazareth and Galilee, Archbishop Joseph Raya, told Jewish and Christian leaders in New York not to 'be mesmerized by the figure of Arafat'. For 'Arafat does not represent the Palestinian people'.[15] The Archbishop was sure that the Palestinian people were tired of war, hatred and division, and were prepared to live in peace and harmony with the Israelis. But they wanted a state of their own, and could no longer remain 'refugees in their own country'.

But this was back in 1974, and nothing that happened in the next six years brought realization of the Archbishop's thoughts any nearer. The Archbishop had asked Israel's Prime Minister, Mrs Golda Meir, if she could not enter into a dialogue with the Palestinians. But Mrs Meir had already, in April 1972, turned down the 'Hussein Plan' for the creation of a federal Jordanian state, in which the Palestinians to the west of the River Jordan would be self-governing. In May 1972 the Israeli Defence Minister, Moshe Dayan, rejected the proposal of the newly-elected West Bank mayors to form a 'Council' which could negotiate with Israel on the area's future. One prominent Israeli military commander, General Mattityahu Peled, wrote that it was Israel's fault if Arafat was recognized as the leader of the Palestinian Arabs, for the people of the West Bank and Gaza had never been given a chance of choosing their own leaders.[16] Another Israeli who was critical of his government's policies was Kollek's Deputy Mayor, Meron Benvenisti. In his view: 'Some of the demands of the Arab population could be satisfied without violating the principle of Israeli sovereignty and the objections of various Israeli bodies to these demands seemed to me to be motivated by outdated or unjustifiable ideas.'[17]

There were two reasons why the Israelis were so hesitant to try to negotiate with representatives of the Palestinians in the West Bank and Gaza. The first was that such representatives would be regarded as traitors by the PLO and the rest of the Arab world. The second concerned Jerusalem, and has been analysed by a leading Israeli administrator, Raanan Weitz.[18] If Israel sought a

'Jordanian solution', he explained, then an agreement over Jerusalem and its holy places could be envisaged. For King Hussein's capital was at Amman, and Jerusalem would not be his capital city. But if there were a 'Palestinian solution', the Palestinians would inevitably need East Jerusalem as their capital. Weitz, surprisingly, tendered the thought of a federal state of nine 'districts'; three of the districts would be Arab (Nablus, Hebron and Gaza) and a unified Jerusalem would be the ninth district, possibly including Bethlehem and Ramallah.

Such a solution would fit well enough with the thoughts of some Palestinian moderates, who might not be prepared to press endlessly and hopelessly for the 'secular and democratic' Greater Palestine from which the PLO would expel a great many Jews. Thus one Arab author believed that the 'actuality' was that 'Palestinians and Israeli Jews are not fully implicated in each other's lives and political destinies'.[19] He wanted the 'productive encounter' between Palestinian Arabs and Jews, which he believed would be to their mutual advantage. But even a relative 'moderate' like this one agreed that he wanted the secular, democratic state at the end of the day. This is just what Israelis fear.

President Sadat, too, ranks as a 'moderate'. Yet during the negotiations up to and following the Camp David Agreements he never ceased to demand the return of Jerusalem to Arab rule, and not just at times when he was being accused of selling-out Palestinian rights. The mystery of why the Camp David Agreements made no mention of Jerusalem was explained only a year after they were signed. At a Jerusalem Chamber of Commerce luncheon the former Israeli Ambassador to Washington, Simcha Dinitz, stated that the first draft of the agreements tabled by the United States referred to Jerusalem as continuing to be an undivided city, open to people of all religious beliefs.[20] This was acceptable to the Israelis but not to the Egyptians. They asked for an alternative version, which referred to the city as undivided but added that a part of it would 'be returned to Arab sovereignty'. This was, hardly surprisingly, turned down by the Israeli delegation. According to Dinitz, President Carter personally intervened, pointing out that East Jerusalem was, like the West Bank, 'captured territory' – the President was even ready to state this in a letter to Sadat. In the event, the letter was not sent and all reference to Jerusalem was omitted from the agreements.

Sadat's awareness of the strength of Palestinian feeling about

East Jerusalem remained constant in the years after the Camp David Agreements were signed. He understood very well that higher living standards, better housing, better municipal government and improved education could not compensate for the loneliness and frustration of East Jerusalem Arabs who were determined to regard themselves as second-class citizens as long as they were under Israeli rule. This almost masochistic attitude was as much responsible for refusal to accept any share of municipal responsibility in Jerusalem as was fear of reprisal for 'collaboration'. But that fear existed too, and with good cause, as this poem by a Palestinian patriot, Rashid Husain, would suggest:

> Give me a rope, a hammer, a steel bar,
> For I shall build gallows;
> Among my people a group still lingers
> That feeds on shame and walks with downcast heads.
> Let's stretch their necks!
> For how can we keep in our midst
> One who licks every palm he meets?[21]

Nor should one forget that the government of an allegedly 'moderate' Arab state, Jordan, made the voluntary sale of land or home by an Arab of East Jerusalem a crime punishable by death. Sadat never ceased to understand that the strength of subjective Palestinian feeling was matched by the undying and equally deep feeling of hurt and affront in most of the Arab world, over the conquest of Jerusalem by a Jewish state.

How to negotiate and work towards a solution of a Jerusalem Question which both Jews and Arabs, for very different reasons and in differing measure too, regard as affecting the core of their being? One view was:

> If and when negotiations take place and reach their climax ... boundary questions will intertwine ideology with expediency. It might be judged worth while to give up a good deal for a secure and recognized base ... But Jerusalem – Zion incarnate as a holy hill – raises deeper issues. Here is where the universal idea and the claim to particular possession meet and, it would seem, confront. What is it about the holy city that the Jewish people feel that they cannot outwardly share to the full? What does it stand for, that they alone must retain the right to defend? Is there some essential that, by sharing, they would lose? Would they sacrifice that essential,

if they shared it? Does its retention, as their very own, further their universal mission, or obstruct it? These are the questions they must in due time answer, and much may hang, for us all, on what they say.[22]

Israel, it has been observed, 'lives with the nightmare of annihilation'.[23] But that nightmare is only peripheral to the issue of sovereignty over Jerusalem, although there is a valid argument that West Jerusalem can probably never again be adequately defended if there is an enemy within the gates, in East Jerusalem and on neighbouring hillsides from which rocket weapons could lay the city waste and prevent planes from taking off from any airfield in Israel.[24] Israel's nightmare about Jerusalem is that realization of what had been a dream can be reversed, and that what seemed to have been a gift from God can be taken or thrown away.

Yet even a good friend of Israel could write: 'Arab demands for self-rule in Jerusalem will eventually have to be taken into account. Kollek is certainly aware of this, and my guess is that he is prepared to consider reasonable proposals for a shared administration. The Arabs know that there is no meanness or arbitrariness in him. He has shown by his fairness that coexistence is possible and desirable. He is Israel's most valuable political asset.'[25]

Kollek, certainly, has never shown any inability to speak for himself. Over the years he showed himself to be open-minded and pragmatic. In London, speaking in the Jerusalem Chamber of Westminster Abbey, he spoke about his stewardship as Mayor of Jerusalem, ever since the city was reunited:[26]

We have given the Arabs independent education; we have allowed them to preserve their Arab citizenship, in this case Jordanian (should in the future a Palestinian entity come into being, it would be Palestinian citizenship); they have the right to vote within the Municipality as foreign citizens and the right to vote for their country, whatever it would be, although they live in Jerusalem; they have the management of their Holy Places; they have free access from the outside and 150,000 people have come every year from Arab countries to the Holy Places; there is an absolute use of the Arab language in the city and you can find arrangements for self-government either through a borough system or through a millet system, or a combination of both.

Within this framework you can find self-rule for Arabs.

But at the same time, Jerusalem is the soul and the heart of the Jewish people. We have waited and continued to pray for it; once it was united, it could not be divided again.

[But:] Despite all our efforts, it is obvious that the Arabs in Jerusalem still do not accept being included within Israel's frontiers. But then it must not be forgotten that the city's Arabs also complained about occupation when the Turks, the British and the Jordanian Bedouin were in control. They called it occupation even then![27]

Kollek believed it a mistake to regard the Jerusalem Question as insoluble, but one 'solution' which he rejected utterly was internationalization. This had failed in Danzig and Trieste, and the Vatican, which had been the leading protagonist of the idea, lost interest when it realized that the Roman Catholic Church would in no event secure a controlling share in running the city. As for the United Nations, with its built-in lobby system and Third World majority: 'Heaven forbid that Jerusalem should be as shabbily treated as the United Nations treats the world's problems.'[28]

In an effective summing-up, he wrote:[29]

We can only look at the situation realistically. If, at worst, Muslim and Jewish differences prove irreconcilable, we will have to live in tension for a long time. All the more reason to care for the city as much as we can, to ensure its welfare and well-being. If, at best, Jews and Arabs find accommodations that are acceptable to the aspirations of all three faiths, no one would argue that what we are doing for Jerusalem today has been irrelevant. We want Jerusalem to remain a multi-cultural city – a mosaic of peoples. There are certainly differences of religion, language, cultural attitudes and political aspirations. But I believe that if the Arabs of Jerusalem are encouraged to feel secure, it should be possible for all to live together in reasonably neighbourly relations.

The bottom line is that Jerusalem must never again be divided ... In this undivided city our objectives are free movement of people and goods, access to the Holy Places for all, the meeting of local needs, reasonable urban planning and development, the reduction of intercommunal conflicts and the satisfaction of international interests.

Within an undivided city, everything is possible, all kinds of adjustments can be made, all kinds of accommodations can be considered, all kinds of autonomy can be enjoyed, all kinds of positive relationships can be developed.

Kollek was never afraid to look at all kinds of possible solutions, or to come up with ideas of his own. As early as 1971 he proposed giving diplomatic status to Christian Holy Places.[30] He did not include the Muslim Holy Places only because their future would have to be regulated within the broader framework of an overall settlement of the Arab–Israeli dispute. Kollek's offer was forwarded to the World Council of Churches, and he would repeat it on a number of occasions thereafter.

At about this time he was carefully considering proposals for creating a 'borough system' in Jerusalem, primarily in order to give the Arabs of East Jerusalem self-government. The borough system was the brainchild of his deputy, Meron Benvenisti, who was asked towards the end of 1968 to come up with plans for the future political organization of the city. He suggested the creation of five boroughs in and around Jerusalem, two of them mixed Arab–Jewish and one of them purely Jewish, within the city's boundaries, along with boroughs of purely Arab Bethlehem and Beit Jalla.[31] The five boroughs would return members to a Greater Jerusalem Council of fifty-one members, thirty-one of them Jewish. This was on a fair proportional basis, as Jews constituted 66 per cent of a total population of just on 300,000.

Benvenisti evidently had two objectives: to develop true coexistence between Arabs and Jews in and round Jerusalem, and to give the city a more ample hinterland. A subsidiary aim may have been to satisfy the Christian world that mainly Christian Bethlehem and Beit Jalla were being looked after. But the Deputy Mayor became the target for all sorts of false accusations, such as inviting the imposition of Jordanian joint sovereignty in the area. The Knesset refused to debate his proposals and the Foreign Minister, Mr Abba Eban, stated that they were of no practical use even though it had been his Ministry which had first requested them. According to Benvenisti himself, he was accused of treason and one member of the Knesset was prepared to ask Parliament to bring him to trial.[32]

His plan, however, was not quite dead. It came up for somewhat haphazard discussion once or twice. Thus Kollek expressed his regret in 1974 that the plan had not been implemented, as it would have led to a real improvement in inter-communal relations.[33] The Mayor admitted that it was probably too late to do anything about it, as few people would dare to support it any more.

It was another five years before the Benvenisti plan, now in much modified form, came before the public again. Benvenisti had in the meantime left the municipal administration. The generally accepted view was that he had differed over policy with the Mayor, but according to one well-informed source it was because 'Teddy had shied an ash-tray at his head once too often'.[34] The Mayor sometimes became impatient, and a good friend of his admitted that on such occasions he might behave 'like a bear'.[35] In any event, what was regurgitated in late 1979, and was under discussion in 1980, seemed to be the ghost of the Benvenisti plan.

What was proposed was to create 'neighbourhood' boroughs in Jerusalem. The use of the word 'neighbourhood' implied a recognized degree of coexistence, which was not in fact there; Jews and Arabs were still living in a state of mutually accepted separation from one another. But there was nothing wrong in pursuing the thought that a borough system, of some kind, could still be created. Benvenisti was himself sceptical; he said that offering the Arabs 'neighbourhood councils' would be unacceptable – it meant asking the Arabs to stick their necks out, in return for next to nothing.[36] Neighbourhood boroughs appeared to be a selected designation for the most modest kind of decentralization, giving citizens a bigger say in their local affairs.

There was more to it than that. Kollek sent a top-level delegation to London in January 1980, headed by the Deputy Mayor, Elad Peled. It spent a week in London, and studied every aspect of urban administration there. This study included the entire basis of administration in London by the Greater London Council and the London boroughs. The mission was a fact-finding one. Only one conclusion could be read into that; Jerusalem wanted to find a pattern of municipal government which could help to solve its own problems.[37] Incongruously, the Likud Party, of Mr Begin's ruling government coalition, challenged Kollek's decision to send a team to London, because it might lead to the re-division of the city.[38] Of course, it implied the exact opposite, and Kollek struck back by declaring his abiding concern in keeping Jerusalem united.

Kollek elaborated his thoughts in a comprehensive interview with the *Jerusalem Post*[39] early in 1980. He told the paper that he envisaged a system with boroughs of 40,000 to 50,000 inhabitants, of which probably three would be mainly or entirely Arab. Arab residents of Jerusalem would have special voting rights; they could vote for their own borough council, for the Jerusalem Municipal Council, and for whatever sort of autonomous administrative authority should be set up on the West Bank. Kollek was in favour of giving Jerusalem's Arabs the option of holding Jordanian citizenship, or, presumably, Palestinian citizenship if this were a feasible alternative. What he called 'a sovereign Muslim flag' could fly from the two great mosques of the Haram, but not as a symbol of sovereignty over the whole of the Temple Mount. The last Haram gate which, for security reasons, was still in Israeli hands, the so-called Mohgrabi Gate, should be handed over to the Muslim authorities. In addition, the rights and prerogatives of East Jerusalem Arabs could be anchored in legislation; thus their right to administer the Temple Mount area, to hold Jordanian citizenship and to use the Jordanian curriculum in their schools.

The powers of the borough councils could be easily and quickly determined; Kollek felt that London could be taken as a structural model for a borough system which would offer the right amount of self-administration to citizens. Above all, he explained, action should be taken soon. 'This should not be the result of American pressures or the demands of Egypt or King Hussein. This is our capital and we have to find solutions that seem right to us ... We have to find a way to live together. I don't want to have here what happened with Israeli Arabs.' And, 'We still have time. In three years the pressures on us will be even greater. Let's do it now.'

Kollek was always well aware that the Arabs wanted to maintain the special character of their parts of the city. This was something that Israel should support, for 'they need a smooth-running economy, so that they can stay here, and so that the tourists will come ... This gives them an Arab-national reason, an almost moral-patriotic justification to safeguard peace and quiet in Jerusalem and be against terrorism.'[40] He saw no discrepancy in doing the best that he could for Jerusalem's Arabs, while pushing ahead with the strengthening of Jewish Jerusalem.

Kollek repeatedly pointed out the nonsense of creating new settlements in the West Bank when the money could have been so much better used in Jerusalem. Thus:

There are 1,000 people living in the settlements north of

here, and 1,000 young couples leave Jerusalem every year
because they cannot afford to buy apartments, and no
apartments are being built. The amount of money wasted on
Yamit (in the Sinai Peninsula) could have solved the housing
problem for the young people of Jerusalem in the past ten
years.[41] [And again:] If anyone says that in order to safeguard
Jerusalem, they have to settle in Hebron, or in Judaea and
Samaria, I sincerely believe that these settlements are
detrimental to Jerusalem. If we want to annex areas, there is
political justification. Otherwise they are a waste of money.
For each family settled in the West Bank there could be three
families in Jerusalem.[42]

Kollek built up an unchallenged reputation for himself as a
realist. He openly admitted that the Arabs of East Jerusalem had
to regard him as an occupier: 'Maybe the best possible occupier,
but an occupier'.[43] He criticized his own government for being
'miserly' over granting the Arabs of Jerusalem their rights,
which he believed should be enshrined in law and not be merely
a matter of administrative practice which could easily be
reversed.[44] But there were signs that efforts would be made by
others to water down the borough plan, soon after it was once
again being publicly aired early in 1980. Thus the *Jerusalem Post*,
examining the plan, suggested that it was less a borough plan
than a 'neighbourhoods plan'; neighbourhoods would have
strictly limited competences and would be 'structured on
location, which would all fit into the general municipal structure
of Jerusalem – the united capital of Israel'.[45] On the other hand,
there was no reason why East Jerusalem Arabs should not retain
Jordanian nationality or send representatives to the
administrative authority of an autonomous West Bank entity.

As the original architect of the boroughs plan, Meron
Benvenisti made his views plain in two long articles contributed
to the *Jerusalem Post* when his plan was taken out of cold storage
early in 1980. These were his most operative thoughts:

At some stage there has to be a meeting of minds, between
Arabs and Jews, over Jerusalem. But at the time of writing, this
was not the case; Arabs believed that East Jerusalem's
annexation was illegal and that it remained a part of the West
Bank, while most Israelis assumed that any connection between
East Jerusalem and an autonomous Palestinian entity would
make the annexation of East Jerusalem null and void. Yet the
successful launching of an autonomous Palestinian entity was

inconceivable, unless East Jerusalem played its part in it.[46]

But Benvenisti saw three reasons for hope. The five-year transitional period allocated to the autonomous Palestinian entity at least postponed 'the inevitable clash over sovereignty' over East Jerusalem; it gave time for 'a variety of constructive suggestions'. Then the Prime Minister, Mr Begin, and his Likud Party insisted that Israeli sovereignty extended to all Arab territories west of the River Jordan which were occupied in the 1967 war. Paradoxically, this meant that the offer of autonomy – limited as it was, and not immediately acceptable to the Arab world – extended in some measure to East Jerusalem too. Finally, for President Sadat it was more important to be able to pray in the El Aqsa Mosque than to regard this right as implying recognition of Israeli sovereignty over the Temple Mount. So Sadat might 'prefer guarantees of the unaltered Muslim and Arab cultural and religious character of Jerusalem, rather than the establishment of a leftist-radical Palestinian capital which will destroy its sanctity'. Therefore Egypt might still be prepared to negotiate practical interim arrangements for Jerusalem, until its final status would be decided along with that of the West Bank and Gaza.

Benvenisti foresaw the following practical steps, which could 'defuse' the Jerusalem issue:[47]

East Jerusalem Arabs who remained Jordanian citizens would be free to vote in elections to the autonomous authority in the West Bank, and be elected to it. The Muslims of Jerusalem and the West Bank would be members of the same religious community, and its courts and institutions would be managed by the Waqf with its headquarters in Jerusalem. The Muslim community would continue to have control of its holy places and its religious life. East Jerusalem Arabs should vote for, and be elected to the municipal administration of the united Jerusalem, which would establish a system of 'local councils'. The East Jerusalem school curriculum would continue to be that of Jordan. The Arab Chamber of Commerce would be fully recognized, and all official printed matter in Jerusalem would be in both Hebrew and Arabic. Finally, there would be no further land expropriations, save for approved town-planning schemes.

Benvenisti pointed out that many of these provisions were already in existence; but they should, for the first time, be formalized, as part of a transitional solution which guaranteed Arab rights. During the interim period which would lie ahead in any event, Israelis would be free to continue to regard autonomy

as functional rather than a matter of territorial independence.
Arabs would be free to regard East Jerusalem as part of the West
Bank. Benvenisti implied that it would be wise to allow them to
differ, during the transitional period in which a measure of real
understanding could be built up. His view about boroughs was
that his original ideas had caused too much controversy, and it
might be wise to devise a more flexible system of 'local councils'.
The essence of his thought was that 'the danger to progress lies in
the impatience of frustrated peace-seekers', and that 'the seeds of
long-term solutions are sown in practical arrangements'.

This philosophy of gradualism was attractive. For 'instant
solutions' of persistent political problems seldom succeed.
Jerusalem has posed one of the most persistent problems in the
world's history, all the worse for having a religious as well as a
political content. Yet it would be unrealistic not to expect clever
and courageous thinkers to come forward with plans for
Jerusalem at a time of intense international uncertainty.
Jerusalem gave the mighty Roman Empire its most desperately-
fought battle when it was dominating the civilized world. It
caused something like a world war at the time of the Crusades,
and provoked a European war in the Crimea in the nineteenth
century. It was intimately involved in the First and Second World
Wars, and in four Middle East wars since 1945. It could be the
focus for the Third World War of modern times. It is hardly
surprising that a growing sense of urgency over Jerusalem's
future steadily developed during the 1970s.

Perhaps the outstanding 'outside' contributor to this sense of
urgency was a British peer, Lord Caradon, who as Mr and later
Sir Hugh Foot, became intimately involved in the affairs of the
Middle East. He served for a time in Palestine as a British colonial
administrator, and came back there often afterwards. As British
Ambassador to the United Nations, he was responsible for the
final framing of United Nations Resolution 242, which produced
guidelines for a solution of the Arab–Israeli dispute, although the
original ideas embodied in that resolution were American rather
than British. The resolution laid down the general precept of the
inadmissibility of acquiring territory by force – implying that
territorial change can only be negotiated – and the more relevant
instruction that there should be secure and agreed frontiers for
the states involved in the Arab–Israeli dispute. Lord Caradon's
views, then, were those of someone with real experience.

In *The Times* in 1974 he defined three 'propositions' on which
he claimed to find all Palestinians united.[48] These were that there

should be a comprehensive settlement of the Middle East dispute, and not one which left them out; that this settlement should not be imposed but freely negotiated under 'international assurance'; and that there should be 'an Arab administration with Arab sovereignty' in East Jerusalem. Caradon claimed that he had found 'growing understanding for the conception of an undivided city with, on one side, an Arab Jerusalem under Arab sovereignty and Arab administration and, on the other, an Israeli Jerusalem under Israeli sovereignty and Israeli administration', with 'freedom of access and movement between the two, freedom of religion and freedom of access to the Holy Sites for everyone under an international statute, and an international presence, not to administer the city but to ensure ... freedom of communication, movement and access'. Caradon wanted a solution of the Jerusalem Question without delay, so that 'everything else would be easier' and 'Jerusalem could become, not a barrier but a gateway to lasting peace'.

Caradon reiterated his views many times thereafter. Thus, in the *International Herald Tribune* he wrote: 'Everything else depends on Jerusalem. If there is no settlement in Jerusalem, Secretary of State Kissinger need fly to the Middle East no more, the Geneva Conference need not meet again. For to ignore or postpone the status of Jerusalem is to deceive.'[49] He asked for an international statute, with an international High Commissioner to co-operate with the Arab and Israeli authorities in a 'twin' city in ensuring freedom of access and worship for the Holy Places. In the *Guardian* he underlined and expanded his thoughts. Everything was dependent on Jerusalem, which had to remain physically undivided; he had told his Arab friends that if barriers were again erected in Jerusalem, he would come to tear them down with his own hands.[50] There would in effect be 'twin cities' in Jerusalem, each an inspiration to its respective community. This would be a 'prize' and a 'blessing', for everybody.

Early in 1977 Caradon came out strongly in favour of the creation of a Palestinian state, with East Jerusalem as its capital.[51] He was critical of Israeli building in East Jerusalem and elsewhere in occupied territories, he found Nablus under curfew and Hebron in a state of protest strike, and he believed that 'the occupation of Arab lands by force has gone on much too long'. He was convinced that without Arab sovereignty over Arab Jerusalem there 'can never be peace'. Two years later he was writing again in the *Guardian*,[52] complaining of 'a conspiracy of silence about the future of Jerusalem' – the city had not been mentioned at Camp David. He repeated his demand for 'two sister cities', and he called on the UN General Assembly to take a new initiative in a four-point plan which would include the demilitarization of Jerusalem and the demarcation of boundaries between its Arab and Jewish sister cities by an international commission. Caradon added his recommendation that the Jewish Quarter of the Old City should be included in Jewish Jerusalem, and that 'an area of Mount Scopus including the Hebrew University should be Israel territory connected with Israel by an open bridge'. This phrase was somewhat ambiguous; in fact, as already pointed out, Mount Scopus was by 1980 connected with the rest of 'Jewish Jerusalem' by a continuous belt of Israeli settlement.

Lord Caradon supported his many letters to the press with a 33-page memorandum, which recapitulated some of Jerusalem's past history and repeated the arguments which he had already aired. Much of the memorandum was written in evocative, even emotional language; its arguments were well marshalled and the urgency of the need for a solution was re-stressed. One argument which was re-stated more than once was that continued Israeli domination of the whole of Jerusalem could only disturb and enrage Arab feelings all the more, the longer it went on. The memorandum was widely circulated in the United States, Britain, the Arab world and Israel, among people concerned with the problem of Jerusalem's future. It represented the outstanding effort, by a single individual, to provide food for thought on a solution of the Jerusalem Question.

Lord Caradon's arguments encountered opposition and criticism, all along the line. His article in the London *Times* of June 1974 was instantly answered by Mr Arthur Goldberg, like himself a former Ambassador (of the United States) to the United Nations. There was a certain piquancy about this; for Arthur Goldberg had been responsible for drafting the basic version of UN Resolution 242, which the British delegation subsequently worked over and then brought to fruition by securing unanimous approval in the UN Security Council. Arthur Goldberg, in fact, operated from the same premises as Lord Caradon in their joint endeavour to achieve a settlement of the Arab–Israeli Middle East dispute, but arrived at different conclusions over method, and even actual aims.

In his answer,[53] Goldberg opposed the 'sister cities' concept on three grounds. Even though it might gain fleeting Arab approval, it would satisfy neither Arabs nor Jews. In any case, this concept had already been given a chance, from 1948 to 1967, when there had indeed been an 'Arab Jerusalem' and a 'Jewish Jerusalem'. It had not worked. Real freedom of access to all holy places had been denied by the Arabs, but readily guaranteed by the State of Israel. So, Goldberg argued, Jerusalem should now remain an undivided city, 'basically under Israeli sovereignty and administration, with Vatican-type enclaves for the Muslim Holy Places and surrounding areas, under Arab sovereignty and Arab civil administration'. He remarked that his proposal was not perfect, but possibly more viable than Lord Caradon's.

There were many other 'answers' to Lord Caradon's proposals, over the years. Teddy Kollek's were strictly relevant. Apart from them, two letters to the press had more than passing significance. First, the two letters. They were both written to the *Guardian*, by the Archdeacon of Oxford and Canon of Christ Church, C. Witton-Davies, who had served for several years at St George's (Protestant) Cathedral in Jerusalem.

In his first letter,[54] the Archdeacon contrasted the freedom of access which Israel guaranteed for all holy places with the sad state of affairs which existed when Jordan was occupying East Jerusalem, and drew attention to Kollek's offer of 'delegated' sovereignty for the Holy Places. 'This', he added, 'would be the limit to which I consider sanctified commonsense should permit any alteration of the status quo.' In the second letter,[55] the Archdeacon had much to say about Lord Caradon's proposals. He did not agree that Jerusalem had been 'occupied' by the Israelis in the 1967 war; it had been 'liberated, opened up, universalized again as it had been before 1948'. Nor did he agree with Lord Caradon's demand for an international authority, whose responsibilities 'should be limited and directed to the Holy Places in Jerusalem and free access to them for everybody'. For this was precisely the situation under Israeli rule, and had been for twelve years past. In the Archdeacon's view, Lord Caradon's 'suggested statute for Jerusalem just will not work'.

Teddy Kollek was equally downright. In his book,[56] he disagreed sharply with Caradon's view that the question of Jerusalem should be tackled first, and everything else would then fall into place. 'I'm afraid that Lord Caradon's proposal is an invitation for us all to bang our heads against the wall', he wrote. He was absolutely positive that a settlement for Jerusalem could come only in the final stages of negotiations and he was equally positive that 'to divide the city up again would be obscene; it would be just as bad as cutting up a living body'.[57] He was moreover sure that division would be the upshot of any plan like Caradon's for 'divided sovereignty would soon mean the same walls, mines and barbed wire'.[58] On a more mundane note, divided sovereignty would make organized administration impossible: 'What could be done about crime? A man could commit a theft in East Jerusalem and get off scot-free by running away to West Jerusalem, and vice versa.'

Between 1917 and 1967, according to Meron Benvenisti, there were more than three dozen different 'solutions' suggested for the Jerusalem Question.[59] In these different solutions Jerusalem was regarded as a canton, an international enclave, a county on the British model, a free city like Danzig, a United Nations trusteeship territory, the home of two capitals, the capital of Israel, or the capital of a unified Palestinian state. Much ingenuity, certainly, has been devoted to the problem of the city's future.

Since 1967 there have been five concrete detailed plans. The Benvenisti Plan (of 1968) has already been mentioned. Teddy Kollek produced his amended version in 1970, with a similar system of boroughs but giving them more limited powers and having them all represented in the municipal council. The even more emasculated borough-plan, also already mentioned, was mooted in 1980. Meanwhile, there had been the Caradon Plan and the less-well-known Pragai–Herzog proposal of 1970.[60] This divided the Old City into three separate sectors, Muslim, Jewish and Christian. The Muslim sector would have had its own authority, the Christian would have been administered by a 'World Central Christian' body, and the Jewish would be a part of the State of Israel. Scarcely ranking as a 'plan' was the widely voiced demand for the re-division of the city, as it had been for only nineteen years of its whole existence, between 1948 and 1967.

Internationalization was not feasible, for it was opposed by both Arabs and Jews.[61] In any case, the United Nations Partition Plan of 1947, which offered a 'corpus separatum', provided for a referendum. This would have almost certainly given a Jewish majority; even if it had not done so, it could not conceivably have given a majority in favour of continuing inter-nationalization.[62]

A condominium would be clumsy and hard to implement. One authority has pointed out that it would lead to a mass of localized problems, of currency, customs duties, civil security, law enforcement, services and so on.[63] And who would be Israel's 'partner' – a Palestinian state or Jordan?

A United Nations trusteeship terrritory would presumably preclude Israel's retention of Jerusalem as its capital, that is, unless Israeli and Palestinian–Jordanian governments operated under an international umbrella. Israel, moreover, long ago became intensely and justly suspicious of the United Nations.

A borough system could hardly be expected to commend itself to Arab opinion and Palestinian aims. Yet there was much to be said in favour of Israel taking unilateral steps. In the opinion of one expert, these could gradually improve the situation, while leaving a final solution open.[64] They could include special legislation for the Temple Mount, a statute or at least some form of solemn declaration for the Christian Holy Places, the establishement of Arab borough councils and an Arab Education Board, a legislative enactment to guarantee Arabs choice of citizenship and voting rights, a firm undertaking to end all further expropriation of Arab-owned land. These would be steps in the right direction, which could be taken at any time.

So much for the views of analysts. The views expressed by informed individuals have been literally legion. There is room only for a few of them.

Those of the total pessimists merit little discussion, for they are unhelpful. Thus one Israeli writer's view was that there was no possibility of a constructive dialogue with the Arabs; so it was actually safer to operate on the basis of 'What I have, I hold'; even a purely 'ocular' concession to the Arabs would be a mistake, for it would encourage them to ask for more.[65] In the *Guardian*, James Cameron was totally despondent: 'There will never in Jerusalem be integration in our time, only morbid coexistence. Or perhaps worse.'[66] A hotel-owner in East Jerusalem was only slightly less pessimistic; the ethnic contours of Jerusalem had been altered by the building of new Jewish quarters, the expropriations of Arab land had been a grievous affront to Arab dignity, and the amounts offered in compensation were often derisory. The only hope, as he saw it, was to give the Arabs as much self-government as possible as quickly as possible, and do everything possible to 'de-politicize' the issues in Jerusalem.[67]

There was a school of thought which believed that an accommodation could be reached over Jerusalem with Jordan. Thus Brigadier Yehosofat Harkabi, former chief of Israeli military intelligence, thought that King Hussein would sooner or later bring his 1972 plan for a federal and democratic Jordanian state out of cold storage.[68] For a state controlled by the Palestine Liberation Organization in the West Bank could be a serious threat to the Hashemite monarchy: it had as much to fear as Israel from what could become a puppet regime of the Soviet Union, ready to encourage a Soviet air-lift into the country. One historian saw an arrangement with Jordan, possibly with the co-operation of outside trustees, as the best of a not very encouraging lot of solutions.[69] It might have been significant that in February 1980 Teddy Kollek and former Foreign Minister Moshe Dayan were holding discussions with Anwar Nusseibeh, the chairman of the East Jerusalem Electric Corporation and a former Jordanian Defence Minister.[70] Nusseibeh argued for dual sovereignty in Jerusalem but against the physical re-devision of the city.

Some Israelis have advised unilateral concessions over the Holy Places – whatever else might be done about Jerusalem. Ex-Foreign Minister Abba Eban would let 'our eastern neighbour, whether Jordanian or Palestinian, fly its flag on the Haram es Sharif, so that El Quds would have an Arab expression'.[71] And the Christian Holy Places should be given 'a diplomatic status similar to that of the embassies'. He pointed out that President Sadat had suggested 'an Arab flag' on the appropriate building in Jerusalem, but that this proposal was rejected by the Israeli Government. Eban agreed that 'this card' should probably be played only in negotiations for permanent peace.

Ex-General Chaim Herzog favoured 'formal confirmation' of the existing status of the Holy Places, which was in practice extra-territorial. This could be linked with a borough system in Jerusalem as a whole, and in the Old City in particular; thus the Armenian Quarter could be a borough.[72] The former head of Israel's Foreign Ministry, Walter Eytan, was explicit on the question of the Haram:[73]

'I have for many years been convinced there is only one solution for the Jerusalem problem – and that is for Israel to make a unilateral, unsolicited offer to give the Haram es-Sharif to an Arab sovereign as his wholly sovereign territory.' Eytan compared this with the 'gift' of the Vatican City to the Pope by Mussolini – it would give 'tremendous dynastic satisfaction' to King Hussein, or King Khaled of Saudi Arabia. For that matter, he added, 'we might make the offer to Sadat, but better a King than a President'. For the Arab world as a whole there would be real religious consolation in seeing the great mosques under 'unfettered Arab sovereignty'.

Somewhat wryly, Eytan has noted that it was a Muslim who murdered Hussein's grandfather, King Abdallah, on the threshold of the El Aqsa Mosque, and that no Saudi monarch troubled to pray there during the nineteen years that it was under Arab rule.[74] Yet it was Saudi Arabia's King Feisal who repeatedly declared that his dearest wish was to pray there before he died, but only after it fell into Israeli hands.

Among a host of other views that of Israel's Minister of Defence, Ezer Weizman, was succinct: Egypt and Israel were both in agreement that Jerusalem must remain united forever.[75] In office, a Minister could say no more than that, at that juncture (December 1979). But two other Israeli opinions deserve to be given in detail.

Ex-General Aharon Yariv was a former chief of military intelligence, for a short time Minister of Information, and in 1980 in charge of Israel's Centre of Strategic Studies. In a letter to the author,[76] he offered 'a short list of theses'. He did not claim that they represented the views of a majority of Israelis, but the probability was that they did just that. They were as follows:

(a) To the Jewish people, Jerusalem has a 'triple meaning' – religious, spiritual and political – which was unique. The city was the one and only centre of the Jewish people. The roots of Arab history and religion are elsewhere.

(b) For nearly 150 years the Jews have been the largest religious community in Jerusalem, and for well over 100 years they have comprised an actual majority of all of its inhabitants.

(c) For practical as well as other reasons, Jerusalem should remain undivided and the capital of the State of Israel.

(d) The Muslim and Christian Holy Places should be given special territorial status. Arrangements should be worked out which conform with existing conditions and long-standing traditions. Christian and Muslim leaders should accept the responsibility for negotiating such arrangements; thus the King of Saudi Arabia might act on behalf of the Arab world.

(e) East Jerusalem should enjoy special municipal status within Greater Jerusalem, on the model of the municipal system of London. There should be some expression there of a 'Palestinian political presence'.

(f) There should be gradual adaptation and adjustment of the present situation in Jerusalem, in consonance with the development of the 'Palestinian political entity' in the West Bank.

So much for Aharon Yariv and his views, always recalling that his was one of the most acute intellects of Israel's remarkable 'military' men, who moved from the defence forces into politics, civil administration, commerce and cultural affairs, and became leaders there too.

The second Israeli opinion deserving detailed treatment was that of Gideon Rafael, former head of the Israeli Foreign Ministry and Ambassador in London.[77] His thoughts arranged themselves in a different order, for his first and most operative premise was that the solution of the Jerusalem Question was indissolubly bound up with a solution of the problems of the 'region' as a whole.

The region, at least initially, was composed of Jordan, Israel and Palestinian Arab territories. Rafael envisaged a 'Middle East Benelux', created by stages. The first stage should be the association of the proposed Palestinian 'entity' (Luxembourg) with Israel (Belgium). Association with Jordan (Holland) would follow in due course.

Jerusalem would become the 'Brussels' of this regional association, with common institutions dealing with trade and industry, communications, ecology and so forth. It would continue to be a unified city and the capital of the State of Israel.

There should be a tripartite religious and ecumenical 'authority' which would safeguard the rights of all religions in the city. It should be accorded the maximum prestige and respect.

The municipal organization of Jerusalem should be revised, in order to give the Arabs in their parts of the city full municipal self-administration.

The essence of his thoughts, Rafael explained, was that there should be maximal 'de-politicization' of the Jerusalem issue, and maximal emphasis on mutual interest in preserving a unique city, in sharing and co-operating in order to do this. He believed that Israel's interest in Jerusalem was primary, while Christian and Muslim interests were derived – thus Christians needed Jesus' descent from 'Royal Jesse', while Muslims 'annexed' Abraham, Moses and even King David, as 'Daoud'.

Rafael rejected, regretfully, a 'Caradon Plan', essentially on grounds of impracticability. For the moment two twin capitals exist, there would be two different political systems, two judiciaries and, in all probability, two competing economic units. But the question of where the Palestinian entity (Luxembourg) should have its capital should, for the time being, be left open.

Interestingly, Abba Eban had also embraced the idea of a Middle East Benelux and a Palestinian Luxembourg in a number of statements to newspapers in 1979–80. Interestingly, too, a supposed 'hawk' like Moshe Dayan was, by 1980, fully aware of the need for flexibility in seeking a solution of the Jerusalem Question. In an interview with the *Jerusalem Post*,[78] he argued in favour of negotiated municipal reorganization, special administrative arrangements for the Holy Places, special voting rights for the Arabs of East Jerusalem, and even the possibility of re-negotiating sovereignty over East Jerusalem at the end of the proposed five-year interim period of Palestinian 'autonomy'.

What emerges from these thoughts, and from a myriad other statements of views, is that something like a national consensus on the future of Jerusalem already exists in Israel. It is based on four precepts. The first is that Jerusalem should remain united; to a man like Rafael, and to almost every Israeli, the building of another 'Berlin Wall' through the middle of the Holy City was 'inconceivable'. The second precept is that Jerusalem should remain the capital of Israel. There is no acceptable alternative, and throughout its long history Jerusalem has been the capital only of a Jewish state, and of no other. The third precept is that everything possible should be done, in the fields of administration and religion, to make the first two precepts palatable to the Palestinians and the rest of the Arab world.

The fourth precept is, perhaps, less clear-cut and is not yet apparent to some Israelis. This is that a solution of the Jerusalem Question can only be achieved within the context of an overall solution for the region as a whole. Within such an overall solution are those elements which can bring true understanding and peace: a shared political as well as religious interest in Jerusalem, a shared determination to maintain its unique values, a shared endeavour to develop the economy and ecology of the region and to improve human existence in it. A Middle East Benelux, then, which could later take in war-weary and torn Lebanon, and other states? A Middle East Common Market, perhaps? At least, nobody should doubt that some form of union is needed for those small states, and their peoples, living between the Arabian Desert and the Mediterranean Sea in a corridor of land down which invading armies from both north and south have marched throughout the thousands of years of its history.

If that is the political 'case', the human case is not less important. It is a case for symbiosis between two peoples who have so much to offer one another. The Arabs have courage, pride, dignity, hospitality and, so often, a sense of humour. The Jews have imagination, industriousness, inventiveness, and that fundamental, golden faith in themselves which has made them the only people in the world's history to defeat dispersion by preserving a sense of unity and identity against all the odds.

Yet, by 1980, the road to Arab–Israeli understanding was as full of pitfalls as ever before. In Jerusalem itself, the latest expropriations of Arab landholders – 1,000 to 1,200 acres of rocky hillside were to be compulsorily purchased at a cost of building and compensation of around £300 million – raised a storm of criticism. King Hussein of Jordan was once again hinting at an 'option on peace with Israel',[79] and his brother and heir was discreetly putting the case for a residual Jordanian interest in Jerusalem and the West Bank.[80] The Palestinians, whose sense of identity had become fully established in the previous two decades, were appealing for justice and were displaying a degree of organization which advertised their determination to obtain it.* The PLO and its leader, Arafat, were still preaching the use of armed force to secure the whole of Palestine and obliterate the State of Israel.† An 'Islamic Revolution' in Iran threatened to spill over into much of the Arab world, and the Soviet invasion of Afghanistan was a frightening reminder of age-old Russian interest in the Middle East and readiness to intervene disastrously in its affairs.

* Thus Jonathan Dimbleby writes of the Palestinian refugees in Lebanon: 'For a decade these people have been portrayed as pitiable refugees ... But there is order here. It is clean. These are no slums. These people are not sick. Nor are they downtrodden ... They resent pity. Their manner is self-possessed. They are refugees, yes, but they have demolished the psychological walls of their prison. There is frustration and overcrowding, yes, but there is also vibrant energy, disconcerting fervour and fierce determination.' (*The Palestinians*, Quartet Books, London, 1979.)

† Yassir Arafat has made it so abundantly clear that he believes in the destruction of the State of Israel by armed force, that literally hundreds of his statements could be quoted. He has never deviated from the phrase used over and over again: 'The popular War of Liberation is the only way to liberate the land'. (Thus on radio 'Voice of Palestine', 1 February 1977.) On CBS (18 July 1979) he proclaimed the need for another war in the Middle East, along with an oil embargo directed against the United States. He added that 'the most violent means against the US and her interests in the region' should be adopted. In the Venezuelan paper, *El Mundo* (11 February 1980), Arafat said, among other, equally inflammatory things, 'We shall not rest until the day when we return home, and until we destroy Israel', and 'Revolutionary violence is the only means for the liberation of the land of our fathers'.

The UN Security Council, for its part, offered a contribution of ultimate irrealism by calling, on 1 March 1980, for the 'dismantling' of 'settlements' in Jerusalem.[81] Jerusalem was indeed mentioned no fewer than seven times in its Resolution 465 and the hawks in the Israel Cabinet were given fresh ammunition for a campaign against compromise and commonsense.

Where, then, lies the solution for Jerusalem? Plenty of voices of non-Jews have been raised on Israel's behalf and in the belief that Israel can be the best trustee of the Holy City. Thus, James Parkes: 'That Jerusalem should remain united and within the political sovereignty of Israel is right and proper; for, though both Christendom and Islam venerate it as a holy city, neither ... has ever had the place in their thought that it has had for nearly three millennia of Jewry.'[82] And John Oesterreicher wrote: 'Men are but tenants. The glory of the Israelis is to have been good stewards, to have been worthy of His trust. Though the Holy City is indeed the symbol of God's universal rule, it is a Jewish city.'[83]

One human story offers confirmation of the views of these two Christian theologians. On 20 October 1979, a forty-year-old Californian Jew, Richard Fogel, arrived in Jerusalem. He was a tough, hard-bitten seaman, taking a year off to amble round the world. He was divorced and had plenty of time to spare, and he was in no sense religiously minded and included Israel in his itinerary only because 'it might just be interesting'. He found a bed in a hostel and someone there suggested he should walk down to the Western Wall.

He came to it from the top of the steps which run down from the edge of the Jewish Quarter to the piazza in front of the Wall. When he saw the Wall, in all its majesty, he ran down the steps and across the piazza. He wanted to touch the Wall, and a great flood of feeling welled up in him when he did so. He began to weep; 3,000 years of history, with its memories of striving and suffering, struck him like a physical blow, with tremendous force:

> I just knew that I was Jewish once more, that my people's whole history was in those stones and that, maybe, my life would begin here all over again. I cried for an hour or more, I guess – I just lost count of time. I had forgotten how to pray, so a rabbi standing beside me gave me a printed sheet with the words. I prayed and prayed, and I came back to the Wall that evening. I knew I must go on coming to it and I thought I might stay there forever.[84]

His story is a reminder that Jerusalem is the heart and core of Jewish belief and Jewish being. Teddy Kollek has written:

> In 1967, when attacked by the Jordanians, the Jews were willing to sacrifice their lives for Jerusalem. They would again. Some would give up ... the Golan, the Sinai, the West Bank. But I do not think you will find any Israelis who are willing to give up Jerusalem. This beautiful golden city is the heart and soul of the Jewish people. You cannot live without a heart and soul. If you want one simple word to symbolize all of Jewish history, that word would be Jerusalem.[85]

A Dominican priest wrote that Jerusalem is 'Yerushalayim', embracing both 'Shalom', peace, and 'Shalem', unity.[86] 'The only language in which the people of the City of Peace and Unity can converse is deep silence; in it, one can hear and respond to the Word which is truth to Muslims, Jews and Christians.' The City of Peace and Unity 'bears witness, to the teaching of God, the Rock of Abraham's sacrifice, the Wall of the Temple, the Rock of Christ's Calvary, the Rock from which Muhammad journeyed to Heaven'.

In those thoughts is implicit the feeling that Jerusalem must be shared by all those who, like the simple seaman from California, believe in it. But Jerusalem still needs a guardian and a steward. Have the Israelis, as Monsignor Oesterreicher believes, been stewards of Jerusalem worthy of God's trust? There are many who would agree with him.

REFERENCES

1. Yaacov Herzog, *A People that Dwells alone*, Weidenfeld, London, 1975.
2. Ibid.
3. Ibid.
4. Ibid.
5. Martin Buber, *On Zion*, East & West Library, London, 1973.
6. Ibid.
7. Michael Adams, *Chaos or Rebirth: The Arab Outlook*, BBC Publications, London, 1968.
8. A. L. Tibawi, *The Islamic Pious Foundations in Jerusalem*, Baskerville Press, London, 1978.
9. Michael Adams, op. cit.
10. A. L. Tibawi, op. cit.
11. Habib Chatti, at London International Seminar on Jerusalem, 3 December 1979.
12. *Jerusalem: Islam's Noble City*, Free Palestine publication, in *New Statesman*, 23 April 1978.

13. *Jerusalem, the Holy*, United Arab Emirates publication, in the *Guardian*, 12 December 1979.
14. Yassir Arafat, *Liverpool Daily Post*, 2 November 1979.
15. Archbishop Joseph Raya, at American–Jewish Committee, New York, 12 November 1974.
16. Mattitiyahu Peled, *Jerusalem Post*, 3 December 1973.
17. Meron Benvenisti. *Jerusalem, the Torn City*, Isratypeset, Jerusalem, 1976.
18. Raanan Weitz. *Self Rule, Shared Rule: Federal Solutions to the Middle East Conflict*, ed. Daniel J. Elazar, Turtledove Books, Ramat Gan, 1979.
19. Edward W. Said, *The Question of Palestine*, Routledge, London, 1979.
20. *Jerusalem Post*, 19 September 1979.
21. Quoted by Eliat Zureik, *The Palestinians in Israel*, Routledge, London, 1979.
22. S. Clement Leslie, *The Rift in Israel*, Routledge, London, 1971.
23. Saul Bellow, *To Jerusalem and Back*, Secker & Warburg, London, 1979.
24. General Mordechai Gur, *Jerusalem Post*, 7 March 1980.
25. Saul Bellow, op. cit.
26. Teddy Kollek, *Jerusalem Perspectives*, ed. by Peter Schneider & Geoffrey Wigoder, Furnival Press, London, 1976.
27. Teddy Kollek, *Foreign Affairs*, July 1977.
28. Teddy Kollek, *For Jerusalem*, Weidenfeld, London, 1978.
29. Teddy Kollek, *Foreign Affairs*, July 1977.
30. Teddy Kollek, *The Times*, 11 August 1971.
31. Abraham Rabinovitch, *Jerusalem Post*, 7 May 1971.
32. Meron Benvenisti, op. cit.
33. Teddy Kollek, *Jerusalem Post*, 29 August 1974.
34. A close friend of both Kollek and Benvenisti in conversation with the author.
35. Saul Bellow, op. cit.
36. Robert Rosenberg, *Jerusalem Post*, 29 August 1974.
37. *Jewish Chronicle*, 25 January 1980.
38. *Jewish Chronicle* News Service, 13 February 1980.
39. Abraham Rabinovitch, *Jerusalem Post*, 1 February 1980.
40. Teddy Kollek, *Jewish Observer & Middle East Review*, 12 May 1977.
41. Teddy Kollek, *Jewish Chronicle*, 31 August 1979.
42. Teddy Kollek, at B'nai B'rith dinner, Jerusalem, 29 February 1980.
43. Teddy Kollek, on CBS TV, as reported in *Jerusalem Post*, 4 March 1980.
44. Teddy Kollek, to American–Jewish Committee, Jerusalem, 11 February 1980.
45. Yehuda Yalon, *Jerusalem Post*, 2 March 1980.
46. Meron Benvenisti, *Jerusalem Post*, 8 February 1980.
47. Meron Benvenisti, *Jerusalem Post*, 22 February 1980.
48. Lord Caradon, *The Times*, 14 June 1974.
49. Lord Caradon, *International Herald Tribune*, 28 November 1974.
50. Lord Caradon, *Guardian*, 25 April 1975.
51. Lord Caradon, *The Times*, 7 January 1977.
52. Lord Caradon, *Guardian*, 27 August 1979.
53. Arthur Goldberg, *The Times*, 3 July 1974.
54. *Guardian*, 20 April 1979.
55. *Guardian*, 18 September 1979.
56. Teddy Kollek, *For Jerusalem*.
57. Teddy Kollek, *Jerusalem Perspectives*.

58. Teddy Kollek, *Time* magazine, 20 November 1978.
59. Meron Benvenisti, op. cit.
60. Saul B. Cohen, *Jerusalem: Bridging the Four Walls*, Yerzl Press, New York, 1977.
61. Meron Benvenisti, op. cit.
62. H. Eugene Bovis, *The Jerusalem Question: 1917–1968*, Hoover Institution Press, Stanford University, Stanford, Calif., 1971.
63. Ibid.
64. Meron Benvenisti, op. cit.
65. Willem van Leer, in personal conversation with the author.
66. James Cameron, *Guardian*, 11 April 1977.
67. This non-Jewish source cannot be named.
68. Yehosofat Harkabi, in personal conversation with the author.
69. Allan Gerson, *Israel, the West Bank and International Law*, Frank Cass, London, 1978.
70. Jewish Telegraphic Agency, 7 February 1980.
71. Abba Eban, in letter to the author.
72. Chaim Herzog, in letter to the author.
73. Walter Eytan, in letter to the author.
74. Walter Eytan, *Israel Digest*, 1 June 1979.
75. Ezer Weizman, in letter to the author.
76. Aharon Yariv, in letter to the author.
77. Gideon Rafael, in personal conversation with the author.
78. Moshe Dayan, *Jerusalem Post*.
79. Moshe Brilliant, *The Times*, 18 March 1980.
80. Crown Prince Hassan bin Talal of Jordan, *A Study of Jerusalem*, Longmans, London, 1979.
81. *The Times*, 2 March 1980.
82. Rev. Dr James Parkes, *Whose Land?*, Penguin, London, 1970.
83. Monsignor John Oesterreicher, *Jerusalem the Free*, Anglo–Israel Association, London, April 1963.
84. Richard Fogel, in personal conversation with the author.
85. Teddy Kollek, *Foreign Affairs*, July 1977.
86. Father Bruno Hussar, in letter to the author.

CHAPTER TEN

Towards a Solution

In a letter written to an American friend[1] at the end of August 1980, the Mayor of Jerusalem, Teddy Kollek, set out some of his thoughts on the future of the city.

He began by admitting, with his usual candour, that he was: 'Not convinced that all decisions taken by the Government of Israel on the subject of Jerusalem have been conceived on the highest level of political prudence and analysis'. Thus, 'The decision to move the Prime Minister's office from West to East Jerusalem, which has been announced so demonstratively, is a case in point. As Jerusalem is one city, the location of the Prime Minister's office ... is irrelevant'.

Then, again, there was the 'recently passed Jerusalem Law'. Kollek wrote: 'Jerusalem is our capital. It has always been the capital when the country was under Jewish rule, but ... this recent piece of declaratory legislation is gratuitous and has merely contributed to the multilateral escalation of rhetoric'. Such rhetoric resulted in interested parties, 'being manoeuvred into the situation of making opposing and extreme statements ... This will not get us anywhere'.

Kollek went on to lay down guide-lines for the future of Jerusalem. First:

As far as territorial sovereignty is concerned, it cannot be fragmented and Jerusalem still remain one city. President Sadat has recently expounded the idea of two sovereignties in an undivided Jerusalem. This is an impossible notion, no matter how attractive and reasonable it may sound on the surface. If a model were required in order to demonstrate the dangers inherent in this suggestion, Berlin is a case in point. The ugly Wall which has divided that city ever since August, 1961, is really the inevitable outcome of two disparate sovereign political systems operating within the confines of one city.

We in Jerusalem have had nineteen years' experience of walls, minefields and barbed wire running across our city, and nobody in his right mind is prepared to return to that situation.

So much for the maintenance of a unified Jerusalem. But 'functional sovereignty' could be shared. Thus, 'The Moslem Holy Places ... are under the control of the Moslem Religious Council which is *de facto* subordinate, not to the Israeli but to the Jordanian authorities. It is Jordan which controls the budget of the Jerusalem Moslem Religious Council and which appoints Moslem judges and clerics'.

The Arab citizens of Jerusalem enjoy what might be described as functional self-determination. They, 'Are nationals of the Hashemite Kingdom of Jordan; they are free to cross the Allenby Bridge any time they wish into territory which is technically in a state of war with us. Yet at the same time, they enjoy full rights as citizens of Jerusalem to participate in municipal elections in the city'. Kollek added, 'Conversely, approximately 200,000 Arabs from countries which are technically at war with us cross the Jordan annually in order to worship at their mosques in Jerusalem'.

Kollek did not believe that the Palestine Liberation Organisation, the self-appointed 'leadership' of the Palestinian Arabs, had any right to a voice in the future of Jerusalem. He wrote:

One of the greatest dangers to the unity of Jerusalem, and indeed to the attainment of peace in the Middle East is the PLO ... Many people tend to accept the PLO as a national liberation movement. The fact is that no Arab country wants the PLO, not the Egyptians, not the Saudis, the Kuwaitis, the Jordanians, the Iraqis. And this is true even more so among the Arabs in Jerusalem, on the West Bank, and in the Gaza Strip. They are proud when Arafat speaks at the UN, but they do not want him here. But everyone is intimidated and does not dare express such feelings.

From my numerous and continued contacts with the Arab population in Jerusalem, I have learned that we are not viewed with affection. But I can confirm with greater emphasis that they are horrified at the prospect of a PLO take-over of their area, because they realise that it would spell the end of their relative well-being, the end to free enterprise, and the end to the right to criticise, oppose and demonstrate to which they have become accustomed under Israeli administration. The older generation among the Palestinian Arabs have not forgotten the reign of terror imposed on them in the 1930's by the spiritual founding father of the PLO, the Grand Mufti of Jerusalem, Haj Amin el Husseini, a reign of terror which lasted until the Grand Mufti backed the wrong horse and went over to the Axis Powers in 1930.

Kollek was certain that true peace could only be reached by mutual agreement between Arabs and Jews:

By logic, the Arabs of Jerusalem, as well as the Arabs on the West Bank in the Gaza Strip, ought to be our natural partners in the search for peace. But what chance do they have as long as the international community, and especially the nine Western European countries, persist in their ... infatuation with the PLO and in extending to that terrorist group a status of political and diplomatic respectability, thus pulling the rug out from underneath the Arabs who live in this area, undermining the peace process, and jeopardising the security of Israel ... There are no instant solutions and no miracle cures to the problems of our area, but I have no doubt that unless the governments of Western Europe and elsewhere desist from their policy of boosting the PLO, this terrorist organisation will continue successfully to intimidate and assassinate the moderate Palestinian elements, thus making peace an even more illusory goal'.

Kollek was well aware that the future of Jerusalem cannot be settled in isolation from the rest of Palestine. Moreover:

The city administration of Jerusalem cannot solve the political problems of our area. However, I feel that by creating in Jerusalem an infrastructure of tolerance and coexistence, in spite of the absence of a political consensus, we ensure the future of our city and we may be creating a model for emulation, once the conditions conducive to peace are in sight. In this respect, I feel we can claim a certain measure of success in spite of the existing political tensions from which Jerusalem, for obvious reasons, is not immune. Ours is a peaceful and tranquil city, and terrorist outrages are fortunately few. The Arab population of Jerusalem, which numbered 65,000 at the time of the reunification of the city in 1967, has doubled since then and continues to grow at a rate of 5.1 per cent per annum. This is an unusually large growth rate, which could not be maintained if the economic, social and cultural conditions in Jerusalem were not as tolerable as they indeed are ... Over thirty different Christian communities, their churches and institutions are once again free to develop and flourish in accordance with their cultural and spiritual heritage. The Moslems, as I have already stated, are in exclusive control over their Holy Places, while the Jews, who were barred from worship at the Western Wall during the nineteen years of Jordanian occupation, once again enjoy unhampered worship there.

In short, Jerusalem is once again an open city and a good place in which to live.

Evidence of progress in the pattern of Arab-Jewish coexistence in Jerusalem was given in an article in an Israeli monthly magazine.[2] Youth clubs have been established all over the city, and Arabs and Jews meet there regularly. In the 'elections' at the 1980 'Youth Town', a seventeen-year-old Arab girl, Abir Allawi, became 'Deputy Mayor' and in her inaugural address said that: 'If we learn how to work together while we are still young, this co-operation will make it easier for us to co-ordinate matters as adults'. The city administration organizes joint art exhibitions, language classes and sports occasions. There are joint discussion groups among teachers as well as students, and at one meeting in 1980 on Mount Scopus on Arab participant, A'isha e-Za'ed, said that Arab-Jewish coexistence had, 'Become a pillar of peaceful modern life in Israel. We have still a long road ahead of us, and we must increase our efforts, but we are all praying for common goals: tolerance, mutual respect, and peace – regardless of our differences'.

There have been other, more mundane signs of inter-community progress. Nearly 10,000 Arabs voted in the third municipal elections held in unified Jerusalem in 1980; and the Mukhtar (communal leader) of the Deir Abu Tor district,

Ibrahim Shweiki, declared: 'We in the Holy City participate in elections despite threats and intimidation. We believe this city should remain united, without being cut off from the Arab world. Coexistence on a daily basis is possible.'

Jerusalem's Arabs have participated very readily in contributing to Israeli National Insurance, and have reaped the benefits. About one thousand Jerusalem Arabs have joined the 'Histadrut' (Trade Unions). Arabs, increasingly, are joining workers' committees in industry. Jewish and Arab taxi-drivers have developed a special sense of solidarity, and have supported each others' strikes. On the other hand, the Arabs still refuse to administer their own schools and join in town planning; no Arab up to the middle of 1980 had been appointed to really senior position in the Municipality; Arabic was still not being used in official correspondence with the Arab minority; there was no Arabic telephone directory; and the Arab minority continued to protest about their lack of housing and the preference shown to Jewish residents.

Obviously the overall picture of life in Jerusalem is not wholly rosy. Indeed, 1980 saw all sorts of troubles descending on Teddy Kollek's head. Early in the year a bitter controversy broke out over the future of the East Jerusalem Electricity Company, Arab-owned and operated and in existence since 1926. Israel's Government decided that the company should be compulsorily purchased and its operations carried out in future by Israel's national Electric Corporation (IEC). An order to this effect was promulgated at the end of February. Later, one writer to the London *Times*[3] would castigate this step as clear evidence of the campaign, 'to erase the last semblance of the Arab character of East Jerusalem'. He claimed it was, 'almost the last public utility of any consequence in Arab hands'.

There was wide condemnation of this step in the outside world. In fact, there were solid reasons for taking it. The East Jerusalem company, according to the Israelis, was literally unable to serve its allotted area – largely owing to the fact that its population had rocketed – and was already buying two-thirds of the electricity which it distributed from the IEC. Then it was unable to extend its operations, and only 50 out of 130 Arab villages on its grid were being supplied with electricity. The East Jerusalem company was using small diesel generators which were not economic, had no funds to replace them, failed to keep properly audited accounts and, above all, failed to maintain efficient standards of distribution.[4]

Nevertheless, the manner and style of the announcement of the impending demise of the East Jerusalem company were unfortunate. Yet, as so often in disputes in Israel, the rule of law emerged as an operative factor. On 7 July Israel's High Court of Justice granted the company a temporary injunction, ordering the Government to show due cause as to why its order should not be rescinded and a negotiated settlement be sought.[5] At least, the matter was put on ice and the Chairman of the company, the former Jordanian Cabinet Minister, Anwar Nusseibeh, called the court's decision 'a step in the right direction' which opened the way to legal redress. But the whole episode was painful for Kollek and the Municipality, concerned as they were only with ensuring efficient electricity supply, without stirring up political dispute.

In March 1980, Kollek and his administration were landed with another unwelcome problem. Israel's Government was reported on 11 March to have ordered the expropriation of, 'about 1,000 acres of land in East Jerusalem to build homes for Jews', a move which 'appears to be the first stage in a plan to seize 5,000 acres of East Jerusalem, most of it Arab-owned'.[6] The purpose of this plan, the report went on, was to, 'extend the ring of modern Jewish suburbs which have been systematically erected in ... East Jerusalem since the area was annexed during the 1967 war'.

In fact, 800 acres were expropriated, but the expropriation of a further 400 acres was authorized under the Government order. The ground in question was along Jerusalem's eastern border, and in the northern part of the city. It amounted to a chunk of barren hillside, mainly on the eastern side of the ridge which runs between French Hill and the Jewish settlement of Neve Yaacov, overlooking and merging with the Judaean Desert which runs down to the Dead Sea and Jordan Valley. There were one or two small Arab houses on these 1,200 acres of land; they were to be left undisturbed.

The Government defended its plan and Prime Minister Begin stated that, 'expropriation of land for public use is done by every country'.[7] About 30 per cent of the land was Jewish-owned, 68 per cent was owned by Arabs and 2 per cent was state-owned. Begin wanted 12,000 flats built in the area in the next four years. There was, of course, a strategic reason for the project; Neve Yaacov was in the extreme north of Jerusalem, an isolated Jewish settlement. The new building project would link it with the Jewish settlement on French Hill, Mount Scopus and the main body of the city of Jerusalem. There was no attempt on the Israeli side to conceal this purpose.

For Kollek this was another supremely uncomfortable episode. According to newspaper reports, he had opposed this building project and had claimed that it could only, 'unduly exacerbate tensions between Jews and Arabs'.[7] Kollek had, in addition, categorically stated on several occasions that the era of massive land expropriations had ended – the shape of the city of Jerusalem, for many years to come, had already been defined. When the expropriation order was announced, Kollek could not actively oppose it – his views had already been overridden and he could not deny that this was a suitable area for a new housing estate. But he pointed out at once that implementation of this plan meant huge investments which, 'are nowhere in sight'.[8] The announcement was an ill-timed exercise in barren diplomacy. It seriously embarrassed Israel's friends in the outside world, turned some of them into enemies and, in a practical sense, achieved nothing. One of Israel's best journalists reported that, 'Even if the Government musters the resources to build in South Neve Yaacov, it would probably take two years before the first houses could be started'.[9] Kollek saved one small trick in the game by asserting that his aim was to ensure that 3,000 Arab homes would be included in the South Neve Yaacov project. He had an additional point to make: 'The Arabs', he said, 'are here by historic right, not because of a right which we have given them'. He brushed aside accusations that he took the side of the Arabs in inter-communal disputes. For he believed that, 'one of these days – in 50 or 100 or 200 years – the Arabs will accept this as the capital of Israel'. His purpose was to encourage them to accept this reality as soon as possible.

In May 1980 Kollek was confronted by strikes which kept shops closed for five days, by sit-down 'strikes' in Arab schools, and by a wave of violence which involved clashes between Arab and Jewish schoolchildren and a number of arrests. He called the situation 'worrisome' but added that there was no need for panic; the 'contagion' of the West Bank was partly responsible.[10] What irked him most was the knowledge that many Arab shopkeepers wanted to open, but were inhibited by threats from gangs of youths, some of whose members were found to be in possession of incendiary bombs when they were arrested. Kollek had spoken out often in the past against social intolerance which brought violence in its train.[11]

In June Kollek had a very different problem on his hands.

Jewish squatters had occupied a hillside in the south of
Jerusalem, claiming that it had remained totally unused for
thirty-two years and that, 'Jews abroad should know the money
they sent there goes only to the rich'.[12] The thirty-eight families
of squatters found themselves confronted by more than one
thousand policemen, who were prepared to use force to evict
them. So they dismantled their tent-city, and left. They had much
right on their side. Many Jewish, as well as Arab families are
living in slums. Yet the Begin Government had shown itself
ready to pour out money to house 'religious' settlers in isolated
places on the West Bank, where their presence was an affront to
Arab villagers. Many of these so-called 'idealists', who claim that
they are only returning to their ancestral homeland, are able to
let their homes in Jerusalem and elsewhere for handsome sums,
while occupying subsidized premises in Arab territories. This was
another difficulty for Kollek to bear; for he had repeatedly
advised against throwing money away on remote and
purposeless settlements on the West Bank, when that money
could have been profitably used in Jerusalem.

There were plenty of other problems. The publication in July
of the long-term city plan, which envisaged raising the
population from 400,000 to 650,000 in the next twenty-five years,
brought sharp criticism.[13] For it might involve the utilization of
thousands more acres of Arab-owned land in north Jerusalem.
In addition, it would mean increased industrialization. By the
end of 1980 Jerusalem's industries represented about 12 per cent
of its overall economic activity, or less than half the proportion
in Tel Aviv. The half-dozen discreetly, even almost
surreptitiously sited 'industrial parks' in Jerusalem must, indeed,
be expanded, if the city is to achieve anywhere near a 'balanced'
economy. Of course, there is a huge, anti-industrialization lobby
in and outside Israel. There are the religious leaders who argue
that industry is 'foreign' to the city of three great faiths. There
are the romantics who would like to preserve the already fading
folksiness of a city of men and women in flowing robes, beggars,
goats, donkeys and the occasional camel. There are the survivors
of the non-Jewish, non-Arab 'élite', who see their own positions
being undermined by the modernization which is the only
alternative to a museum in mothballs. The answer to all such
people is that a modicum of industrialization, carried out with
the discretion which has already been practised – one is only
aware of the 'parks' when one is being shown round them – is
both natural and inevitable. Kollek, in the meantime, has to bear

the brunt of blame for 'changing the character' of Jerusalem.

The Mayor's two principal problems in 1980, however, had to do with circumstances utterly outside his control and so far only briefly mentioned. These were the law to declare Jerusalem to be the capital of Israel and the statement of the Prime Minister, Mr Menahem Begin, that he intended moving his office to Arab East Jerusalem.

The preliminary reading of the Jerusalem Law took place in the Knesset (Parliament) in May. The Law, consisting of three short paragraphs, was initiated by Ms Geula Cohen, the representative of the extreme right-wing 'Tehiya' party. By the time Knesset committees had finished with it, the Law had been expanded only to four short sections, which said nothing new whatever. A united Jerusalem was the capital of Israel, and the seat of its President, legislature, executive and Supreme Court. The Holy Places would be protected, and access to them guaranteed. Government would co-operate in developing Jerusalem and making it prosperous. All of this had been said before, very often.

The three readings of the Bill promulgating the Law went through without much opposition, for Government supporters could hardly oppose it and the Labour Opposition was manoeuvred into an awkward position – its members would be accused of lack of patriotism and of 'deserting' Jerusalem if they opposed the Bill. In the third reading only fifteen members of the Knesset had the courage to oppose, while three abstained; ninety-nine members supported it. The Labour Opposition evolved its own forumla; it would support the Bill purely perfunctorily, as a mark of its disdain. Plenty of governments would welcome such easy accommodation. Kollek managed to get two short paragraphs added; they laid down that special economic, financial and other priorities should be granted to Jerusalem by all state authorities, and that the Government should set up bodies to implement this. Addressing the Knesset Committee, he said that there ought to be a, 'supreme co-ordinating committee' chaired by himself and a minister, that two annual financial grants should be calculated on the city's budget and its population, and that the Law should contain express provisions for the Holy Places and their administration. The Law, in fact, should promote Jerusalem's welfare, instead of being an ideological démarche.

Early in August 1980 Begin announced that his office would be moved to East Jerusalem. He had stated his intention of doing this when coming to power in 1977, but suggestions that a move was planned were officially denied as late as June. The site chosen was in an Arab-inhabited area, and the foreign press later reported that three Arab families had been served eviction orders but had refused to move or to accept compensation.[14] Several Cabinet ministers expressed their doubts about the wisdom of the move and the timing of the announcement, while the Chairman of the World Zionist Organisation, Arye Dulzin, called it, 'an act of great folly'.[15] Almost simultaneously, it was announced that the Ministry of Housing, too, would move into the Sheikh Jarrah quarter of East Jerusalem.

Begin would later announce that 'warning letters' sent to the three Arab families had nothing to do with eviction, but a spokesman of the Israel Lands Administration rebutted this by inference, in a statement in which it admitted that the 'warning letters' had been intended as 'pressure' on the families and (almost unbelievably) that it had not 'considered the timing' of its actions, which were dictated by the desire to complete an expropriation order which dated back to 1968. The fat, at all events, was already in the fire. Begin's two moves were bound to provoke serious repercussions.

The most serious was the effect on foreign governments which had embassies in Jerusalem. They numbered only thirteen; most countries with diplomatic relations with Israel decided to pay lip-service to the original United Nations Partition Plan of 1947, which declared Jerusalem to be a 'corpus separatum'.* So the great majority of foreign embassies and missions have always been in Tel Aviv.

Ironically, the Begin Government actually thought that the Jerusalem Law would end uncertainty and encourage foreign countries to bring their embassies to Jerusalem. There would be obvious advantages for them; most of their work was done in Jerusalem, they would get better and cheaper accommodation, and they would live in a far preferable environment. But the exact reverse occurred. All thirteen embassies, twelve of them Latin American and the thirteenth that of Holland, were withdrawn from Jerusalem. Venezuela, Uruguay and Ecuador were the first to go, Guatemala and the Dominican Republic the last. The Dutch departed after bitter heart-searching and were more honest than the others in admitting that they had been put

* Footnote: Thus one found the strange paradox of Spain, which had no diplomatic relations with Israel, continuing to maintain a Consulate in East Jerusalem after the 1967 war and its annexation by Israel.

under threat of oil-blackmail by the Arab League. Arab pressure
continued, and Israel's trade with the Latin Americans, worth
$227 million in 1979, was put in jeopardy. They were among
Israel's best customers for arms and helped to give Israel's arms
industry an adequate base. Worried questions were asked by
some of the smaller Latin American states as to how they would
be able to find buildings in the Tel Aviv area and to afford the
immensely higher rents for them.

Jerusalem lost its 'diplomatic being' in one fell swoop. There
were other minor, negative developments. Turkey closed its
consulates in both West and East Jerusalem and only after some
hesitation decided to maintain diplomatic relations with Israel.
Switzerland refused to sign an agreement on mutual pension
rights in Jerusalem, although prepared to sign it either in Tel
Aviv or in Berne. The Government took a very serious view of
this decision not to to transact government-to-government
business in the capital; it was reminiscent of the state of affairs in
the early period after Israel won its independence. Wisely, the
Government did not upbraid Holland and other countries for
withdrawing their embassies from Jerusalem, but the acme of
stupidity was achieved by a colleague of Ms Geula Cohen,
Professor Yuval Neeman, with his remark: 'Better no embassies
in a Jerusalem which is Jewish, than 140 embassies in a Jerusalem
which is not Israel's'. The Jerusalem Law made the city no more
Jewish than before, and there was no compensation for the
removal of the embassies.

There was an instant reaction to the Law in the United
Nations. On 30 June the Security Council had voted 14–0 for a
resolution denying Israel's right to change the status of
Jerusalem, and calling on Israel to end its, 'prolonged occupation
of Arab territories, including Jerusalem'. Worse by far, the
United States did not veto the resolution, but merely abstained.
Israeli anger was only partly assuaged by President Carter's
admission that this was a mistake. Now, on 20 August , the UN
Security Council censured Israel for declaring Jerusalem to be its
capital and called on all nations to remove their embassies from
Jerusalem – an empty enough gesture of itself. But, once again,
the United States abstained, and Secretary of State Edmund
Muskie sadly admitted that:

> The status of Jerusalem cannot simply be declared; it must be
> agreed to by the parties. That is a practical reality. We have
> encouraged all parties to refrain from unilateral actions

which seek to change the character or status of Jerusalem. In line with this position we will not vote against the resolution as presently written.

Muskie added that the US would,

Continue firmly and forcefully to resist any attempt to impose sanctions against Israel. That step is contained in a draft resolution to be presented here but not to be voted upon. We are unalterably opposed to it. We will vote against any such resolution'.

This was some compensation, but it did not obliterate the heightened fear that Israel could be left without a single friend in the UN. The American press was scathing. *Time* magazine asked, 'Whom did it help?' and headlined, 'The Knesset concludes a pointless exercise in pointless provocation',[16] and in the *International Herald Tribune* Dial Torgerson decided that, 'The government of Menachem Begin is busily passing ammunition to its enemies, saying, in effect, "Why not? They'll shoot at us anyway" '.[17] The same paper called Israel's actions over Jerusalem 'capital folly'.[18] Israel had been 'reckless' to play upon passions which were so easily aroused over Jerusalem; what Israel needed was, 'Not aggressive militancy but aggressively offered peace terms that promise more than the endless occupation of land bearing a million hostile Arabs. Israel also needs Sadat, who has provided the time and the diplomatic framework for dissolving the enmities of a generation. He, too, is isolated, and it is folly to humiliate him'.

Sadat, for his part, had already broken off peace talks with Israel as early as 15 May, shortly after the legislation on Jerusalem had been introduced in the Knesset. In July he repeated his belief that East Jerusalem was 'Arab and an inseparable part of the West Bank',[19] and in August his Government praised the UN vote censuring Israel for its Jerusalem Law. A correspondence between Sadat and Begin in August seemed to have fizzled out, but peace talks began again a few weeks later and limped along thereafter. Reactions elsewhere in the Arab world were predictable; King Hussein of Jordan called for Israeli withdrawal from all Arab territories, including Jerusalem;[20] Saudi Arabia and Iraq threatened to cut all economic and diplomatic ties with countries which accepted Israel's annexation of East Jerusalem;[21] the Islamic Conference's Jerusalem Committee urged a total boycott of states which approved of Israel's annexation;[22] finally,

both the Conference and Prince Fahd of Saudi Arabia called for a
'jihad' or Muslim Holy War against Israel. These declarations
were declamatory and rhetorical, lacking in substance or in a
sense of steady purpose. But one should remember that in the
past the Arab trade boycott of Israel frightened a great many
reputable business firms from trading with Israel, and today the
threats of any Arab state with oil resources frighten the life out of
otherwise competent and composed heads of government in the
outside world.

There were religious reactions. The Vatican is a law unto itself,
and has always been sincerely and intimately concerned with the
future of Jerusalem. Under the present Pope, one can expect that
this pristine interest will be translated into terms of especially
acute commonsense and educated thought. The interest of the
Roman Catholic Church, with its following of a majority of the
truly committed Christians of the world, should not be
underestimated. Once upon a time, the Vatican pronounced, in
limbo; today its words are weighed.

Pope John Paul II doubtless felt instinctively that 1980 could be
a crucial year for Jerusalem. In April he spoke of Jerusalem as a
'very delicate issue' and called for, 'A new effort, to find a new
approach ... to translate into action a very fundamental
brotherhood and attain, with God's help, a solution, possibly
original, but close, definitive, respectful of everybody's rights'.[23]
At the end of June he was quoted in a statement by the Roman
Catholic Church's Secretariat of State as saying that the
Jerusalem question was 'pivotal to a just peace in the Middle
East'.[24]. He added that the Christian, Jewish and Muslim religious
communities should be 'partners in deciding their future'.

This Vatican statement was interpreted in some quarters as
meaning that 'any power which comes to exercise sovereignty
over Jerusalem' would be accepted, provided that it would agree
to the establishment of 'an appropriate juridical system
guaranteed by a higher international body'.[25] The desire for
some type of international guarantee was not, of course, new; it
was made by Pope John Paul II's predecessor, Pope Paul VI.
Mainly as a matter of form, the Vatican statement asked,
additionally, for religious liberties for all three faiths in
Jerusalem, for the protection of their historic rights and
institutions, for the maintenance of their social and educational
roles, and for the three religions to be treated on a basis of
equality. All these questions, as it happened, had already been
dealt with satisfactorily by the Israeli authorities.

The Vatican, needless to say, was disturbed by the promulgation of the Jerusalem Law. But the Pope showed tact in speaking thereafter in general terms and a minor key. On 18 September he appealed for all possible efforts to make Jerusalem truly a city of peace in these words:

> It is my hope and prayer that your attention and research on the Biblical and spiritual significance of Jerusalem, the city of the Weeping Wall, the city of the rock, the city of the Resurrection, where the Church suffers bitterly its divisions and the spiritual heirs of Abraham still face each other painfully, should contribute to making it really the holy city, and the city of peace.[26]

The Pope's advisers doubtless realized that any declamatory condemnation of Begin's Jerusalem policies could have a counter-productive effect – Israel's Prime Minister is combative to a fault, regarding all outside criticism as unwarranted interference in the internal affairs of his country. But it is doubtful whether he had the support even of a majority of Israeli citizens or of the Jews of the Diaspora in his actions over Jerusalem. Almost all Jews, everywhere, believe that Jerusalem should remain united and the capital of Israel. But this was so, and could remain so, without the passing of superfluous legislation or the moving of the Prime Minister's office into Arab East Jerusalem. Jewish reactions to Begin's actions were mainly negative.

Thus *The Jerusalem Post* called the Bill which led to the Jerusalem Law 'a travesty',[27] and the proposed transfer of Begin's office 'a reckless move', which, 'was calculated to underline the city's division rather than its unity, and to help raise to a crescendo the chorus of international disapproval of Israel's very reunification of the capital'. One of Israel's veteran diplomats, Walter Eytan, spelled out the total absurdity of the office move:[28]

> If Jerusalem is Israel's single, undivided and indivisible capital, under all-encompassing Israeli sovereignty, it surely makes no difference where, within its city limits, the Prime Minister's office is located. The only things that should count are the adequacy of its premises and the Prime Minister's convenience.
>
> At present his office lies within easy distance of the Knesset and the main Government departments. What sense is there in moving it three or four kilometres away, with one-way

streets and downtown traffic they way they are? The proposed transfer suggests uncertainty, a hidden fear that we may yet lose East Jerusalem, and a belief that the chances of this loss would be reduced if the Prime Minister worked there. There is no sound ground for believing any such thing.

Teddy Kollek was quoted in a West German newspaper as saying that 'I would feel safer in my skin if this Law didn't exist. It has a purely declamatory character and only stirs up superfluous questions ... Parliament's decision impedes the peace negotiations with President Sadat unnecessarily. It plays into the hands of Israel's enemies'.[29] Moshe Dayan made this the occasion for calling for a firm but enlightened national leadership – he wanted all religious and municipal issues in Jerusalem thrown open to discussion without precondition and he favoured a statement of equal rights for all religions and clear-cut definitions of areas under their control. The Jerusalem Law, in his view, was a blunder and the Government should never have allowed it to get through the committee stage.[30]

In London, *The Jewish Chronicle* – perhaps the most influential organ of Jewish opinion in the world, outside Israel itself – called the Law, 'Another of those incredible tactical errors by which an extremist element has forced the Government (with the reluctant but inevitable support of the Opposition) into taking a position designed further to alienate her from her friends and confirm the worst calumnies of her enemies'.[31] But the paper's editorial stressed that only Israel was capable of safeguarding the rights of all of Jerusalem's citizens and administering the city fairly, and that 'Israel's right to hold Jerusalem in trust for all mankind is well-established'. Back in Jerusalem, the leading English-language paper said that Israel needed the Law 'like a hole in the head' and expressed disgust over Begin's evident 'panic' and 'hysterical' analogy between passage of the Law and Europe's surrender to the Nazis in World War II.[32]

Israeli humour is rich in irony and one writer, Philip Gillon, had this to say:

> So successful has the Jerusalem Law been that I am thinking of another coup for our august Knesset to consider. They could end all that nonsense of our being criticised in that glass building on the East River (the United Nations) by a simple but brilliant manoeuvre. They could simply pass a law declaring that New York is the undivided second capital of Israel and the Jewish people, now and forever more.[33]

Begin's actions sparked off an endless discussion in the world press, one which will not die down until there is a final peace settlement in the Middle East which takes care of the Jerusalem question. Much of it, understandably, covered old ground. Thus Lord Caradon, in *The Guardian*,[34] renewed his plea for a Jewish and an Arab Jerusalem to live side by side in a united city, which could become 'not an impediment but the gateway to a lasting peace'. The old idea of internationalization was discussed in the columns of the London *Times*, and in one letter, a former British Ambassador to Cairo, Sir Harold Beeley, suggested that Jerusalem needed to be divided, not into two parts but three – the capital of Israel, the capital of Arab Palestine, and the Old City under international control.[35] Lord Caradon advanced his formula in the same paper and was answered by another correspondent, who pointed out that however attractive the concept, there were obstacles of a practical nature:

> For instance, if Jerusalem is to be an open city there could be no ordinary frontier arrangements between the two sovereign states that share it. Relations between Israel and her Arab neighbour (Palestinian or Jordanian) would be required to switch overnight from those of hostility to those of extreme cordiality and mutual trust. No doubt human ingenuity could devise ways and means of coping with the difficulties, but to do so goodwill and determination would be required in great and unusual quantities.[36]

Abba Eban, once Israel's Foreign Minister and widely regarded as the country's greatest foreign affairs expert, reasserted the need to keep Jerusalem undivided:

> It is the law of history that peace never divides cities. Wars divide cities and the functional association between the idea of a divided Jerusalem and the idea of war is too emphatic to be ignored. Those who advocate the division of Jerusalem should understand that they are proposing something more akin to war than to peace.[37] ... This does not mean that universal or Arab interests in Jerusalem should be set aside. In the heart and centre of the city there is a wonderful testimony to the legacy of Islam. The Aqsah Mosque and the Haram el Sharif express an aesthetic perfection and a spiritual grace the like of which no extant edifice in Jerusalem proclaims in such coherent form.
> There is every reason to accord them a special status and

jurisdiction under those who hold them sacred. There is also good cause to acknowledge the special ties of the Arab inhabitants with the Arab world by flexible arrangements about citizenship and access. But the kind of division that marked the two decades before 1967 should be dismissed from memory and consciousness, never to be renewed.

I asked an Israeli diplomat perhaps second only to Eban in experience, lucidity of thought and eloquence for his views on a solution to the Jerusalem question. Gideon Rafael is a former head of the Israeli Foreign Office, and served as Israel's Ambassador both at the United Nations and the Court of St James. He saw four elements in the Jerusalem situation. The first was the need to maintain the city's unity, in every practical sense. The second was the division of authority and responsibilities, with a measure of decentralization, by creating a system of boroughs: Arab, Jewish and, possibly, 'mixed'. The third was the securing of joint co-operation between Arab and Jewish bodies, and between Arabs and Jews in the running of the municipality. The last was the promotion of a degree of religious extra-territoriality.[38] By this was meant a special status for Arab and Christian Holy Places.

Rafael laid down certain conditions for working out a solution on these lines. It should be sought steadily and purposefully; there could not be 'a solution in one'. Maximum use should be made of the five year interim provided for under the terms of the Camp David Agreements, in order to resolve Israeli-Palestinian differences. Diplomatic processes should be set in motion, and movement towards a solution of the Jerusalem question was bound up with that of the whole region and was a key element; it could not be settled in isolation.

Guide-lines like these indicate how much positive and constructive thought is going on in Israel – the image of an embattled, inflexible, Prussianized people is a false one. In particular, Rafael drew attention to the possibility of a framework of social and communal co-operation by decentralizing and creating partly self-administering 'boroughs'. The idea was not new, and had been aired by Kollek's Deputy Mayor, Meron Benvenisti, years earlier. It was shelved, but never dropped, as Teddy Kollek made plain to me in personal conversation.[39] The idea, he said, remained in essence a good one. If it could be implemented it could bring Arab participation in running the affairs of the city, first on this lower level and then perhaps in the Municipality. Here, then, was an avenue towards social harmony and the 'sharing' of Jerusalem in a practical sense.

In an interview with *The Jerusalem Post*,[40] Kollek was explicit. Greater London, he said, offered a structural model of a borough system which gave a large measure of self-government to its inhabitants. A London borough might have upwards of 200,000 inhabitants; for Jerusalem, something like 40,000 would be more appropriate. This would give Jerusalem perhaps ten to twelve boroughs (of which several would be predominantly Arab or 'mixed'). Given municipal harmony, Kollek would allow the Arabs of Jerusalem to vote in elections for a West Bank governing authority and, presumably, in subsequent Jordanian or Palestinian elections. He would allow Muslim flags to fly over the great mosques of the Temple Mount – privately he remarked to me that the late Levi Eshkol had suggested this when he was Prime Minister, and that Mr Begin was a member of Eshkol's National Government at the time. Semi-jokingly, Kollek remarked:

> We should behave towards the Arabs no worse than we do towards the Natorei Karta (the ultra-orthodox Jews of Jerusalem). They run their own educational system, we close their streets to traffic on the Sabbath, and the Natorei Karta even curse the State. Why are the Arabs any worse than they?

Kollek's ideas were examined by one writer in *The Jerusalem Post*.[41] He found them perfectly practicable. The boroughs would be, 'units structured on location, which would all fit into the general municipal structure of Jerusalem'. Of course, 'Extreme Arab nationalism still exists, and is likely to continue to exist, regardless of how the city of Jerusalem may be organized for municipal purposes', but, 'The question is how legitimate – not extreme – Arab national feelings can be satisfied within the Jerusalem context'. Jerusalem's Arabs should be allowed to vote in the West Bank, for, 'Why try to separate Arab Jerusalemites from the natural population to which they belong ethnically?'.

A borough system could ease, even banish localized communal tension. It could – and this is much more important – open the way to full Arab participation in the administration of Jerusalem. It could help to break up the log-jam of Arab-Jewish enmity – but it could not do this on its own, only within the wider framework of a solution to the Jerusalem question. New thought is needed for a solution of that.

There were in 1980 two small but significant hints of a new spirit of mutual concession. The first came from President Sadat of Egypt. When the Egyptian seven point plan on Palestinian autonomy was published in May,[42] Sadat tried to keep off the problem of Jerusalem, as far as possible. Only the fifth point of the plan referred to it, stating that East Jerusalem was 'an integral part' of the West Bank, and that its inhabitants should participate in elections for a Palestinian representative body. But two months later Sadat was accused of having offered East Jerusalem as a gift to Israel.[43] His plan for Jerusalem was announced in Cairo on 19 July. It stated that Jerusalem should never again be divided, but should have one elected Mayor, 'Arab or Israeli, according to the wishes of the populace'. In separate interviews with the Israeli papers, *Ma'ariv* and *Al Hamishmar*, Sadat was quoted as saying that Jerusalem could remain the capital of Israel, if Muslim flags could fly over Muslim Holy Places. Sadat said that the 800 million Muslims who had a vital interest in Jerusalem would accept his plan.

Sadat was reported to have failed to consult Muslim leaders before making this plan public, and of having grieviously offended the PLO. The plan was not, as reports tended to indicate, a blue-print; its real importance lay in the indication of readiness to compromise. The phrase 'one elected Mayor' suggested that the Municipality of Jerusalem had an intrinsic importance, over and above the complexities of the overall Arab-Israeli Middle East dispute.

The second hint came from Teddy Kollek. In a letter to *The Jerusalem Post*,[44] he asked that Jerusalem should be given a, 'Special status, which would enable it to deal with all its most complicated problems, from housing to education, from health to social welfare, quickly and efficiently ... without interference by the Government in every little detail'. This status could 'be formulated in a special Jerusalem Law', and there could be a 'Minister for Jerusalem'. Kollek concluded: 'Jerusalem, which has singular problems, needs a special status'.

This letter of Kollek's was written before the first reading of the empty and purposeless Jerusalem Law which did Israel so much diplomatic damage. Kollek was apprised of the contents of the Law and was seeking to divert interest and effort into more useful channels. Possibly, his initiative was mainly diversionary, therefore, but the underlying thought implicit in it was more far-reaching. Its trend was towards a radically new solution of the Jerusalem Question, or at least consideration of such a solution.

One must reconsider some of the basic elements of the Jerusalem question. Israel wants the city to remain undivided and the capital of the State. The Arab world is mainly in favour of the re-division of the city, with an Arab East Jerusalem becoming the capital of a Palestinian or Palestinian-Jordanian entity. Many Arabs agree that city with so unique a role should not be physically re-divided, whatever happens to it politically. The Christian world continues to express an abiding interest in Jerusalem. On the whole, most Christians who actually *know* Jerusalem would not want it once again divided, and would admit that Israel has been an efficient guardian of the city since its reunification in 1967. Other Christians are necessarily more vague. Why, some ask, cannot the city simply be 'shared' between Jews and Arabs, with Christian religious rights guaranteed? Or could a part of the city be internationalized? Or, again, could the whole city have some undefined, but 'special' status?

The objections against re-dividing Jerusalem are virtually unsurmountable. It would seriously damage the character of the city. It would re-erect barriers of all kinds, physical but political and spiritual as well. In a divided Jerusalem there would be not the slightest impetus towards the Arab-Israeli reconciliation and co-operation which are needed if there is ever to be real peace in the Middle East. On the contrary, the city would remain an object of continuing, bitter dissension. In addition, a new line of demarcation between East and West Jerusalem would be impossibly difficult to fix; the population has increased immensely since 1967 and has flowed across the frontiers. Leaving aside such facts as the huge majority of Jews in Jerusalem's population and the age-old pre-eminence of the city in Jewish thought and belief, re-division would be retrograde and archaic.

There are equally valid objections to internationalisation. For one thing, neither side wants it; nor does anyone else, save theorists who are totally unaware of what it means to live under an alien regime. An international authority would be an unhappy and impotent referee. Its presence in Jerusalem would ensure that Arabs and Jews would be kept apart and that there would be no chance of endemic, damaging Arab-Jewish enmity being gradually broken down. On the contrary, a Jerusalem internationalised and probably subjected to 'divisions of convenience' – to spare the international authority trouble would remain a bone of deadly contention.

The 'Caradon Plan', and similar proposals, would preserve the illusion of an undivided Jerusalem. But it would be split between two completely different governments, one Arab and one Israeli. Some political commentators have suggested that this might not be too bad; the sentimental phrase of 'sister cities' has been coined.[45] Sisters, particularly of different faiths, can be deadly enemies; Mary and Elizabeth Tudor provide a case in point. The 'Caradon Plan', too, would keep Arabs and Jews apart, although it represents an altogether honest endeavour to find a solution.

A huge majority of Israelis, and most Jews in the outside world, would readily settle for a continuation of the present status quo – if in some way this did not turn out to be an insuperable hindrance to a final Middle East peace settlement. Unfortunately, there has been no sign that the Arab world could ever accept the present status quo, even if there were some useful minor modifications, such as the flying of flags over the Muslim mosques, or built-in rights for East Jerusalemites to vote on the West Bank or retain Palestinian-Jordanian citizenship.

Let one prominent, level-headed Palestinian speak for himself: Anwar Nusseibeh, ex-Minister of King Hussein's Government in Jordan and a resident of East Jerusalem, told Teddy Kollek and Moshe Dayan in February, 1980, that Jerusalem should remain physically united but should contain 'two separate sovereignties'.[46] He did not explain how this could be made possible. In June he wrote to *The Jerusalem Post*, asserting that he was not concerned with turning Jerusalem into 'a political or temporal capital'. His interest in Jerusalem was religious; it was 'the fulcrum of my faith' and 'a city that God has graced, and described in the Koran as holy'.

These statements might seem to be slightly at variance, but Nusseibeh had explained his feelings at much greater length to the author of a short book on Jerusalem, J. Robert Moskin. He had the following to say:[47]

> In Jerusalem we had barbed wire; we had walls. But at least we felt that we were not completely disinherited from a city we regarded as our own. In 1967, even the little that we had was taken away; and instead of living as a sovereign people, now we live under conditions that are imposed by the Israelis and in the shaping of which we have no say. I have to pay tax which I cannot afford. I have to watch the confiscation of my land. I am a lawyer but I don't practice law because I do not accept Israeli occupation and annexation. I was a member of

the Jordanian Parliament, but I do not operate in the administration because I do not recognise the laws of Israel.

I want real peace between Jews and Arabs – peace on a human level – a real reconciliation. It can happen only over time. It is very simple. Either Arabs and Jews can coexist within the same society on a basis of compatibility, in which case there is no need to re-divide the country, but in which case the refugees would have to be repatriated or compensated – or to divide the country cleanly ... Jerusalem would have to be part of the same pattern. We do not want to fragment it. No, we want to grant to it the dignity to which it is entitled, but recognising that it is as holy and dear to Christians and Moslems as it is to the Jews. The 1967 line was perhaps not ideal, but it was better than what we have today.

The city is divided. All right, Teddy Kollek doesn't want to divide the city. Then unite it in the context of a city in which Jews and Arabs live side by side in an atmosphere of self-respect.

Once again, there are contradictions, for in a different place in the interview Nusseibeh said that Arab sovereignty should be restored in East Jerusalem. But his hope that Jerusalem could stay physically united, with Jews and Arabs living side by side in an atmosphere of self-respect, is a reminder that there are influential Palestinians who, emancipated from the PLO doctrines of war to the death and total conquest of Palestine, are looking for agreement and compromise over Jerusalem. At the same time, Nusseibeh and other Arab 'moderates' cannot for one moment accept the present pattern of total Jewish control of Jerusalem.

It would be idle, at this stage of history, to present a 'blueprint' for a solution of the Jerusalem problem. Meron Benvenisti once wrote that 'no fewer than forty plans for ultimate solutions have been officially presented', since Jerusalem became recognized as an international problem sixty years ago.[48] Many of these plans were lucid, even brilliant; all of them were unacceptable to one side or the other, or to both. This gave the dispute over Jerusalem a 'zero sum nature'. So Benvenisti contented himself with five pointers to constructive thinking: only issues relevant and essential to the peace-making process should be dealt with. Both sides should openly acknowledge the sensitivity of the Jerusalem problem. Both sides should declare their willingness to negotiate on it. Interim arrangements should be agreed, in order to prevent the conflict from worsening. Finally, both sides should agree on a joint statement of irreproachable general considerations, such as safeguarding of holy places, free access to them, and maintenance of the city's physical unity.

Benvenisti added another consideration, which he seemed to think was a mere generality. This was the restoration of a unified municipal administration. From this can be evolved the germ of an idea which may be of more operative value than a blue-print.

Kollek and others have talked of a special status for Jerusalem, with extended municipal powers. Why, then, should Jerusalem not be given 'administrative sovereignty', with full control over its own affairs? West Berlin manages very well with this and, it might be added, a unified Berlin would manage much better. The capital of Israel would remain in Jerusalem, for its Government and Parliament are situated there. But there would be no reason why Jerusalem should not house the government of a Palestinian entity, or of the Palestinian component in a Jordanian-Palestinian Federation.

Such a 'sovereign administration' would be very different from an internationalized 'free state', as for instance Danzig once was. For Danzig was administered by an alien authority, resented by the vast majority of its German inhabitants. The people of Jerusalem, all of them, would be given the chance to govern their own city, and that government would involve the participation and co-operation of Arabs and Jews in the most crucial meeting-place of these two hitherto warring peoples. Coexistence, as the Soviet Union has shown, has little real content, when all that it consists of is negotiations at arms length and a temporary agreement not to go to war. True coexistence implies a working partnership; in Jerusalem, Jews and Arabs have a unique chance of putting true coexistence to the test and setting an example which could be the saving of the Middle East. What better way than by joining in self-rule, in the interests of all, in their own city?

Naturally, there would be objections, from both sides. Some Israelis would argue that the establishment of a sovereign administration in Jerusalem would weaken and water down Israel's claim to total sovereignty over the whole city. As it happens, there is a built-in Jewish majority in Jerusalem, which is the real gauge of Israeli sovereignty in an area of dispute. That majority, given an efficiently operated borough system, would persist, for boroughs would look after their own housing and settlement. The reality of Israel's trusteeship of Jerusalem would remain. It might be argued, too, that Israel would forfeit exclusive control over the affairs of Jerusalem. But has Israel ever sought such exclusive control? On the contrary, Kollek and others have clearly indicated their desire for Arab participation in the administration of the Municipality. That participation, based on the principle of sharing, has to be implemented if the Jews and Arabs of Jerusalem are ever to live together as neighbours and friends.

In addition, Israel would explicitly remain both trustee and 'protecting power' for Jerusalem. Under present circumstances, there could be no alternative to this. The Camp David Agreements provide for the five-year interim during which Palestinian rights will be consolidated and developed. The modalities of Jerusalem's future status and system should be given an equal interval of time to be worked out, for this – as already explained – can only be done within the framework of an overall peace settlement. This can be done; the real obstacles to settlement are political and psychological, not functional. Jerusalem's is not an isolated problem; it is at the heart of the whole Arab-Israeli dispute.

Arabs would claim they are not being given enough. That has been their traditional posture during the entire course of the Middle East dispute, for they could have had a unified Palestine in the 1920s and were actually given their Palestinian State – which they refused – under the United Nations Partition Plan. Their share in the administration of Jerusalem would be a fair one, in proportion to their numbers. The meeting of their needs would follow automatically, for true coexistence can only be based on the spirit of concession on both sides (since the West makes concessions and the Soviet Union does not, East-West coexistence is *not* working). Concessions which could reasonably be made might include total Muslim control of Muslim holy places, the flying of Muslim flags over them, the right to Jordanian (or Palestinian) citizenship of East Jerusalemites, and their right to vote in elections in neighbouring Arab countries.

A commensurate Arab share in the administration of Jerusalem, and Arab control over their own holy places, should at least help towards repairing the damage done to Arab dignity and pride by the loss of wars and territories, against an enemy people whom they have treated sometimes benevolently, but more often with contempt, ever since the Koran first warned against the wiles and wickedness of the Jews. It is a little paradoxical that Arabs have made so much play with the accusation that Israel has treated them as second-class citizens, when Jews were regarded exactly as that throughout most of the Arab world for fourteen centuries.

The Christian world should scarcely object to any arrangement which encourages both Arabs and Jews to share productively in the administration of Jerusalem, and which offers a chance of turning it at long last into a city of peace. It can be argued, of course, that all sorts of difficult problems 'on the ground' will remain to be worked out, but it should not be beyond the wit of man to regulate mere modalities. There is the Camp David five-year interim in which to devise full working arrangements. As already stated, these five years constitute a desperately needed breathing space in which to work out terms of a settlement which must be intimately related to the security of the region, to its economic circumstances and needs, and to the problems of the two already existing states in the immediate area, Israel and Jordan. At the end of the road, there could be something like a Middle East 'Benelux', consisting of Jordan, Israel, whatever Palestinian entity has evolved and, hopefully, Lebanon. Here, indeed, would be a unit of assured survival, prosperity and peace. The creation of such a unit would, of course, need to be the result of organic phased growth – and not a part of an 'instant solution'. Instant solutions should be treated with deep distrust.

The Christian world has a vested interest in the creation and development of a peaceful and prosperous region, and the Vatican's request for a statute for Christian holy places is surely no problem. The Israelis have already given the Christian shrines autonomy and protection; there can be nothing against dressing these facts up in truthful and appropriate words.

Indeed the arguments in favour of meeting the Vatican's request halfway are very strong. A sincere statement on the guaranteed rights in Jerusalem, in perpetuity, of both of the two great faiths – Christian and Islamic – could only do good. What could do more to recommend and enhance Israeli trusteeship of Jerusalem's Holy Places than a statement of this kind? What more effective reminder could there be of Israel's role so far as their guarantor and protector?

The political climate of the Middle East in 1980 was as threatening as it has ever been in the past. The purposeless Iraqi-Iranian war was fresh proof of the instability of the whole region. The Soviet invasion of Afghanistan posed a new danger, of Russian military intervention along the oil-rich shores of the

Persian Gulf. Another new threat was that of the development of an Iraqi nuclear weapon. The weaknesses of the Saudi Arabian regime were dramatically exposed by the attack on the Great Mosque of Mecca. Meanwhile, the old disputes – between Syria and Iraq, between the South Yemen and Oman, between Egypt and Libya – grumbled on. So did the civil war in Lebanon.

The Arab League continued to denounce all peace-making efforts, from UN Resolution 242 of 1967 onwards.[49] The PLO remained utterly intransigent. In a statement made in Amman in March,[50] the organization's spokesman on foreign affairs, Farouk el Kadoumi, said, 'The PLO will *not* accept any measures which specifically guarantee the security of Israel. This is one of the contents of 242, which the European countries recognize but we do not.' In July the PLO demanded the closure of the Jordan bridges, which have been kept open to Arabs and their goods ever since 1967; only at Jordan's insistence was the PLO resolution turned down by a majority of the Arab League states.[51]

Nothing in the demeanour of the PLO's leader, Yassir Arafat, justified the belief, engendered by Soviet propaganda and by the wishful thinking of statesmen in the western world, that he has become a 'moderate'. One of his favourite analogies is between the Israelis of today and the Crusaders of the past – the Jews, he has said repeatedly, will be thrown out of the land which is Arab by right just as surely as the Crusaders were seven centuries ago. In one purple passage, Arafat spoke of the capture of Jerusalem. When the Crusaders took the city, he said, 'the blood of its defenders reached the hocks of their horses. That was in the days of cavalry heroism ... We will offer one martyr after another for every inch of the road to Palestine, and for every inch of land in Palestine'.[52] He was speaking, inappropriately, at the funeral of one of his followers, who had been murdered by Iraqi agents. But his visions of blood have not faded, and they are primarily of the blood of Jews.

Yet the mouthings of Arafat and his lieutenants should not blind anyone to the fact that there *is* a possibility of achieving coexistence between Israelis and Palestinian Arabs, and a possibility, too, of extending that coexistence to Jerusalem in the positive sense of the word, and not in terms of uneasy and mainly wary contiguity. One young Palestinian Arab told me openly and boldly, in front of others who were present, that his people – given a real chance – could find common ground with Israel.[53] It was, he believed, a singular paradox that his people could coexist more easily with the Israelis than with fellow-Arabs. For what had the latter done to help the Palestinians? The Jordanians had killed 3,600 of them. The Lebanese Christians had fought them tooth and nail. On the West Bank they had been asked to be heroes, and in the Gaza Strip the PLO became the most terrible predators in the entire history of the area. That left Syria, and its leaders had never dropped their territorial claim to the whole of Palestine (and the Kingdom of Jordan, too) as being nothing more than 'Southern Syria'. Israel had conquered much of their land and had fought and won wars which had resulted in hundreds of thousands of Palestinians becoming refugees. Israel, as this young man saw it, could help now by talking to them seriously and giving them a sense of real hope. Israel, he might have added, cannot live in a state of perpetual war – this has already caused a deterioration in the underlying realities of life in Israel.

What he said could be true, in whole or in part. The Jerusalem problem remains at the heart of the matter. In the context of a peace settlement, it is the trickiest problem of the lot. Its solution will have to be 'original' as Pope John Paul suggested. It will require flexibility and compromise, as Eban and Sadat have indicated. It presupposes Arab-Jewish co-operation in a unified city and municipality, as Kollek, Rafael and many others have urged. Jerusalem is a unique city, and a solution of the Jerusalem question, too, may need unique characteristics. That solution will probably need to be the last piece of the mosaic of Arab-Jewish agreement, leading to future understanding and friendship, to be fitted into place. But the fitting has to be planned in advance, and it will take a great deal of time. Why not start planning it, now?

REFERENCES

1. Letter of 25 August 1980, from Mayor Kollek to Mr S. P. Doron, of Rhode Island Avenue, Washington.
2. 'Thirteen Years: Common Ideas Emerge', by Gideon Weigert, in *Israel Scene*, May 1980.
3. Lord Ballantrae, in *The Times*, 23 May 1980.
4. Terence Prittie, in unpublished letter to *The Times*, written 23 May 1980.
5. David Richardson, in *The Jerusalem Post*, 8 July 1980.
6. Christopher Walker, in *The Times*, 12 March 1980.
7. Ibid.
8. Statement by Kollek to *The Jerusalem Post*, 17 March 1980.

9. Abraham Rabinovich, in *The Jerusalem Post*, 17 March 1980.
10. *The Jerusalem Post*, 9 May 1980.
11. Thus in a statement to a Press Conference in Jerusalem on 6 December 1979, Kollek said that he supported protest, but not violence. He added: 'We've worked hard to develop Jerusalem's reputation as a city of tolerance, but I can assure you that the televised pictures of tire-burning in Jerusalem looked to those outside the country the same way that the Teheran or Pakistan demonstrations appear'.
12. Christopher Walker, in *The Times*, 18 June 1980.
13. Thus in *The Sunday Telegraph*, 27 July 1980.
14. Eric Silver, in *The Guardian*, 30 August 1980.
15. *Jewish Chronicle* News Service, 12 August 1980.
16. *Time* magazine, 11 August 1980.
17. *International Herald Tribune*, 5 September 1980.
18. *International Herald Tribune*, 4 August 1980.
19. President Anwar Sadat, speaking to the National Democratic Party, 22 July 1980.
20. King Hussein, speaking at the Arab League Conference in Amman, 6 July 1980.
21. Joint Saudi-Iraqi communiqué, issued in Taif, 6 August 1980.
22. Islamic Conference statement, Casablanca, 18 August 1980.
23. Pope John Paul II, in conversation with King Hassan of Morocco, 9 April 1980.
24. Vatican statement of 30 June 1980, circulated to members of the UN.
25. *Jewish Chronicle*, 4 July 1980.
26. Pope John Paul II in Castelgandolfo Palace, 18 September 1980.
27. *The Jerusalem Post*, 29 July 1980.
28. Walter Eytan, former head of Israel's Foreign Office, in *The Jerusalem Post*, 29 July 1980.
29. In the *Nürnberger Nachrichten*, 2 August 1980.
30. In *The Jerusalem Post*, 8 August 1980.
31. *Jewish Chronicle*, 8 August 1980.
32. *The Jerusalem Post*, 25 August 1980.
33. In *The Jerusalem Post*, 5 September 1980.
34. *The Guardian*, 12 July 1980.
35. *The Times*, 16 September 1980.
36. Keith Kyle, in *The Times*, 19 September 1980.
37. In *The Daily Telegraph*, 8 September 1980.
38. Gideon Rafael, in conversation with the author, 14 April 1980.
39. Teddy Kollek, in conversation with the author, 28 April 1980.
40. *The Jerusalem Post* Magazine, 1 February 1980.
41. Yehuda Yalon, in *The Jerusalem Post*, 2 March 1980.
42. *The Jerusalem Post*, 5 May 1980.
43. Irene Beeson, Cairo correspondent of *The Guardian*, 21 July 1980.
44. *The Jerusalem Post*, 4 May 1980.
45. Thus in *The Yorkshire Post*, 11 August 1980.
46. The meeting was reported by the Jewish Telegraphic Agency on 7 February 1980.
47. 'Report from Jerusalem', J. Robert Moskin, Institute of Human Relations Press, New York, 1977.
48. Meron Benvenisti, in the *Jewish Chronicle*, 17 October 1980.

49.   Arab League Conference, Amman, 10 July 1980.
50.   *The Daily Telegraph*, 19 March 1980.
51.   *The Jerusalem Post*, 8 July 1980.
52.   Yassir Arafat, at the funeral of Al-Din Qalaq in Paris, 9 August 1978.
53.   Conversation at an Atlantic College (South Wales) forum, October 1979.

Bibliography

AAMIRY, A. M. *Jerusalem: Arab Origin and Heritage.* London, Longman, 1978.
AL-TAL, Abdallah. *Disaster of Palestine.* Cairo, 1959.
ADAMS, Michael. *Chaos or Rebirth. The Arab Outlook.* London, BBC publications, 1968.
ANTONIUS, George. *The Arab Awakening.* London, Hamish Hamilton, 1938.
ASHTOR, Eliahu. *Jerusalem in Muslim Thought.* Jerusalem Jerusalem Keter, 1973.
ATIYAH, Edward. *The Arabs.* London, Pelican, 1955.
BELLOW, Saul. *To Jerusalem and Back.* London, Secker & Warburg, 1976.
BEN-GURION, David. *Israel: Years of Challenge.* London, Blond, 1966.
BENVENISTI, Meron. *Israel. The Torn City.* Jerusalem, Isratypeset, 1976.
BERLIN, Isaiah. *Chaim Weizmann.* London, Weidenfeld & Nicolson, 1955.
BOVIS, H. Eugene. *The Jerusalem Question.* Stanford (Cal), Hoover Institution Press, 1971.
BUBER, Martin. *On Zion.* London, East & West Library, 1973.
CAMERON, James. *The Making of Israel.* London, Secker & Warburg, 1976.
COHEN, I. *A Short History of Zionism.* London, Frederick Muller, 1954.
COHEN, Saul B. *Jerusalem. Bridging the Four Walls.* New York, Nerzl Press, 1977.
COOK, Stanley. *An Introduction to the Bible.* London, Cambridge Press, 1945.
DAYAN, Moshe. *The Story of my Life.* London, Weidenfeld & Nicolson, 1976.
DOUGLAS-HOME, Charles. *The Arabs and Israel.* London, Weidenfeld & Nicolson, 1967.
DRAPER, Theodore. *Israel and World Politics.* London, Secker & Warburg, 1968.
EBAN, Abba. *An Autobiography.* London, Weidenfeld & Nicolson, 1978.
FISCH, Harold. *The Zionist Revolution.* London, Weidenfeld & Nicolson, 1978.
GERSON, Allan. *Israel, the West Bank and International Law.* London, Cass, 1978.
GOICHON, A. M. *Jérusalem. Fin de la Ville Universelle?* Paris, Maisonneuve & Larose, 1976.
GLUBB, Sir John Bagot. *Peace in the Holy Land.* Hodder & Stoughton, London, 1971.
GLUBB, Sir John Bagot. *A Soldier with the Arabs.* Hodder & Stoughton, London, 1957.

GILBERT, Martin. *Jerusalem. Illustrated History Atlas.* New York, Macmillan, 1977.

GILBERT, Martin. *The Jews of Arab Lands. Their History in Maps.* London, Furnival, 1975.

GULSTON, Charles. *Jerusalem. The Triumph and the Tragedy.* Grand Rapids (Mich), Zondervan, 1978.

HASSAN, Crown Prince, bin-Talal of Jordan. *A Study on Jerusalem.* London, Longman, 1979.

HERZOG, Chaim. *Who Stands Accused?* London, Weidenfeld & Nicolson, 1978.

HERZOG, Yaacov. *A People that Dwells alone.* London, Weidenfeld & Nicolson, 1975.

HOLLINGWORTH, Clare. *The Arabs and the West.* London, Methuen, 1952.

HOLLIS, Christopher & BROWNRIGG, Robert. *Holy Places.* London, Weidenfeld & Nicolson, 1969.

KEDOURIE, Elie. *Diplomacy in the Near and Middle East.* Princeton (NJ), Van Nostrand, 1956.

KHATIB, Rouhi Al-. *The Judaization of Jerusalem.* Amman, 1979.

KIRK, George. *A Short History of the Middle East.* New York, Praeger, 1964.

KOLLEK, Teddy. *For Jerusalem.* London, Weidenfeld & Nicolson, 1978.

KOLLEK, Teddy. *Jerusalem Perspectives* ed. Peter Schneider & Geoffrey Wigoder, London, Furnival, 1976.

KOTKER, Norman. *The Earthly Jerusalem.* New York, Scribner, 1969.

KUTCHER, Art. *The New Jerusalem.* London, Thames & Hudson, 1973.

LACQUEUR, Walter. *The Road to War.* London, Weidenfeld & Nicolson, 1968.

LANDAU, Jacob. *The Arabs in Israel.* Oxford University Press, 1969.

LESLIE, G. Clement. *The Rift in Israel.* London, Routledge, 1971.

LEVIN, Harry. *Jerusalem Embattled.* London, Gollancz, 1950.

LUTTWAK, Edward & HOROWITZ, Dan. *The Israeli Army.* London, Allen & Lane, 1975.

MCNEISH, James. *Belonging.* London, Collins, 1980.

MCINTYRE, Ian *The Proud Doers.* London, BBC Publications, 1968.

MILLER, William. *The Ottoman Empire and its Successors.* London, Cambridge Press, 1923.

NARKISS, Uzi. *La Bataille pour Jérusalem.* Paris, Hachette, 1979.

NIBLEY, Prof. Hugh. 'Jerusalem in Christianity', from Jerusalem. Keter, Jerusalem, 1973.

NOEL, Gerard. *The Anatomy of the Catholic Church.* London, Hodder & Stoughton, 1980.

PARKES, Rev Dr J. M. *Whose Land?* Harmondsworth, Penguin, 1970.

PARKES, Rev Dr J. M. *The New Face of Israel.* Leeds, University Press, 1964.

PARKES, Rev Dr J. M. *Arabs and Jews in the Middle East.* London, Gollancz, 1967.

PRITTIE, Terence. *Israel. Miracle in the Desert.* New York, Praeger, 1967.

PRITTIE, Terence. *Eshkol of Israel.* New York, Pitman, 1969.

RABIN, Yitzhak. *The Rabin Memoirs.* London, Weidenfeld & Nicolson, 1976.

SAID, Edward. *The Question of Palestine.* London, Routledge, 1979.

SAMUEL, Maurice. *Blood Accusation.* London, Weidenfeld & Nicolson, 1967.

SCHWARZ, Walter. *The Arabs in Israel.* London, Faber, 1959.

SCOTT-JAMES, Bruno. *The Letters of St. Bernard of Clairvaux.* London, 1953.

SHALEM, Diane & SHAMIS, George. *Jerusalem.* Jerusalem, 1970.

SNOW, Peter. *Hussein.* London, Barrie & Jenkins, 1972.

STEIN, Leonard. *The Balfour Declaration.* London, Valentine & Mitchell, 1961.

TEKOAH, Yosef. *Barbed Wire shall not return to Jerusalem.* New York, Israel Information Services Publication, 1968.

TIBAWI, A. L. *Jerusalem: Its Place in Islam and Arab History.* Beirut, Institute of Palestine Studies, 1969.

TIBAWI, A. L. *The Islamic Pious Foundations in Jerusalem.* London, Baskerville Press, 1978.

VESTER, Bertha Spafford. *Our Jerusalem.* Beirut, Middle East Export Press, 1950.

WEIGERT, Gideon. *Israel's Presence in East Jerusalem.* Jerusalem, 1973.

WEISGAL, Meyer & CARMICHAEL, Joel (Editors). *Chaim Weizmann. A Biography by Several Hands.* New York, Atheneum, 1963.

WEITZ, Raanan. *Self Rule, Shared Rule: Federal Solutions to the Middle East Conflict.* Ramat Gan, Turtledove Books, 1979.

WEIZMANN, Chaim. *Trial and Error.* London, Hamish Hamilton, 1949.

WEIZMAN, Ezer. *On Eagles' Wings.* London, Weidenfeld & Nicolson, 1976.

ZANDER, Walter. *Israel and the Holy Places of Christendom.* London, Weidenfeld & Nicolson, 1971.

ZUREIK, Eliat. *The Palestinians in Israel.* London, Routledge, 1979.

Index